HAMBURG

Also in the series

HAMBURG

A Cultural History

Matthew Jefferies

Interlink Books

An imprint of Interlink Publishing Group, Inc.
Northampton, Massachusetts

First American edition published in 2011 by

INTERLINK BOOKS
An imprint of Interlink Publishing Group, Inc.
46 Crosby Street, Northampton, MA 01060
www.interlinkbooks.com

Library of Congress Cataloging-in-Publication Data
Jefferies, Matthew.
Hamburg : a cultural history / by Matthew Jefferies. -- 1st American ed.
p. cm.
Includes bibliographical references and indexes.
ISBN 978-1-56656-846-3 (pbk.)
1. Hamburg (Germany)--Civilization. 2. Hamburg (Germany)--History. 3. Hamburg (Germany)--Intellectual life. 4. Hamburg (Germany)--Buildings, structures, etc. 5. Historic buildings--Germany--Hamburg. 6. Historic sites--Germany--Hamburg. I. Title.
DD901.H247J44 2011
943'.515--dc22
2011013251

Printed and bound in the United States of America

To request our complete, full-color catalog, please call
1-800-238-LINK, visit our website at www.interlinkbooks.com or write to us at:
Interlink Publishing, 46 Crosby Street, Northampton, Massachusetts 01060
email: info@interlinkbooks.com

Contents

Preface & Acknowledgments

I first visited Hamburg in the winter of 1981. I was on my gap year travels and, in truth, my initial impressions were far from positive: the place seemed cold, raw and uninviting, distinctly lacking in German *Gemütlichkeit*. It would be another three years before I fell under the city's spell, when an undergraduate year at Hamburg University gave me the opportunity to experience life in the north German metropolis first hand. Back then, before the age of cheap air travel and continental city-breaks, my journey took the best part of two days, with a tortuous cross-country train ride to Harwich followed by 22 turbulent hours at sea. It was all too easy to imagine the relief felt by generations of sailors as the city's spires, cranes and warehouses finally came into view.

The welcome feel of dry land underfoot, the animated bustle on the landing stages and the pervasive aroma of sizzling *Bratwurst*, potato pancakes and roast almonds quickly served to lift my mood. My home for the next nine months was a white room on the eighth floor of a high-rise student hostel, with panoramic views of the city from the east. Within weeks I was negotiating the S-Bahn network like a native, jumping night buses and reviewing Hamburg gigs for the *New Musical Express*. Even the university's crowded lecture theaters had a certain exotic charm.

Yet one memory of those early weeks stands out above all others. I had been befriended by a family from the city's suburbs and was taken on a late-night tour of St. Pauli. The dapper headteacher and his pharmacist wife not only showed me the notorious Reeperbahn, with its strip-clubs, casinos and brothels, but even the shadowy backstreets near the wholesale fish market, where truck drivers parked for the night and teenage prostitutes shivered on street corners. This eminently respectable middle-aged couple strolled up the Reeperbahn as if on a Sunday walk in the park, while I followed a short distance behind, desperately trying not to gawp.

I learned that night that the residents of Hamburg are difficult to shock. Indeed they take pride in their worldliness and their urbanity. Their cool sobriety may sometimes seem like metropolitan arrogance, but there are in fact few places where I have experienced such generous hospitality. In particular I am indebted to the Giersch family, whose spare room I have been returning to for the past 27 years. Anja Seddig and Frauke Dünnhaupt have been friends for nearly as long, while at Hamburg University I owe much to my "mentor" Professor Hermann Hipp, whose knowledge of Hamburg's architecture is unrivaled. Two academic colleagues, Mark Russell and Maiken Umbach, kindly read and commented on the manuscript. Finally, I must thank the Alfred Toepfer Stiftung FVS for awarding me a two-year Hanseatic Scholarship in the late 1980s, and for a host of invitations thereafter. The foundation exists to promote "understanding between the countries of Europe"; this book represents my own small contribution to that task.

Introduction

A Cultural History of a "City without Culture"?

Hamburg has never been a city noted for its culture. Despite its size and importance, it was slow to develop the cultural infrastructure of a major urban center. The absence of a royal court meant that Hamburg not only missed out on palaces and pleasure gardens, but also on the theaters, galleries and grand avenues which came to grace even the smallest capital cities. It did not even have a university until 1919. Hamburg's proud republican traditions left other monuments, of course, but as a city of work and of trade, commerce always came before culture.

Moreover, what Richard Evans calls the "celebrated philistinism" of the patrician families who for centuries controlled Hamburg's fortunes meant that the city appeared to take an almost perverse pride in the absence of cultural fripperies. The architect Fritz Schumacher (1869-1947), who came to the city in 1909, wrote that a "feeling of great loneliness is the likely lot of anyone who works as an artist in Hamburg." A few years earlier the director of the city's art gallery, Alfred Lichtwark (1852-1914), had bemoaned: "a million people—and is there a poet, a composer among us who makes his living from his art? A million people—and where are the painters, the sculptors, the architects who correspond to this economic flowering?"

No building, however grand or venerable, was allowed to stand in the way of progress, especially if it was draining the money-minded city fathers of hard cash. The city's giant thirteenth-century Gothic cathedral was pulled down in 1804-7, partly because it was under the jurisdiction of the Archbishop of Bremen, and partly to make room for a new grammar school, but mostly due to the high maintenance costs of the crumbling structure. Five more medieval churches followed between 1807 and 1837. "No other city in the world has ever developed such a lust for self-destruction as Hamburg. Hamburg could have been the city of the Renaissance, the Baroque and the Rococo—yet all these treasures were consistently and enthusiastically sacrificed in the name of commerce," Lichtwark lamented. Yet not all Hamburg's architectural wounds were self-inflicted: the "Great Fire" of May 1842 destroyed over 750 acres of built-up land and nearly all the city's major public buildings. A century later, Allied bombing in Operation Gomorrah led to the devastating firestorm of 1943, which left much of the city a gutted shell.

Today, few buildings date back more than two centuries, and those that do—such as the five major churches—are in large part reconstructions. Far from wallowing in self-pity, however, the city has always sensed opportunity in catastrophe, continuing to expand and prosper at a time when similar port cities across Europe were declining and contracting. With a population of nearly two million, Hamburg is one of the largest cities in the European Union not to enjoy the status of a national capital. It is a fascinating and highly livable metropolis, full of color and contrast. Above all, as Germany's "gateway to the world," it is a cosmopolitan city, whose culture has been shaped by those passing through, as much as by those who stayed: Dutch sugar refiners; English textile merchants; French bakers; and Greenland whalers, whose skill at extracting oil from blubber ensured it was one of the first places to enjoy the benefits of street lighting.

When the lawyer and art collector Gustav Schiefler (1857-1935) first began writing a cultural history of this "city without culture" a hundred years ago, it seemed like a bold act indeed. The Germans may have become known in the late eighteenth century as an inward-looking nation of "poets and thinkers," but Hamburg's self-image was very different: cool, rational and open to the world, so long as there was a profit to be made. When the poet Heinrich Heine remarked that in Hamburg "the customs are English," this is what he was getting at. But just as England was never really a "land without music," so Hamburg was not quite as philistine as its reputation suggested. On the contrary, when the publisher Cotta brought out the collected works of the recently deceased writer and philosopher Johann Gottfried Herder in 1805, there were more sub-scribers in Hamburg than anywhere else in Europe. Similarly, Cotta's thir-teen-volume collected works of Goethe found 221 subscribers in Hamburg, compared to just 70 in Berlin and 51 in Leipzig. While it long suited the city to be considered a hard-headed, no-nonsense kind of place, this did not mean it was especially hostile to the arts. Many of the city's merchants and traders were prepared to offer the same kind of cultural pa-tronage that monarchy or the aristocracy provided elsewhere. They were anxious to demonstrate that money can produce culture just as breeding can: to this day Hamburg has more charitable foundations—more than one thousand in total—than any other German city.

In fact, Hamburg's historic contribution to the arts was considerable. In music, for example, the first public opera house in the German lands was opened there in 1678. Georg Friedrich Händel was a member of the Hamburg Opera orchestra before he became the court composer of George I; Liszt and Wagner conducted there too; and Mahler was its musical director for six years. Europe's first periodical of music criticism, *Critica Musica*, was published in the city in 1722. It was the work of Johann Mattheson (1681-1764), a German-language opera composer who started a second periodical called *Der musicalische Patriot* in 1729. Then in 1783 Carl Friedrich Cramer founded the *Magazin der Musik in Hamburg*. As Celia Applegate (2005) observes, "Vienna may have been the place to which aspiring musicians went to play and to write music, but it was in the cities of northern Germany where people wrote about it." Carl Philipp Emanuel Bach (1714-88), who in the eighteenth century was more famous than his father Johann Sebastian, worked as a music director in Hamburg for many years. J. S. Bach had himself come to Hamburg in the hope of becoming organist at St. Jacob's Church.

The city produced its own composers too: Mattheson; George Philipp Telemann (1681-1767), who is listed in the *Guinness Book of World Records* as the most prolific composer of all time; Reinhard Keiser (1674-1739); Felix Mendelssohn (1809-47); and the great Johannes Brahms (1833-97), one of the first composers able to live off royalties alone. Admittedly, Brahms enjoyed his greatest success in Vienna and had a sometimes difficult relationship with his home town, but he was the first artist to be honored with the freedom of the city (1889), and always remained fiercely proud of his roots. As he once wrote in a letter: "I have always had a longing for Hamburg. My most treasured, if melancholic, hours are when I'm sitting alone in the evening and thinking back."

A similar story can be told in literature. Four of Germany's leading eighteenth-century poets spent time in the city: Barthold Hinrich Brockes (1680-1747), Friedrich von Hagedorn (1708-54), Matthias Claudius (1740-1815) and Friedrich Klopstock (1724-1803). The latter lived for many years at Poststrasse 36 in the center of the city, and when he died some 50,000 people turned out to pay their respects as his cortège headed for the cemetery at Ottensen. Two decades later a frequent visitor to Klopstock's grave was another poet with a popular touch, Heinrich Heine (1797-1856), who spent a total of around six years on the Elbe. He had his first poems published in the journal *Hamburgs Wächter* (1817) under the pseudonym "Sy Freudhold Riesenharf."

Germany's leading dramatist of the Enlightenment, Gotthold Ephraim Lessing (1729-81), may have only lived three years in the city, but in that time he ran an ambitious National Theater on Gänsemarkt, staged the première of *Minna von Barnhelm*, and wrote his influential *Hamburgische Dramaturgie*. When the theater failed for lack of finance he moved to a librarian's post in Wolfenbüttel, but he wished he could have stayed longer. The young theater director Friedrich Ludwig Schröder (1744-1816) followed in Lessing's footsteps and became the first man to introduce performances of Shakespeare anywhere in German-speaking Europe, even if he did have to add happy endings to *Hamlet* and *Othello* to make them acceptable to a Hamburg audience. If all this seems a little too masculine, one could also mention Elise Reimarus (1735-1805), "the Muse of Hamburg," who was a prolific author of children's literature as well as the hostess of a lively literary salon.

Hamburg's historic contribution to the visual arts might appear more modest, but two of the most important German painters of the late medieval period—Master Bertram (*c.*1345-*c.*1415) and Master Francke (*c.*1380-*c.*1440)—both worked in the city, and a culture of art collecting and dealing had become well established by the seventeenth century at the latest. In 1817 the city became home to Germany's first public *Kunstverein* (art association), whose maiden exhibition highlighted the work of the Romantic artists Caspar David Friedrich (1774-1840) and Philipp Otto Runge (1777-1810). The latter had first come to Hamburg as an apprentice and, after studying in Copenhagen, returned to live in the city. As well as his own mystical and richly allegorical paintings, Runge left an important body of theoretical work for German Romanticism. To this day Hamburg's Kunsthalle (art gallery), which opened in 1869 on Glockengiesserwall, owns many fine examples of both artists' work, along with Bertram's "Grabow Altarpiece" (from Hamburg's St. Peter's church) and parts of Francke's "St. Thomas of Canterbury Altarpiece."

The jewel in the crown of Hamburg's cultural life in the late eighteenth and nineteenth centuries, however, was the Patriotic Society: a "society for the advancement of the arts and useful trades" founded in 1765 (although dating back in an earlier incarnation to 1724). In this usage, to be a "patriot" meant simply to be a "friend of the city," and included those—such as Jews—who did not yet enjoy full civic rights. The society, whose motto was *Emolumento publico* ("for the public good"), was a vital conduit for Enlightenment ideas in the city, and its membership included not only architects and scientists, but merchants and traders too. Its contribution to the development of civil society in Hamburg was huge: the city's first lightning conductor (1775), poor relief scheme (1778), savings bank (1778), public baths (1792) and post box (1858) were just some of its achievements. Its members were also instrumental in establishing the Art Association, the Museum of Arts and Crafts, the College of Visual Arts, and the College of Applied Sciences. The Patriotic Society was the first organization of its kind anywhere in the German lands, and offers compelling evidence that a cultural infrastructure did develop in Hamburg, despite the absence of royal patronage. Writing in 1789, the Danish poet Jens Immanuel Baggesen (1765-1826) observed that while Hamburg was no temple of the muses, it was a guesthouse in which they sometimes lodged. The city was, he concluded, "after Rome and Paris perhaps the most interesting in Europe."

Chapter One
A Brief History of Hamburg

Although signs of human habitation have been found in neighboring Holstein dating back to the Stone Age, there is no reference to a settlement called "Hammaburg" until the ninth century AD. Archaeological evidence points to the existence of a Saxon trading post some two centuries before this, but it may only have been occupied on a seasonal basis. It is known that in the early ninth century the army of the Holy Roman Emperor Charlemagne ventured further north than ever before, and established a permanent settlement in the Hamburg area in the year 808. Some histories of the city describe this Carolingian fort, with its palisades and ditches, in considerable detail. It stood, it is suggested, on what would later become the site of the Gothic cathedral: a ridge of slightly higher land overlooking the confluence of the Alster and Bille rivers. Yet much of this remains conjecture. In 2006 archaeologists undertook a major dig of the Domplatz ("Cathedral Square," just south of the Petrikirche, or St. Peter's Church), confident of unearthing the city's earliest remains, but apart from the crypt of the former cathedral remarkably little was found. This does not necessarily mean that Hammaburg was located elsewhere—wooden structures from the ninth century seldom leave many traces—but one should be wary of all too colorful descriptions.

The first documented reference to Hammaburg (*Ham* being an Old Saxon term for "land on riverbank" or "marshland"; and *Burg* meaning castle or fortress) comes in the Latin manuscript *Vita Anskari*, written by the theologian Rimbert (*c.*830-88). It tells how, in the year 831, a Benedictine monk called Ansgar from the monastery at Corvey was sent north by Emperor Ludwig the Pious to become the first Bishop of Hammaburg, with a missionary role to convert the heathen peoples of Jutland and Scandinavia. Just one year later Pope Gregory IV raised Ansgar to the status of an archbishop. Ansgar oversaw the building of a wooden chapel dedicated to the Holy Mother, but his time in Hamburg ended abruptly when the settlement was ransacked and burned to the ground by Viking raiders in 845. He managed to flee to Bremen, from where he continued his mis-

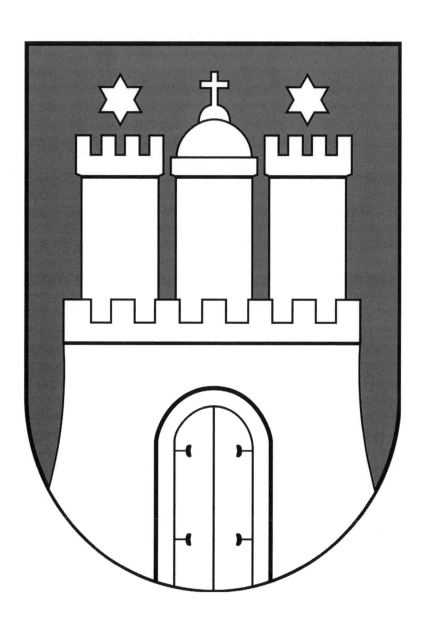

The city's coat of arms, unchanged since the thirteenth century

sionary activities until his death. He was succeeded as Archbishop of Hamburg-Bremen by Rimbert, his former student.

Ecclesiastical documents record one other event which is of interest for the early history of Hamburg. In 965 Pope Benedict V was deposed by the power-hungry Holy Roman Emperor Otto, who banished him to Hammaburg. Later he was beatified and his bones returned to Rome (999). An empty tomb found during the 2006 dig is believed to have been his. More interesting, however, is what the episode says about Hammaburg's status in the tenth century. Hermann Hipp suggests it tells us two things: first, that the settlement was considered to be at the end of the world; but also that it was big enough to accommodate a person of some importance.

The tenth and eleventh centuries saw almost permanent conflict between the area's secular rulers, the Church and outside raiding parties. The wooden Carolingian fort was not immediately replaced, but in the course of the eleventh century three substantial stone structures were erected: a fortified tower house, built as a residence for the Archbishop Bezelin Alebrand (*c.*1035); the "Alster castle," on the site of the present Rathausmarkt (*c.*1040); and the "new castle," close to today's Nikolaibrücke (*c.*1060). The Hamburg coat of arms, which was first adopted in 1241 and remains largely unaltered today, depicts a stylized version of these three castle towers and a city gate. They are presented in white against a red background, with a cross over the central tower and a white star over each of the flanking towers. In the eleventh century, however, even the presence of three castles and a defensive barrier (the "heathen wall") could not prevent frequent raids on the settlement, and in 1072 another archbishop had to flee to Bremen. Although cathedrals continued to be built—including the first stone structure around the middle of the eleventh century—it was Bremen which became the archbishop's permanent residence. Hamburg would not again be the seat of a Catholic archbishop until 1995.

Between the eleventh and thirteenth centuries Hamburg began to develop into a proper medieval town, with a population of around 4,000, weekly markets, craft and trade guilds (known in Hamburg as *Ämter*) and several churches. It boasted a harbor, two water mills and a network of dykes to prevent flooding. It also gained its first hospitals, both of which were located outside the city gates: a leprosy hospital to the east in St. Georg (1220) and the Holy Ghost Hospital to the west (1247). For most of this period the rulers of Holstein (and hence of Hamburg) were the Saxon Counts of Schauenburg, although for a short time during the early thirteenth century it fell under the control of the Danish crown. The biggest Schauenburg contribution to Hamburg's history was undoubtedly made by Count Adolf III, who in 1188 launched a plan for a separate Neustadt (new town) on the western side of the Alsterfleet canal, on the site of the ruined "new" castle. To attract merchants and craftsmen he offered a range of financial incentives, including freedom from duties anywhere under his jurisdiction. The plan took off and soon the Neustadt formed its own parish centered on the Nikolaikirche (St. Nicholas' Church). Despite this, however, Adolf III was not well liked in Hamburg, and there were already indications of the city's growing independence from princely rule: the adoption of its own coat of arms was one sign; the banning of the Counts of Schauenburg from owning land in the town was another; but perhaps the clearest sign yet of the town's growing autonomy was the introduction of a written civil and criminal law code, naming the Hamburg *Rat* (Council) and not the ruler of Holstein as the supreme legal authority (1270).

AN HISTORIC FORGERY

The principal source of Hamburg's self-confidence was the prosperity of its merchants, who were prepared to go to great lengths to protect their interests. Nowhere was this more apparent than in the acquisition and maintenance of Hamburg's precious free port status. For centuries, the city's chroniclers have told how Count Adolf III sought an audience with the Holy Roman Emperor Friedrich Barbarossa, while both men were setting out on a crusade to the Holy Land in 1189. Adolf requested Barbarossa's support for the new town project, and he was rewarded with a string of promises: that Hamburg citizens were to be spared imperial military service; that they were free to fish anywhere on the Lower Elbe; and above all, that they were free to trade without tolls and custom duties between the city and the sea. The emperor's *Freibrief* (license) subsequently became an almost sacred document for Hamburg: the basis on which its long tradition as a free port rested. It was the focus of elaborate 800th anniversary celebrations in 1989, and it is still marked for three days every May by the city's *Hafengeburtstag* ("harbor birthday") fair.

It has been known since 1907, however, that the charter in the city's archives, dated May 7, 1189, is a forgery. Historians today believe that the document was secretly commissioned by the Council in the thirteenth century, long after Barbarossa had drowned in the Anatolian River Saleph on the 1189 crusade. The exact date of the forgery is, however, disputed: Bracker (1989), Plagemann (1995) and Krieger (2006) all put it "around 1225," but it was more likely to have been around 1260, when, as Schnee (2003) notes, there was both an immediate need for a document (to resolve a legal dispute with a Bremen archbishop who was blockading the Elbe at Stade) and evidence of extraordinary payments totaling over 10,000 Marks in silver (1259). With the help of the forgery Hamburg finally won its legal case in 1265. Of course, we will never know for sure whether the Hohenstaufen emperor actually made his promises or not, but Hamburg's leaders clearly decided that the rights in question were simply too valuable to lose for the sake of a piece of paper.

The crusade of 1189 was to have a second indirect impact on the city's fortunes. Barbarossa's death prompted his enemy, the Guelph duke known as Henry the Lion, to return from exile in England. Although Hamburg's leaders were wary of the duke, whom they rightly suspected of having designs on the city himself, they knew he needed allies. Hamburg offered its support to Henry, who in return not only confirmed the rights granted by Barbarossa, but extended them to include much of the Upper Elbe too. This opened up a large new hinterland to the east: Magdeburg, Dessau, Dresden, and beyond. Events at the end of the twelfth century then moved quickly: Count Adolf III returned from the Holy Land to defeat Henry the Lion in 1192, but was himself defeated by the Danish King Knut IV in 1201, bringing a temporary end to Schauenburg rule. Following the Danish interregnum it was restored in 1227, but thereafter the counts had little appetite for intervening in Hamburg's affairs.

Whatever the legal or moral status of the "rights" extracted by Hamburg from two of Germany's most powerful rulers in the late twelfth century, they were to have a hugely beneficial impact on the city's fortunes. Hamburg's harbor became an important *entrepôt* for textiles from Flanders and dairy products from Holland; from the south came wine and ceramics; and from the east furs, grain, honey and wax. The city's proximity to the Baltic port of Lübeck meant it could also profit from traffic between the Baltic and the North Seas. Indeed, in 1230 Hamburg signed an alliance with Lübeck which sought to guarantee the trade route between the two cities (a notorious spot for highwaymen) and to introduce a common currency. This was the start of Hamburg's gradual integration into the Hanseatic League, which was completed a century later. The city was still Lübeck's junior partner in the League, which united some 170 towns and cities, as well as groups of individual traders. Yet Hamburg was already the third biggest in terms of population after Lübeck and Cologne, and with the "discovery" of America its more westerly orientation would eventually enable it to surpass its Baltic neighbor.

Within the city itself, the population was becoming more diverse. Krieger (2006) notes that in 1376 it included 84 merchants from Flanders, 40 from Lübeck, and 35 from England; it also included trades such as weavers, hatters, cobblers, tanners, saddlers, smiths and more than 450 brewers, who were not subject to the same guild restrictions as the other trades. Hamburg's beer was already being exported to Holland, Denmark and England. Indeed, the city was often referred to as the "brewery of the Hansa." The large presence of Dutch, Flemish and English speakers in the city was to have a lasting effect on the local accent and vocabulary. The total population, which had doubled from 5,000 to 10,000 in the first half of the fourteenth century, was cut in half by the impact of the 1350 Black Death, but rose again to around 16,000 in 1450. It was around this time, in 1465, that Hamburg became a fully walled city for the first time, but the city fathers also began to acquire territories some distance from the city: at the mouth of the Elbe (the later Cuxhaven), for instance, or further up river at Geesthacht, which it administered jointly with Lübeck.

A FREE CITY?

In 1459 the last of the Schauenburg line, Adolf VIII, died. The following year the estates of Schleswig and Holstein gathered to elect their new ruler and chose King Christian I of Denmark. This proved problematic for Hamburg as the king wanted to play a more active role in the city's affairs than that to which Hamburg had grown accustomed. For the next three centuries the question of whether Hamburg was just a large town in Holstein (as the Danish crown argued), or a Free Imperial City of the Holy Roman Empire (as the city fathers hoped), failed to find a satisfactory resolution. If it was the latter, then Hamburg would not be subject to any ruler except the Holy Roman Emperor himself, but the greatest legal minds of the day were divided on the issue. Historical precedent did not offer any clear answers either, since Hamburg had on occasion been treated as a free city—by being invited to attend the imperial *Reichstag* (diet) in 1472, for instance—and sometimes not.

At the Augsburg diet in 1510, the Holy Roman Emperor Maximilian I decreed that Hamburg should be regarded as a Free Imperial City. At the time this decision was not welcomed by the city fathers with quite the enthusiasm that one might imagine—being "free" brought with it substantial financial obligations to the emperor, particularly in time of war—but when Danish claims on the city were reasserted in the early seventeenth century, Hamburg was happy to have its status confirmed in 1618. By now the Hanseatic League was in decline, but Hamburg was economically and politically strong enough to survive its demise. The city possessed a stock market (1558), a central bank (1619) and its own currency—the Mark Banco and Mark Courant (sixteen Schillings to the Mark; twelve Pfennigs to the Schilling)—which remained legal tender until 1873. It was also the first city in Europe, from 1676, to have a public system of fire insurance. Above all, it was the city's free port and free city status which were seen as the dual guarantee of its prosperity. The two elements have been central to the city's identity ever since.

In the early seventeenth century (1615-26) the Dutch military engineer Johann van Valckenburgh was entrusted with the task of designing a new set of fortifications for the expanding city, whose population rose from about 25,000 in the middle of the sixteenth century to 78,000 a century later. In line with the military orthodoxy of the time, Valckenburgh proposed neither a circular nor an orthogonal set of defenses, but a more complex geometric pattern, resembling a giant star. His plan allowed for a doubling of the city's area (to about 920 acres), guarded behind a wall, embankments, ditches and moats. There were 21 bastions and 263 canons. In W. G. Sebald's novel *Austerlitz* (2001) the mysterious character of the same name observes:

> No one today… has the faintest idea of the boundless amount of theoretical writings on the building of fortifications, of the fantastic nature of the geometric, trigonometric and logistical calculations they record, of the inflated excesses of the professional vocabulary of fortification and siegecraft, no one now understands its simplest terms, escarpe and courtine, faussebraie, réduit and glacis, yet even from our present stand-

point we can see that towards the end of the seventeenth century the star-shaped dodecagon behind trenches had finally crystallized, out of the various available systems, as the preferred ground-plan: a kind of ideal typical pattern derived from the Golden Section... In the practice of warfare, however, the star-shaped fortresses which were being built and improved everywhere during the eighteenth century did not answer their purpose, for intent as everyone was on that pattern, it had been forgotten that the largest fortifications will naturally attract the largest enemy forces, and the more you entrench yourself the more you must remain on the defensive.

In Hamburg's case, however, the defenses did at least protect the city from the devastating effects of the Thirty Years War (1618-48), in which it remained neutral. Valckenburgh's handiwork was put to the test again in 1686 when the city and its five main gates—Dammtor, Steintor, Deichtor, Millerntor and Haftentor—were besieged by the Danes. Although the gates are now long gone, the neoclassical Millerntor guardhouse (1819) still stands, and the names of other gates live on in today's street names. Valckenburgh's fortifications are also evoked by streets with names such as Sternschanze and Glacischaussee. As for the Danes, it was not until the Gottorp Treaty of 1786 that they finally recognized Hamburg's status as a free city. The neighboring Holstein town of Altona—nowadays part of Hamburg—remained in Danish hands from 1640 until 1864, and grew from a small fishing village to become the Danish crown's third biggest city.

Early modern Hamburg possessed a strong sense of civic morality and identity. Ostentatious displays of wealth were regarded as incompatible with the city's republican ideals, which emphasized the *Gemeingeist* (communal spirit) and the common good over the rights of the individual. These were the values that underpinned the founding of the progressive Patriotic Society in 1765 (see Introduction). In the late eighteenth century educated Hamburgers continued to argue that their version of communitarian republicanism was superior to the revolutionary models emanating from America or France. Indeed, both Matthias Wegner (1999) and Katherine Aaslestad (2005) portray this as a "golden age," ended only by the French occupation of the city in 1806, and the spread of laissez-faire individualism in the nineteenth century. In truth, however, there were

Map of Hamburg, 1730

signs of a shift in attitudes some time earlier: a burgeoning "culture of display," exemplified by banquets, balls and conspicuous consumption; and a growing reluctance among the elite to support the city's poor. As the title of a book by Mary Lindemann (1990) suggests, eighteenth-century Hamburg was already a city of both "patriots and paupers."

In 1750 the youngest of the city's parish churches, St. Michael's in the Neustadt, was hit by a lightning bolt and burned to the ground. Its successor, constructed between 1751 and 1762 to designs by Johann Leonhard Prey and Ernst Georg Sonnin, was to become one of the city's most loved landmarks. With its distinctive 433-foot copper-clad tower and elevated position overlooking the Elbe, the "Michel" was a welcome sight for any returning traveler, though its opulent white and gold late Baroque interior must have struck many Lutherans as unnecessarily florid. When he died in 1788 C. P. E. Bach was buried in the church's crypt, alongside his godfather and fellow composer Georg Philipp Telemann.

In 1798 the poet and radical thinker Samuel Taylor Coleridge (1772-1834) spent a few days on the Elbe. He did not comment on the Michel but was impressed by the "vast ramparts of the city," which were like "huge green cushions, one rising above the other, with trees growing in the interspaces, pledges and symbols of a long peace." As for the citizens of the city, "Pipes and boots are the first universal characteristic of the male Hamburgers that would strike the eye of a raw traveller," he noted. The reason why all Hamburg men wore boots soon became apparent:

> The streets narrow; to my English nose sufficiently offensive, and explaining at first sight the universal use of boots; without any appropriate path for the foot-passengers; the gable ends of the houses all towards the street, some in the ordinary triangular form, and entire, as the botanists say, but the greater number notched and scalloped with more than Chinese grotesqueness. Above all, I was struck by the profusion of windows, so large and so many, that the houses look all glass... a conflagration would, I fear, be the previous requisite to the production of any architectural beauty in Hamburg: for verily it is a filthy town. I moved on and crossed a multitude of ugly bridges, with huge black deformities of water wheels close by them. The water intersects the city everywhere, and would have furnished to the genius of Italy the capabilities of all that is most beautiful and magnificent in architecture. It

might have been the rival of Venice, and it is huddle and ugliness, stench and stagnation.

Most visitors commented on Hamburg's "stench," a mixture of ship's tar, whale oil (from the street lamps), horse droppings, roast beef and rotting fish. Yet the stench and stagnation grew much worse in 1801, when the city was briefly occupied by the Danish army; and then in November 1806, when Napoleon's armies moved in. For once Hamburg's efforts to remain neutral, including a hasty attempt to dismantle its fortifications, had failed. Any resistance from its miniature defense force—a citizens' militia consisting of just 1,800 infantrymen, 100 artillerymen, and 85 dragoons—would clearly have been futile. The occupying army did not only consist of Frenchmen, of course: in 1807-8 some 15,000 Spaniards were quartered in the city. In the 1790s Hamburg had been an economic beneficiary of the revolutionary wars, but now the Elbe was blockaded as part of Napoleon's Continental System, and Hamburg suffered particularly from the loss of trade with Britain. When many of the city's merchants tried to circumvent the blockade by smuggling, 300 extra customs officials were sent to the city. They had only limited success—not least because of widespread corruption—and in December 1810 Napoleon decided that the city should be fully incorporated into the French Empire as the Département des Bouches de l'Elbe. This came into force on January 1, 1811 and "Hambourg" remained French until May 30, 1814.

The so-called *Franzosenzeit* under Marshall Davout is regarded as one of the lowest points in the city's history, less because of any sense of national humiliation—German nationalism remained the sole preserve of a few intellectuals at this time—but because the city was prevented from doing what it did best. Some 300 ships sat idle in the harbor, and large quantities of confiscated British produce were destroyed by the French in giant bonfires. To make matters worse, in 1813 when it looked as if the Russian winter had brought Napoleon's reign to an end, Hamburg was then occupied by Russian Cossacks. As we know, however, the French emperor was able to stage a remarkable comeback and the city was taken by his forces for a second time. Hamburg had to meet the crippling costs involved in maintaining a garrison of around 42,000 men, of whom 8,000 were wounded. To make matters worse, Napoleon levied a fine of 25 million francs on the city for having displayed "disloyalty": they should not, he suggested, have let the Russians in. As food supplies dwindled in the winter of 1813-14, Napoleon's soldiers took priority, and many Hamburg citizens fled the city or died of malnutrition. The troops fared little better: around 10,000 of Napoleon's men were buried in mass graves at St. Georg, where Hamburg's main railway station now stands.

Following Napoleon's final defeat at Waterloo, Hamburg became part of the new German Confederation agreed at the Congress of Vienna (1814-15), though this only served to strengthen the city's sense of independence. Like many other European states in the restoration era, Hamburg embarked on an extensive program of nation-building measures, acquiring a "national" anthem ("City of Hamburg on the banks of the Elbe," by Albert Gottlieb Methfessel, 1829), "national" monuments and a female patron saint. Where Great Britain had Britannia, and France had Marianne, Hamburg had Hammonia. She was to become an important part of the city's iconography in the nineteenth century. The city's determination to survive and prosper as an independent city-state in the "age of nations" was also reflected in the new, self-proclaimed title it first used in 1815, and which it adopted officially from 1819 onwards: the "Free and Hanseatic City of Hamburg." The regularity with which the word "free" appears in the city's rhetoric should not, however, be misunderstood: civil and political rights were very limited until the mid-nineteenth century, and democracy did not arrive until after the First World War.

The origins of Hamburg's system of government date back to the thirteenth century. In 1270 Jordan von Boitzenburg compiled the *Ordeelbook*, which codified civil, criminal and procedural law in the city. It was the first such document ever written in the German language. Real power resided with the twenty-man *Rat* (Council), where appointments were determined by a small number of merchant families, and lasted for life. The Council was executive, legislature and supreme court in one. Not surprisingly, dissatisfaction amongst the wider citizenry (*Bürgerschaft*) surfaced periodically. Following riots in 1410 the city gained its first proper constitution, the *Rezess* (an archaic term meaning written settlement or agreement). After a series of violent uprisings, and outside mediation by the Dutch and English envoys, a new constitution (*Hauptrezess*) was more or less imposed on the city by the Holy Roman Emperor in 1712.

The *Hauptrezess* stated that power did not rest with the Council alone, but should be exercised jointly with the propertied citizenry, who participated in the legislative process via *Konvente* (assemblies of qualified citizens). At this time, however, the citizenry comprised less than 1 percent of the population: debt-free male property owners who resided within the city walls; had paid a substantial citizenship fee; and had sworn a citizens' oath as Lutherans. It was not until the constitution of 1860 that they were granted an elected parliament or Citizens' Assembly, also known as the *Bürgerschaft*. Thereafter the electoral system remained subject to regular and blatant jerrymandering in a desperate attempt to halt the rise of socialism in the city. As a result the first truly democratic assembly elections did not occur until 1919, and promptly ceased again in 1933, before recommencing after the Second World War.

The city's reputation for religious tolerance had its limits too. The Reformation formally arrived in Hamburg in 1529, but criticism of the Church had been growing for decades. While the city was no longer the seat of an archbishop, it did have a cathedral, twelve churches, two monasteries, two convents, around 170 altars and 350 priests. No doubt there were sincere and pious men among them, but there was also considerable corruption, both financial and moral. In 1524 Martin Luther's friend Johannes Bugenhagen had been turned down for the pastor's post at the city's main church, St. Nicholas', but by 1529 the majority of the city's population and the Council had been won over by the Reformer's message. Bugenhagen was invited back to draw up a new set of religious ordinances for the city. Services were henceforth to be in German rather than Latin; the monasteries and convents would be closed; and of course the authority of the pope was no longer recognized. In fact, Bugenhagen's *Kirchenordnung* affected much more than just matters of faith, and not only because church parishes were an important part of the city's administration, responsible for welfare, education and even the defense of the city walls. The law, which was passed unanimously and remained in place until 1870, united the Lutheran Church and the Hamburg state. From now on, the Church would have a say in the passage of legislation, and only Lutherans could become full citizens of Hamburg. Although large numbers of immigrants were subsequently allowed to settle in the city, including some escaping from religious persecution elsewhere in Europe (Sephardic Jews from Spain and Portugal, French Huguenots, Calvinists from the Spanish Netherlands), they could only practice their religions within the privacy of their own homes, and could not become citizens of Hamburg without first converting.

It would be a mistake to assume that the next 300 years were marked by the gradual growth of religious freedom. Rather, phases of comparative tolerance and intolerance alternated, usually in line with the city's fluctuating economic fortunes. So, for example, a Jewish prayer room was permitted for the first time in 1628, but 21 years later pressure from the citizenry led to the expulsion of all the city's Jews. Most moved to nearby Altona, and many later returned. By 1800 Hamburg had the largest Jewish population in the Holy Roman Empire, totaling around 6,500, but they continued to be excluded from citizenship. It was not until 1818 that Catholics and other Christian confessions were able to become members of the Council; Jews had to wait until 1860.

Just as Lutheran Hamburg was slow to relax its grip on matters of conscience, so the physical growth of the city was constrained by Valckenburgh's seventeenth-century corset. Admittedly, the city's remaining fortifications were removed in the 1820s, but at four of the city's five main gates uniformed watchmen continued to control the passage of people and goods right up to 1860. While suburbs such as St. Georg and St. Pauli were expanding at a rapid rate—the city's population rose from 130,000 in 1800 to 170,000 in 1840—the medieval core of the city remained horribly cramped. Moreover, in 1840 it still possessed neither a main water supply nor a sewage system. The last outbreak of plague may have been in 1715, but other killer epidemics such as chickenpox spread quickly through the narrow medieval streets, and cholera was a regular visitor right up to the end of the century (in 1822, 1831-2, 1848, 1859, 1866, 1873 and 1892). The 1892 epidemic alone cost 8,600 lives. The predominantly wooden framework of most of the city's buildings also meant that fire was a permanent risk. In many respects, therefore, the Great Fire of 1842— which caused 70,000 people to flee and left 20,000 homeless—was a disaster waiting to happen, but it presented the city with some valuable opportunities too (see Chapter Four).

As in many parts of Europe, the 1840s were a decade of increasing politicization in Hamburg, and the events of 1842 only added to the growing clamor for change. Although 1848 did not bring full-scale revolution, Hamburg's leaders were sufficiently concerned to announce elections for a constituent assembly. Its task would be to replace the *Hauptrezess* of 1712 with a more modern constitution. In the event its recommendations were too progressive for the city fathers, and the new constitution which finally came into effect in 1860 retained many features of Hamburg's earlier system of government. Nevertheless there were some significant reforms. While there was no formal separation of Church and State, the Church did lose its role in the legislative process, and citizenship was now open to men of any faith. The Council, which became known as the *Senat* (Senate), lost its judicial role and became a little more like a modern executive, elected by the Citizens' Assembly. Somewhat anachronistically, however, senators continued to be elected for life. "The problem," Richard Evans (1987) observed, "was not so much that the Senators were old; it was more that most of them, whatever their age, were incompetent, because incompetent Senators were never removed from office."

Evans characterizes Hamburg's governance in the nineteenth century as "amateurish," and certainly compared to neighboring Prussia—which was effectively governed by a full-time professional bureaucracy—it was a ramshackle operation. Even so, a weak executive did not lead to paralysis or stasis on the Elbe. On the contrary, the 1860s witnessed other important changes too: the removal of the remaining city gates (1860-61); the lifting of medieval guild restrictions on the city's trades (1865); the abolition of the citizens' militia (1868); and the opening of Hamburg's first man-made dock, the 3,300-foot long Sandtorhafen (1866), with its 19 steam cranes. For, despite its domestic difficulties, Hamburg's growth as a port had continued unabated through the middle decades of the nineteenth century.

It was now considered the leading port on the European mainland, second only to London in the volume of its trade. Trade with Britain and America was particularly important, though "colonial goods" from Africa and Asia also played an increasingly significant role. The quantity of imports and exports going through the harbor doubled between 1846 and 1850 alone. By the 1850s nearly 500 ships were sailing under the Hamburg flag, and the "Free and Hanseatic City" had its own consulates in 172 countries (even today, Hamburg maintains a network of overseas consulates, and reciprocates by hosting more foreign consulates than any city except New York and Hong Kong). The port added a further string to its bow in the mid-nineteenth century in the form of transatlantic passenger traffic. The migration of millions of Central Europeans to the New World was a lucrative business for two Hamburg shipping businesses in particular: the Sloman line, founded by the Norfolk-born Robert Miles Sloman (1783-1867); and the Hamburg-American-Packet-Transport-Company (HAPAG), which was founded in 1847 and began a regular passenger service to New York a year later (see Chapter Seven).

HAMBURG'S LOSS OF INDEPENDENCE

One reason for the growth of emigration in the 1860s was the absence of peace in much of Central Europe. The three wars fought between 1864 and 1870, which would later (and rather misleadingly) become known as the Wars of German Unification, did not leave Hamburg untouched. The victory of Prussia and Austria against Denmark in 1864 meant that Holstein returned to "German" hands. The two leading German states initially agreed to administer the territory jointly, but in 1866 war broke out between them. Hamburg was left in a precarious position. Its first instinct, in line with Hanseatic tradition, was to remain neutral, but when it became clear that this would almost certainly mean Prussian occupation and maybe a loss of free-city status too, Hamburg joined Lübeck and Bremen on Prussia's side. In fact, the "Six Weeks War" was over before the Hamburg battalions even reached the front, but Prussia's rapid victory led to its annexation not only of Holstein but of Hanover too.

Now surrounded by Prussian territories, Hamburg had little option but to join Bismarck's North German Confederation in 1867. It was clear to the city fathers, however, that this would mean a considerable loss of independence: Hamburg would no longer be able to pursue an independent foreign policy; its citizens' militia would be consigned to the history books; and its merchant fleet would have to lower the three-tower flag for the last time. On the other hand, for the growing number of German nationalists in the city, Prussia's victories brought the dream of a new German Empire one step closer. When that day arrived—sooner than anyone had expected—in 1871, the founding of the *Kaiserreich* (Empire) was greeted enthusiastically in the city, and was marked by carefully choreographed celebrations in front of the town hall.

From now on, Hamburg's fortunes would depend increasingly on decisions taken in landlocked Berlin, and its male citizens would have to serve in the Prussian army, albeit in designated "Hanseatic" regiments. As one of three city-states in the empire, it did retain a degree of sovereignty over matters such as education, policing and income tax, and it was able to negotiate one other important concession: despite joining the German Empire, it did not yet have to become a member of the German *Zollverein* (Customs Union), which meant that the city was effectively a kind of giant duty-free shop. In the end it was able to remain a free port for a further 17 years, and when it did finally become part of the German Customs Union in 1888, it was still allowed to retain a small free port area within its harbor (see Chapter Three).

In these years of declining real autonomy, the symbolic trappings of independence became more important than ever. The symbolism of the new town hall was central to this (see Chapter Two), but there were a number of "invented traditions" too. The most eye-catching was the re-introduction of a kind of historical fancy dress, known variously as the *Habit, Ornat* or *Stalt*, for members of the Senate to wear on state occasions. As Evans notes, the new uniform was more ornate than the original, and was "improved" by the addition of a sword. In Thomas Mann's classic novel *The Magic Mountain* (1924), Hans Castorp's grandfather served as a Hamburg senator:

> He wore the black coat, cut full like a robe, more than knee-length, with a wide trimming of fur all round the edge; the upper sleeves were wide and puffed and fur-trimmed too, while from beneath them came the narrow undersleeves of plain cloth, then lace cuffs, which covered the hands to the knuckles. The slender, elderly legs were cased in black silk stockings; the shoes had silver buckles. But about his neck was the broad, starched ruff, pressed down in front and swelling out on the sides, beneath which, for good measure, a fluted jabot came out over the waist-coat. Under his arm he held the old-fashioned, broad-brimmed hat, that tapered to a point at the top.

It was also in these years that the city experienced its most dramatic growth, with the population rising from 300,000 in 1870 to around 700,000 in 1900, and more than one million in 1910. By the 1900s only half the resident population had actually been born in the city. It should also be noted that large parts of the Hamburg conurbation remained under Prussian jurisdiction and were not included in these figures. It was not until after the First World War that plans for a Greater Hamburg, including its suburbs and satellite towns, were developed. The Greater

Hamburg Law of 1937 saw the city incorporate the former Prussian towns of Altona, Wandsbek and Harburg-Wilhelmsburg, together with a number of other communities, but in return it lost its outlying territories of Geesthacht and Cuxhaven to Prussia. Overnight, the city's population rose from 1.19 to 1.68 million. The 1937 borders were kept with the establishment of the Federal Republic of Germany after the Second World War.

Hamburg's spectacular expansion in the imperial era was inevitably accompanied by growing social tensions. Demands for social and political reform were principally articulated through the Social Democratic Party of Germany (SPD) and the free (socialist) trade union movement, both of which developed strongly in the late nineteenth century and would turn Hamburg into a red bastion for much of the twentieth century. Hamburg's free-port status had encouraged many high-quality manufacturers to settle in the harbor area, where they could import raw materials, work them into finished goods and export them again without paying any duties. Jewelry, furniture, medical instruments and many other products were manufactured in this way. Skilled or semi-skilled workers employed in such businesses formed the backbone of the Hamburg labor movement in the nineteenth century, along with more traditional trades such as coopers, turners and cigar-makers. In 1890 there were no fewer than 84 different trade unions active in the city, with around 40,000 members.

It was a comparatively poorly organized group of workers, however, which undertook Hamburg's most high-profile industrial action pre-First World War: an eleven-week strike by more than 16,000 dock workers in 1896-7. British dockers contributed generously to the strike fund, but when Tom Mann of the Federation of Ship, Dock and Riverside Workers arrived in Hamburg to show solidarity with his German counterparts, he was promptly arrested. The strike, which became increasingly bitter and prompted a typically bombastic intervention from Kaiser Wilhelm II, had a profound impact both locally and nationally. Although it ended in a crushing defeat for the dockers—500 were fined or imprisoned for their actions and few retained their jobs—union membership grew rapidly in the years thereafter. Even so, much of Hamburg's working class remained outside the subculture of the organized labor movement, living from occasional casual work and petty crime, which was rife in the slum quarter between the city center and the docks. Karl Marx, who visited the city in 1867 to sign a book contract with the publisher Otto Meissner, referred

to such people as the *Lumpenproletariat*. There is now no trace of the publisher at Bergstrasse 26, but Marx's book went on to become one of the most famous of all time: *Das Kapital*.

One of Hamburg's biggest firms was the Blohm & Voss shipyard, which employed over 13,000 men on the eve of the First World War. In the mid-nineteenth century, HAPAG and Sloman had been happy for their ships to be built on Humberside or the Tyne, but that all changed in the 1880s. By the 1900s, Blohm & Voss were operating the largest floating dock in the world, and were building massive ocean liners for HAPAG which were designed to cross the Atlantic in just six days. The London *Daily News Leader* suggested that the new German liners represented an even greater threat to British supremacy on the high seas than Tirpitz's naval battleships. On May 23, 1912 Kaiser Wilhelm came in person to Hamburg to launch another HAPAG liner, the *Imperator*, built at the Vulkan yard. With the loss of the *Titanic* just a month earlier, the *Imperator* was now the world's largest ship of any type: a twelve-story floating hotel, with a commodore, four captains, 83 lifeboats, and capacity for 4,594 paying guests, not to mention the figurehead of a fearsome bronze eagle protruding from her bow, proudly bearing the HAPAG company motto *Mein Feld ist die Welt* (literally, "my field is the world").

Yet the confident optimism of the May 23 celebrations was soon to fade. On its initial sea trials the ship had barely made it out of the docks before it ran aground on a sandbank near Altona. The ship proved unstable in heavy seas—American wags dubbed it the "Limperator"—and marble had to be stripped out of the First Class bathrooms to lower its center of gravity. When, in 1914, the *Imperator*'s figurehead lost its wings in an Atlantic storm, some saw it as a worrying omen. The outbreak of war just a few months later was to have a devastating effect on Hamburg and its people. With the Royal Navy blockading the German Bight, the city's harbor fell silent. Bread rationing was introduced as early as February 1915, and other foodstuffs soon followed. The size of the rations dwindled steadily and the black market prices soared. Only the rich or the criminal could maintain an adequate diet. The historian Percy Ernst Schramm, who came from a wealthy upper middle-class family, even recalled eating a paste made from Hamburg's much-loved Alster swans. In February 1917 the first food riots took place, with shops plundered in many parts of the city. In addition to the 40,000 citizens of Hamburg who perished in action, many more died at home from the effects of malnutrition, exacerbated by the fact that the British blockade of German ports continued for nearly a year after the supposed end of hostilities.

TURBULENT TIMES

As the events of 1914-18 indicate, the history of Hamburg in the twentieth century cannot be separated from the triumphs, terrors and traumas experienced by Germany as a whole. The Elbe, it is true, continued to flow, and the needs of the port remained paramount for political leaders of all persuasions, but in other respects it was a period characterized by violent change and sudden ruptures. After a largely peaceful revolution in 1918, in which just eight soldiers and two civilians lost their lives, there followed a failed revolution from the left in 1923; the Nazi "seizure of power" in 1933; the deportation of the city's remaining Jews in 1941; the devastation wrought by Allied bombing in 1943; and the arrival of thousands of refugees from the east in 1945.

A mutiny of sailors in the naval ports of Wilhelmshaven and Kiel triggered the German revolutions of November 1918. On November 6, sailors from Kiel occupied Hamburg's main railway station, the Elbe Tunnel and other strategic buildings. A workers' and soldiers' council hastily set up a provisional government for the city under the leadership of the historian and Independent Socialist Heinrich Laufenberg (1872-1932). After initial hesitation on both sides, the existing Senate agreed to cooperate with the provisional government "in the spirit of the new age." Similar events took place in Berlin, Munich and the Reich's other capital cities. As the kings and grand dukes departed, so Germany effectively became more like Hamburg. Few tears were shed for the loss of the Prussian monarchy, for while the Kaiser had always been warmly welcomed on his visits to the city, the monarchy had not been able to put down deep roots on such richly republican soil. Under the Weimar Republic Hamburg remained a city-state with significant autonomy, but still surrounded by the vast land mass of Prussia, which survived the threat of a break-up under Germany's new model constitution.

In Hamburg the first truly democratic Citizens' Assembly, elected by women as well as men, met in March 1919 and approved a new constitution in January 1921. The Senate was henceforth elected directly by the city's parliament. It was controlled between 1919 and 1933 by an alliance of the SPD and the bourgeois German Democratic Party (DDP), although it continued to include notables without party affiliation such as Werner von Melle (1853-1937), the city's first post-war mayor. Hamburg's coalition government, which also enjoyed the support of the center-right German People's Party from 1924 onwards, proved more stable and successful than the national cabinets in Berlin, although it did require the help of General Lettow-Vorbeck's right-wing *Freikorps* to protect it during the so-called *Sülzeunruhen* or "Brawn Disturbances" of June-July 1919, when the discovery that a city firm had used rancid meat in its products led to days of rioting and looting.

In October 1923, the year of Germany's infamous hyper-inflation (when the price of a loaf of bread in Hamburg reached 17 million Marks), an attempt by communists under Ernst Thälmann (1886-1944) to stage a second revolution in the city led to more than 100 deaths, of which 17 were police officers. As a result 1,400 communists were arrested, and relations between social democrats and communists were poisoned irrevocably. In fact, the only beneficiaries were the parties of the right, whose lurid tales of "reds under the bed" now seemed to have some basis in fact (even though Hamburg's 14,000 communists had no realistic prospect of ever achieving power). Larissa Reissner (1895-1926), a young communist from the working-class district of Schiffbek—where the fighting on the barricades had been fiercest—described one woman's experience of the "Hamburg Uprising" in a book first published in 1925:

> On that dreadful day there stood in the forecourt of Schiffbek police station in rows of three, four, or five, lorries loaded with captured workers lying on their backs, heaped on top of each other.
>
> The rebels! They had fought in open battle according to all the rules of honest warfare, pitting life against life with an adversary a hundred times stronger, yet still sparing prisoners and letting the wounded go. After the defeat they were of course treated like hunted ruffians, renegades standing outside the law. The police pounded their feet on those rows of bloody, gasping bodies heaped upon each other. Dying men crushed by their comrades on top lay underneath with faces squashed against the coal-smeared boards while above the *Wachtmeister* (sergeants) of the Reichswehr tugged hair out, and with their rifle butts cracked the napes of the immobilized men who then lost consciousness...

The Hamburg region was hit hard by the stipulations of the Versailles Treaty of 1919: not only were parts of Schleswig lost to Denmark following an enforced plebiscite in 1920, but the confiscation of nearly all Germany's merchant fleet meant that the number of vessels registered in the port fell from 15,073 in 1913 to just 2,234 in 1923. The *Imperator*, for instance, which had spent the entire war at anchor, was commandeered as an American troop ship and then sold to the Cunard line, who renamed it the *Berengaria*. Under the circumstances, it was remarkable how quickly the fortunes of the city's shipping interests recovered. A deal between Mayor Carl Petersen (DDP) and the Prussian Minister President Otto Braun (SPD) brought an end to the centuries-old rivalry between the port of Hamburg and those of its Prussian neighbors in Altona and Harburg. A new joint port authority now had scope to expand Hamburg's port facilities to the south and west. Meanwhile work on the construction of new vessels began, such as the "Ballin Class" liners for HAPAG.

Away from the docks, Hamburg undertook a massive building program of social housing, with vast new estates constructed at Jarrestadt,

Dulsberg and Barmbek-Nord. The city also invested heavily in new schools, hospitals and other public buildings. Hamburg's City Architect Fritz Schumacher exerted a strong influence on the appearance and layout of these new developments (see Chapter Five). An increase in leisure time led to a boom in sport, recreation and the cinema, which had first come to Hamburg in 1900 and now became a truly mass medium. In 1929 the city became proud home to what claimed to be Europe's largest cinema: the UFA Palace on Valentinskamp boasted 2,665 seats and a screen measuring 91 by 42 feet. Many Hamburgers also developed a taste for jazz, swing and other kinds of dance music, as clubs with names like the Schieber and the Bieberdiele opened in St. Pauli and the city center. By the late 1920s even the venerable Alster Pavilion had become a "Temple of Swing." This was the freer, less inhibited Hamburg visited by the young British poet Stephen Spender (1909-95). In his memoir *World within World* Spender recalled his time on the Elbe in 1929 as an exciting if self-indulgent whirl of "everything that was free: sun, water, friendship [and] bodies."

Before the war, the art gallery director Alfred Lichtwark had invited a number of prominent artists to come and paint in the city, including the French Impressionists Pierre Bonnard (1867-1947) and Edouard Vuillard (1868-1940). Now the city began to develop a small but lively artistic avant-garde of its own. The Hamburg Secession, founded in 1919, became a center of Expressionism, with painters like Erich Hartmann (1886-1974), Eduard Bargheer (1901-79) and Karl Kluth (1898-1972), developing a style reminiscent of the Norwegian Edvard Munch.

It would be a mistake, however, to take the term "the Golden Twenties" too literally. Unemployment remained a problem throughout the Weimar period, and only a small proportion of the city's population were able to enjoy the sort of lifestyle experienced by Spender, or appreciate the art of the Secessionists. Dissatisfaction with the Weimar "system" was growing well before the Wall Street Crash of October 1929. The fact that three members of the NSDAP (Nazi Party) were elected to the Citizens' Assembly for the first time in 1928 indicates as much. In fact, nationalist, racist and anti-Semitic groups had enjoyed significant support in the city for several decades. By the autumn of 1931 Hamburg was facing bankruptcy, unable to meet the welfare bill for the city's 35,000 unemployed. By the end of 1932 the total would reach 164,000: 40 percent of the working population. In a feature on "The Unemployed" for the periodical *Die Tat* in 1933, Heinrich Hauser (1901-55) wrote:

> An almost unbroken chain of homeless men extends the whole length of the great Hamburg-Berlin highway. There are so many of them moving in both directions, impelled by the wind or making their way against it, that they could shout a message from Hamburg to Berlin by word of mouth. It is the same scene for the entire two hundred miles, and the same scene repeats itself between Hamburg and Bremen, between Bremen and Kassel… All the highways in Germany over which I traveled this year presented the same aspect.
>
> The only people who shouted and waved at me and ran along beside my automobile hoping for a ride during their journey were the newcomers, the youngsters… but most of the hikers paid no attention to me. They walked separately or in small groups with their eyes on the ground. And they had the queer, stumbling gait of barefoot people, for their shoes were slung over their shoulders. Some of them were guild members—carpenters with embroidered wallets, knee breeches, and broad felt hats; milkmen with striped red shirts, and bricklayers with tall black hats—but they were in a minority. Far more numerous were those to whom one could assign no special profession or craft—unskilled young people for the most part who had been unable to find a place for themselves in any city or town in Germany, and who had never had a job and never expected to have one.

Hamburg's immediate crisis was solved by a bridging loan from the Warburg bank, but the city was unable to repay it and would have been insolvent had the Reich Finance Ministry in Berlin not stepped in. Damaged by such events, as well as by national factors, the SPD lost its status as the largest party in the Citizens' Assembly to the NSDAP in 1932. The Nazis now held 51 out of 160 seats. It is important to remember that even at their height in March 1933 Hitler's party obtained only 38.8 percent of the Hamburg vote at national parliamentary elections, compared to 43.9 percent across Germany as a whole. Nevertheless, with 18 percent of the vote going to the communist KPD, there was clearly little faith in a democratic solution to the crisis. Political battles were now being fought on the streets as well as at the ballot box. One particularly violent confrontation took place in Altona on July 17, 1932 ("Bloody Sunday"), when fighting between Nazis, communists and the police left 18 dead and more than 300 injured.

DARKEST HOURS

The Nazis never achieved an outright majority in Citizens' Assembly elections, but it is unfortunately a myth that the city was more sceptical about National Socialism than other parts of Germany. The first Nazi Senate was appointed by the Citizens' Assembly on March 8, 1933, after the incarceration of all KPD deputies and the intimidation of those from other parties. Of twelve senators, only six were members of the NSDAP; the others were conservatives and technocrats. While this did much to reassure "respectable" Hamburg opinion, it soon became clear that real power lay neither with the Senate nor Mayor Carl Krogmann, but with the NSDAP *Gauleiter* for Hamburg, Karl Kaufmann (1900-69), whom Hitler also appointed *Reichsstatthalter* (regional governor) in 1933. Kaufmann, a Catholic from the Rhineland who had been too young to serve in the Great War but joined a *Freikorps* battalion soon after, had been a Nazi party member since 1922. Although not a leader with many obvious gifts, Kaufmann's loyalty was highly valued by Hitler, and he was able to build up a position of almost absolute power in the city. With all political parties except the NSDAP banned, the Citizens' Assembly met for the last time on June 28, 1933; a powerless Senate existed nominally until 1938.

In March and April 1933 some 1,200 political opponents of the Nazis were arrested. A temporary concentration camp was opened at Wittmoor, a bleak peat bog in the northwest of the city, in April 1933, but this was soon replaced by a larger facility at an existing prison in Fuhlsbüttel, close to Hamburg airport. The camp operated until 1936, but Fuhlsbüttel continued in use as a prison long after that date. Today it serves as a youth detention center. The largest and most notorious concentration camp in the Hamburg area, however, was opened at a brick factory near the village of Neuengamme on the Elbe marshes, to the southeast of the city, in 1938. In total some 106,000 prisoners were held in the camp: communist and social democratic opponents of the regime, gypsies, homosexuals and the supposedly "asocial," together with prisoners from Germany's occupied territories. Around half died from the effects of forced labor—making bricks for prestigious building projects in Hamburg and digging

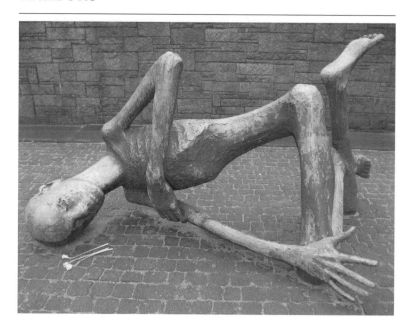

trenches—or from illness and malnutrition. In addition two groups of Russian prisoners of war were gassed there in 1942. Despite this, Neuengamme was largely forgotten in Hamburg after the Second World War, and it was only after protests by former French prisoners and some citizens' action groups in the 1970s that a memorial was erected on the site. Several other monuments have followed, and in 2005 a new exhibition hall was opened, making Neuengamme a somber but rewarding place to visit.

As elsewhere in Germany, Hamburg underwent the process of *Gleichschaltung* ("bringing into line") in 1933-4, affecting every area of public life. There was little apparent resistance, either from within the city administration or from other institutions, such as the university or the Church. The city's left-of-center newspapers were banned, and bourgeois publications such as the *Hamburger Nachrichten* and the *Hamburger Fremdenblatt* were brought under Nazi control. Yet with unemployment remaining high well into the mid-1930s, initial enthusiasm for Hitler was probably not as great as in many other parts of the Reich. In the August 1934 plebiscite called by Hitler to legitimize his uniting of the roles of chancellor and president, 20 percent of electors in the city bravely voted "no," compared to around ten percent nationally. Nazi hostility to the outside world and its desire for self-sufficiency or "autarky" did not bode well for a trading city whose very existence was predicated on the open exchange of goods, people and ideas.

In the end it was another central policy of the National Socialist regime, rearmament, that got the city's economy back on its feet: most of Hitler's new battle fleet was to be built in Hamburg's six shipyards, which meant a quadrupling of shipbuilding jobs in the city in just three years. Germany's biggest ever battleship, the *Bismarck*, was among the vessels built by Blohm & Voss on the Elbe and launched by Hitler on February 13, 1939. Shipbuilding was also stimulated by the *Kraft durch Freude* ("Strength through Joy") program, which promised luxury cruises for loyal German subjects. Although much of this remained in the realm of propaganda, cruises did sail regularly from the city in the late 1930s.

Hitler was a frequent visitor to Hamburg (a total of 33 visits between 1925 and 1939), and was made an "honorary citizen" in 1933. He took little interest in Hamburg's trading fortunes, but was considerably more exercised by the question of the city's future architectural development. In 1937 Hamburg was elevated to the special status of a *Führerstadt*, along with Munich, Berlin, Nuremberg, and the Führer's home town of Linz. Amongst the features planned for the city, which was to be rebranded as the Reich's "Gateway to the World," was a giant suspension bridge to carry a new motorway over the Elbe, an assembly hall to hold 50,000 spectators and a monumental boulevard to run from the Bismarck Monument to Altona town hall, which would be flattened and replaced by a skyscraper to house the Nazi party regional headquarters. High-rise building had hitherto been anathema for right-wing architectural commentators, but Hitler felt Hamburg could be made an exception, since the city had "something American" about it. The architect Konstanty Gutschow (1902-78) was chosen to oversee the project. Few of Gutschow's plans made it off the drawing board, but the foundations for his suspension bridge were laid. The German-Jewish writer Arnold Zweig (1887-1968) described the scene in his sprawling novel *The Axe of Wandsbek* (1947):

> On November 1st, under a tall scaffolding hung with tarpaulins to keep out the rain, the Reichstatthalter dug the first ceremonial spadefuls of

earth from a new foundation for the Elbe suspension bridge, this time in Finkenwerder. The menacing ochrous waters of the Elbe, flecked with white foam, swept past both sides of the island, like a huge, devouring dragon plunging down from the snowy uplands of the Rübezahl Riesengebirge. It was now to be subjected to the will of the Führer, the power of the new Reich. It was true that the hydraulic engineers had only reluctantly accepted the scheme, urging that a substructure of rock was indispensable. But the embodied genius of the Reich, whom Providence had not in vain bestowed upon the German people, would witness the fulfilment of his desire… And so, in his Rhineland accent, the supreme official of the state of Hamburg pronounced the address composed for him by his secretary, and the only unrehearsed item was the storm which cast something of a gloom over the proceedings.

As Frank Bajohr (1995) observes, the belated revival of the city's economy gave Karl Kaufmann a degree of popularity among ordinary Hamburgers, especially as he sometimes seemed to take the little man's side in conflicts with the ever-growing Nazi bureaucracy. Over 150,000 citizens took to the streets on May Day 1939 to celebrate the regime's achievements. Later, Kaufmann's decision to hand the city over to the British in May 1945, rather than to defend it street by street as Hitler and the German military had demanded, meant he was able to portray himself as some kind of unlikely resistance fighter, a "good Nazi" who had done his best for the city. Thus, despite his personal involvement in the deportation of thousands of Jews, Kaufmann was only interned for a short time and never faced a trial. In the 1950s he developed business interests in insurance and chemicals, but also remained active in right-wing politics as a member of the so-called Naumann Circle. For a time he was monitored by the British secret service, but he was ultimately able to live out a comfortable middle-class existence.

Until the early nineteenth century the center of Jewish life in Hamburg had been in the Neustadt, but with the rapid growth of the city a new Jewish quarter developed between Grindelallee and Rothenbaumchaussee, just to the north of the present university campus. In 1933 more than one third of the city's 24,000 Jews lived in this Grindel quarter, or "Little Jerusalem," as it was sometimes known. The philosopher Ernst Cassirer even called it "the new Zion." Many shops here were affected by the national boycott of Jewish businesses staged on April 1, 1933, and by subsequent acts of random brownshirt violence. All Jewish businesses were closed down or "Aryanized" by 1939, including major department store chains such as Tietz, which occupied the Alsterhaus site on Jungfernstieg. There were several large synagogues in the Grindel quarter, including the New Dammtor Synagogue (1895), which was located on the west side of what is today called Allende-Platz, and the main Synagogue on Bornplatz (1906).

Hamburg's main synagogue was a monumental domed structure in the Romanesque style, accommodating some 1,200 worshippers. Like so many German synagogues it was destroyed in November 1938's *Kristallnacht* pogrom, and later replaced by an air-raid bunker. Its outline is commemorated by a cobbled pavement mosaic on Allende-Platz and Joseph-Carlebach-Platz—the latter named after Hamburg's Chief Rabbi who was shot by the Nazis in 1942. Other traces of Jewish life in the area are hard to find, although the Talmud Torah school (1911) on Grindelhof 30, which closed in 1939, has been restored for use by the city's Jewish community. To the surprise of some, this now totals over 3,000 men, women and children, largely due to immigration from the former Soviet Union. Nearby, the building which houses the Hamburg Kammerspiele (studio theater) at Hartungstrasse 9-11 was once a focal point of Jewish cultural life in the city, with a theater troupe continuing to perform right up to 1938.

The Grindel district was home to a number of Jewish writers. One was Heinz Liepmann (1905-66), who lived at Grindelhof 62 until 1933. He wrote the very first exile novel of the Nazi period under the title *Das Vaterland*, published in the Netherlands in late 1933 and much admired by Bertolt Brecht. It tells the story of a fishing boat which leaves Hamburg at Christmas 1932 and does not return until March 28, 1933, having had no contact with the outside world in the intervening months. It is an eminently readable tale, but unfortunately not available in an English translation. Other Hamburg-born Jewish authors include Justin Steinfeld and Robert Muller (1925-98), both of whom left for Britain in the 1930s. The latter's acclaimed novel *The World That Summer* (1959), which was also made into a film, recounts the author's experiences as a half-Jewish boy growing up during the Olympic summer of 1936. Another writer with a Jewish mother and an "Aryan" father, Ralph Giordano (born 1923), stayed in Hamburg and survived by hiding in a cellar for much of the war. His semi-autobiographical family saga *Die Bertinis* (1982) was made into a popular German television series in 1988.

By 1941 two-thirds of Hamburg's Jews had, like Steinfeld and Muller, left the city. Many others had committed suicide. The fate of the persecuted minority that remained—who had already been herded into so-called "Jew houses" to free up accommodation for bombed-out "Aryans"—was sealed in late 1941, when they were summoned to gather on a grassed area between Edmund-Siemers-Allee and Moorweidenstrasse (opposite a freemasons' lodge and next to Hamburg University's main building). In total some 3,200 Jews were transported from here to the ghettoes of Eastern Europe, such as Lodz, Riga or Minsk, and then to the death camps. The last train of Jewish deportees, with 194 people on board, did not leave Dammtor station until February 14, 1945. Since 1989 the Moorweidenstrasse site has been formally known as the "Place of the Jewish Deportees."

All the inhabitants of Hamburg, whether "Aryan" or not, experienced regular bombing raids from May 1940 onwards. Indeed, the numerous giant concrete air-raid bunkers— the biggest is to be found on the Heiligengeistfeld—are the most obvious legacy of the Third Reich still visible today. Even so, some 40,000 people died as a result of Allied bombing in the last week of July 1943 (see Chapter Four). The last bombing raid on Hamburg took place on April 29, 1945, and the city was handed over to British forces four days later. In total Hamburg lost around 70,000 men at the front, 45,000 people in bombing raids and nearly 8,000 murdered Jews. Many others had emigrated or moved into the surrounding countryside to try to escape the Allied bombs.

NEW PEOPLE AND NEW HOPE

The shortfall in Hamburg's population was soon made up by refugees from Germany's eastern territories, who calculated that British occupation would be preferable to that of the Soviets. Even so, life in Hamburg in the immediate post-war period was grim, with housing, food and fuel all in short supply. Around half the city's housing stock had been destroyed, and only one fifth remained undamaged. In order to accommodate the 200,000 refugees who arrived in the city between 1945 and 1949, vast numbers of corrugated tin Nissen huts were erected, although these offered

little protection against the harsh winters of the late 1940s, when temperatures fell as low as -18°F (-28°C) and the Alster froze over for weeks on end. Some 51 million square yards of rubble had to be removed before roads could reopen and new homes be built. Much of modern Hamburg, from the foundations of the widened Ballindamm and the Kennedy-Brücke to the Volkspark, with its HSV football stadium, is built on rubble. It is perhaps appropriate, therefore, that the literature of the immediate post-war period is often referred to as *Trümmerliteratur* ("rubble literature"). One of the prime examples of the genre, *The Man Outside* by Wolfgang Borchert (1921-47), was written in eight days and premièred at the Hamburg Kammerspiele in November 1947, just a day after the author's death. Despite being seriously ill with hepatitis, Borchert had walked nearly 400 miles to return to his native city after escaping from a French prisoner of war convoy. His expressionistic play captures the sense of shock, guilt and desperation felt by many soldiers who returned from the front to find a less than hearty welcome.

Lieutenant-General Sir Evelyn Barker, the British military governor for Hamburg and Schleswig-Holstein, attempted to re-establish democratic rule in the city by appointing respected figures from the pre-Nazi period as mayor and deputy mayor; he then put together a Citizens' Assembly from representatives of the churches, Chamber of Commerce, and trade unions, as well as from four political factions. This body agreed on a provisional constitution, including a British-style "first past the post" electoral system. As a result, the SPD swept to power in the October 1946 elections, winning 83 of the 110 seats and easily defeating the new center-right party, the Christian Democratic Union (CDU), which picked up only 16. As in 1919, however, the SPD sought to build a broad coalition, including three liberals from the new Free Democratic Party (FDP) and one communist in the new twelve-man Senate.

In 1949 Hamburg retained its city-state status in the newly founded Federal Republic of Germany. It opted, however, to adapt its electoral system once again, to reintroduce an element of proportional representation. Hamburg's hopelessly complex electoral law has been subject to numerous "reforms" ever since, including at least four changes since 2000 alone, largely as a result of legal challenges. Currently it operates a "personalized proportional representation" system, with voters casting no fewer than six votes on two separate ballot papers. Although not continually in power, the SPD largely shaped the governance of Hamburg in the second half of the twentieth century, personified by figures such as Max Brauer (1887-1973) and Helmut Schmidt (born 1918), who served as a Hamburg senator before becoming West German chancellor in the 1970s. So far in the twenty-first century things have been very different: the CDU has governed the city since 2001 in coalition with a variety of smaller parties, from the right-wing populist PRO to the Greens.

The 1950s saw a building boom, with new apartment blocks being the main priority. Already by 1953 over 100,000 new apartments had been built. Perhaps the most striking example was the estate of twelve high-rise blocks built between the flattened Grindel quarter and the bourgeois district of Harvestehude, which had been commandeered by the British army. Heavily influenced by Le Corbusier's architectural theories, the eight- and fourteen-story Grindelberg towers (1946-56) were surrounded by parkland, and contained not only apartments but also offices, shops and communal facilities. The Jewish writer and journalist Kurt Hiller (1885-1972), who had escaped Germany in 1934 but returned in the early 1950s, was a prominent resident of block 6, and unlike many such developments the Grindelberg towers have remained a popular residential location.

Hamburg's docks were badly affected by wartime bombing, but most of the damage was done to buildings and cranes rather than the quays themselves. Once the debris of 3,000 wrecked ships had been cleared, the harbor could re-open, even if many of the outgoing goods were in the form of reparations to the Soviet Union. As the Cold War intensified and the Iron Curtain descended across Europe—just thirty miles east of Hamburg—the city lost much of its traditional hinterland. Nevertheless a growth in trade with Western Europe more than compensated for this, and by 1955 the volume of trade had once again reached pre-war levels. Shipbuilding, for the merchant fleet at least, was able to resume in 1951. Like other parts of West Germany, Hamburg experienced a rapid growth in prosperity during the 1950s and 1960s. Whether or not it is accurately characterized as an "economic miracle," the port certainly flourished while its continental rivals struggled. It was helped by an almost total absence of labor disputes, and by heavy investment in the latest technologies. It was, for instance, at the forefront of moves towards "containerization" in the late 1960s (see Chapter Three).

Although best remembered as a time of growing consumer spending—on cars, electrical appliances and travel—the post-war era also saw a revival of Hamburg's cultural life. New journals such as the highbrow weekly *Die Zeit* (1946) and the news magazine *Der Spiegel* (1947) were founded in the city, as were two new orchestras: the NDR Symphony Orchestra (1945) and the Hamburg Symphony Orchestra (1957). The Hamburg State Opera re-opened in a glass-front building on the Dammtorstrasse in 1955, and enjoyed great critical acclaim under the artistic directorship of Rolf Liebermann (1910-99). The Schauspielhaus (Playhouse) remained in its home on Kirchenallee, but also managed to attract a big name as artistic director: the controversial actor-director Gustaf Gründgens (1899-1963), who was able to draw large audiences to his interpretations of the German classics. For those born under Hitler, however, it was the new American classics which began to exert a greater fascination: for instance, the work of James Dean, Elvis Presley and Bill Haley, whose 1958 concert in the city led to a mini-riot. The city authorities' deep suspicion of youth culture would continue for several more decades, as the Beatles were soon to discover (see Chapter Six).

Authoritarian residues notwithstanding, Hamburg became a comfortable, tolerant and attractive place to live in the second half of the twentieth century. Despite structural changes to the city's economy—such as the severe contraction of the shipbuilding industry in the 1980s—the majority of Hamburgers grew accustomed to a high standard of living. While the harbor remained important, Hamburg was no longer solely dependent upon it, with multinational firms such as Airbus, Siemens, Unilever and Holsten making up for some of the thousands of jobs lost in the docks. Hamburg was now an important media city, with major publishing houses, television stations, record companies and film studios. It also developed as a congress and trade fair center, and as a retail destination, with a series of upscale shopping malls built in the heart of the city. Meanwhile the rapid growth of the city's higher education sector brought in thousands of students from other parts of Germany and around the world.

When the travel writer Bill Bryson visited in the early 1990s, he was uncharacteristically generous in his praise: "There was no whiff of arrogance," he wrote, "just a quiet confidence, which was clearly justified by the material wealth… The people had made their city, and even themselves, rich and elegant and handsome through their cleverness and hard work, and they had every right to be arrogant about it, but they were not."

Of course, there were some easy targets for his barbed wit—a shabby hotel room, aging prostitutes and women with unshaven armpits—but, he concluded: "What a perfect life you could lead in Hamburg."

As the new millennium dawned, Hamburg had every reason to feel pleased with itself: after some very dark days in the twentieth century it had succeeded in becoming a cosmopolitan, open and multiracial community, in which churches and synagogues, temples and mosques enjoyed a peaceful coexistence. Such complacency was shattered, however, by the events of September 11, 2001. While the terrorists' targets were on the other side of the Atlantic, their plot had been at least partly hatched on the banks of the Elbe. As news of al-Qaeda's "Hamburg cell" filtered through, many simply could not believe that Mohamed Atta and his fellow conspirators had lived for several years in their community, in a three-bedroom flat at Marienstrasse 54, close to the Technical University in Harburg where Atta studied Town Planning.

In fact, all the key members of the "Hamburg cell" were enrolled on courses in the city: Marwan al-Shehhi, who piloted the second plane into the World Trade Center, came to Germany in 1996 on a grant to study Shipbuilding; Ziad Jarrah, who was at the controls of the United Airlines plane that crashed in Pennsylvania, studied Aerospace Engineering; Ramzi Binalshibh, who failed to obtain a visa to take his pilot's training in the USA, was enrolled on a German language course; and the first man to go on trial in connection with the attacks, Mounir el-Motassadeq, was studying Electrical Engineering. The men, and up to 25 other radical Islamists, were said to have met three or four times a week in the Marienstrasse flat, which has since become an unlikely tourist destination.

The relevance of Hamburg to the "Hamburg cell" has been the subject of much debate in the German media and law courts. Some have argued that as the group was externally financed, coordinated and trained—first in Afghanistan, and then at flight school in the USA—it should not be considered a Hamburg group at all. On the other hand, it seems clear that the core members of the group did undergo their initial radicalization at the Al-Quds Mosque, which opened in 1993 at Steindamm 103 in St. Georg. The reasons for this radicalization appear to have been global rather than local, but this has not prevented a good deal of Hanseatic soul-searching. The episode has certainly led to an increase in racial tensions, but also to efforts to build bridges between the different faith communities. While there are no grounds for complacency, Hamburg today remains more welcoming to outsiders and more tolerant of difference than at any time in its 1,200-year history.

Chapter Two
HISTORY LESSONS IN STONE

Many of the historical episodes and personalities sketched in the previous chapter are commemorated in the Hamburg townscape; most obviously and directly by statues or other monuments, but in other more subtle ways too: in the iconography of a building, for instance; or the name of a park; or even in a particular natural feature. The many "Bismarck Oaks," or the glacial boulder dedicated to the poet Hans Henny Jahnn in Nienstedten, are examples of the latter. Hamburg's monuments range from the very big, like the 111-foot Bismarck Monument in St. Pauli; to the very small, such as the so-called *Stolpersteine*, which measure just 1.5 square inches. It requires no special insight to observe that the biggest gestures are not always the most effective, for while the Bismarck Monument has become virtually invisible, the *Stolpersteine* are truly unavoidable. For those as yet unfamiliar with the concept of *Stolpersteine* (the name literally means "stumbling blocks"), an explanation is in order. In the 1990s the Cologne-based artist Gunter Demnig (born 1947) came up with the brilliantly simple idea of commemorating individual victims of Nazism—whether Jews, gypsies, homosexuals, Jehovah's Witnesses, political opponents or "euthanasia" victims—in front of the houses from which they were taken. The first stones—actually cubes of concrete with a brass plate attached to the top—were planted illegally in Berlin in 1997. The first Hamburg stone was laid in 2002, and so far 2,400 others have followed. Sunk into the pavement, they record the name and dates of each victim. In some residential districts almost every apartment block has a *Stolperstein* outside; some have four or more.

In 2003 the *Stolpersteine* were still opposed by some of Hamburg's conservative politicians, but the project has now gained widespread acceptance, spreading to more than 400 towns across Germany and Central Europe. By providing a specific name and place, they succeed in making the abstract notion of Nazi terror chillingly tangible. There are, of course, other ways of commemorating the victims of oppression, and some will be featured in this chapter, along with a variety of other monuments and me-

morials, including those in the largest municipal cemetery in Europe. We start, however, right at the heart of the city, at the Rathaus or town hall.

THE RATHAUS

Hamburg's present town hall, the sixth in the city's history, was officially opened by Mayor Johannes Versmann on October 26, 1897, having taken eleven years and eleven million Marks to build. The granite and sandstone building sits on 3,997 wooden piles, which have to be kept permanently moist: if the water table sinks, water is pumped into the cellars from the Alster to prevent them from becoming brittle. The Rathaus is located at the city's geographic and symbolic heart, on a plot once occupied by the eleventh-century Alster castle. Between 1290 and 1842, however, Hamburg was governed from a site next to the Trostbrücke—the historic bridge which linked the old and new towns. This medieval town hall—a two-story structure which had been extended and remodeled on several occasions—was blown up in a vain attempt to stop the Great Fire from spreading (although not before the statues which had adorned it since 1649 were safely removed: they were later incorporated into the façade of the Museum of Hamburg History). A provisional town hall was quickly opened in an orphanage on the Admiralitätsstrasse, and that remained the home of the Senate until 1897. A new headquarters for the Patriotic Society was built on the old town hall site in 1845-7; it was in these rooms that the Constituent Assembly met in 1848, and the first elected Citizens' Assembly in 1860.

A new town hall on the present site, adjacent to the Stock Exchange (1839-41), was already envisaged in the first post-fire city plan of 1842. The Rathausmarkt ("Town Hall Square") was christened in 1843. Yet if a consensus was quickly reached on where it should be built, its precise shape and dimensions remained subject to intense debate. An initial design competition was held in 1854-5, and was won by the architect of London's St. Pancras Station, George Gilbert Scott (1811-78). An economic downturn and opposition from local architects meant Scott's design was never likely to be carried out, even if he was already in the process of building Hamburg's Nikolaikirche (1846-74). A second competition followed in 1876, this time only open to German architects, but this did not stop Scott from publishing two designs of his own, one in the Gothic and another in the German Renaissance style. The Frankfurt partnership of

Mylius and Bluntschli emerged victorious from the contest, but once again none of the entries made it off the drawing board. In 1880 a group of ten Hamburg architects—later reduced to seven—under the leadership of Martin Haller (1835-1925) made their own proposal, and this was finally accepted four years later. The plans of the self-styled *Rathausbaumeister-bund* ("League of Town Hall Architects") bore a strong similarity to Scott's 1876 proposals, but at least Hamburg now had a design around which its architects could unite.

Although the idea of "design by committee" is easily ridiculed, the town hall's long and tortuous gestation had its benefits. The picturesque views one obtains of the building from a wide variety of angles are no happy accident, but the result of careful calculation. In town-planning terms, the layout was clearly modeled on St. Mark's Square in Venice, but there is more to it than that. The building's dimensions—it is 364 feet long and its tower 367 feet high—were, for instance, only arrived at after much debate on the precise height and length needed to produce a harmonious design, something that other contemporary projects, such as the new Cathedral in Berlin (1894-1905), often got badly wrong. If the choice of the neo-Renaissance style was in some senses predictable—the savage critical reception of Berlin's new "red Rathaus" (1861-9) had effectively ruled out a brick neo-Gothic design, while the neo-Baroque was deemed too aristocratic for a republic like Hamburg—it also came with risks.

On the one hand, it evoked a golden age of city-states and seemed to fit in with the ethos of the nineteenth century. As the philosopher Wilhelm Dilthey (1833-1911) wrote at the time: "the forms of the Italian and German Renaissance seem very familiar to us, since the cultural conditions of the fifteenth and sixteenth centuries are analogous to our own age: the spirit of the bourgeoisie; the joy of life's pleasures; life's secular splendour, which speak out from the most beautiful works of that time, is our own." Yet as educated Hamburgers knew only too well, city-states like Venice and Florence had subsequently declined. The challenge for the architects, and the politicians who worked with them, was to prevent their hometown from suffering the same fate. It was a challenge made more pressing by its timing: as real power slipped away from Hamburg, the need for symbolic expressions of independence grew stronger.

In part, their answer was to combine typical features of the Italian Renaissance with more specifically North German elements, such as gables in the style of the so-called Weser Renaissance and the copper-clad roof. Hipp (1996) refers to this as "a Faustian synthesis of Nordic and Classical elements." More interesting, however, was their decision to "customize" the building with a host of specifically Hamburg-related details, which give the building a strongly didactic tone; a lesson in both history and civics. With regard to the latter, the building's structure reflects the city-state's 1860 constitution, which had undergone a limited reform in 1879 but continued to leave the majority of adult men without a vote. Under the constitutional principle of *inseparabili nexu coniunctim*, law-making in Hamburg was shared equally between the *Bürgerschaft* and *Senat*: this is reflected in the building, with the left (south) half given over to the Citizens' Assembly, and the right (north) half to the Senate. The mayor, as president of the Senate, has his parlor is in the right-hand corner, on the first or main floor (the *piano nobile*).

The two halves unite in the tower, which projects forward of the main façade and soars toward the sky. It provides the building's public entrance, which unusually has no steps, as if to emphasize the absence of feudal distinctions. A mosaic of Hammonia in a lunette on the tower is flanked by allegorical figures representing the qualities of a good citizen: courage, piety, wisdom and unity. The tower is further adorned by the city's coat of arms, a phoenix rising (an obvious reference to the Great Fire of 1842), and the Latin inscription LIBERTATEM QUAM PEPERERE MAIORES DIGNE STUDEAT SERVARE POSTERITAS ("may the liberty which the ancients struggled to achieve be preserved for posterity"), which had previously been engraved on the Millerntor gate.

In the keystones of the arched windows on the rusticated ground floor—symbolizing the firm foundation on which Hamburg's government rested—are the coats of arms of the leading senatorial families: the Amsincks, Burchards, Sievekings and so on. Senators may have been elected rather than appointed since 1860, but the Senate remained in the hands of a small patrician elite. Where an important senator did not possess his own coat of arms, as in the case of Mönckeberg, a new crest was specially created. Although the imagery of the façade is emphatically republican, bronze statues of twenty kings and emperors can be found in the niches between the first-floor windows. This was no act of sycophancy towards the new German Empire—Kaiser Wilhelm I was conspicuous by his absence—but an acknowledgment of debts of gratitude to those who had

helped the city in the past. The initial selection of monarchs was criticized by the Association for Hamburg History, prompting numerous attempts to rank the city state's definitive "top twenty." In the end, pride of place went to Charlemagne and Barbarossa, who are accommodated on the central tower. Yet even these almost mythical figures are themselves over-shadowed by the aforementioned personifications of the civic virtues. Also placed above the statues of the emperors are the coats of arms of other famous city-states, which can be seen in the tympana of the pediments over the first-floor windows.

On top of the gables in the four corners of the building are statues rep-resenting the saints of the old city parishes. Further saints, associated with the city's former monasteries and suburban parishes, take their place on the intervening gables. Also striking a religious note, but significantly relegated to the internal façades facing the courtyard between the town hall and the stock exchange, are stone statues of the churchmen and aristocrats who had most impact on the city's history, from Bishop Ansgar to the Counts of Holstein. At the center of the internal courtyard is a fountain with a statue of Hygieia, a female allegory of hygiene, which was added in 1895 to commemorate the 8,600 victims of the cholera epidemic in 1892. Indeed, a cynic might suggest that the cholera victims are the only "ordinary" people to feature in the town hall's architecture. This is not quite true. Above the pediments of the first-floor windows are busts representing 28 different trades and professions, chosen to illustrate the diversity of Hamburg's population. The individual busts, by the Tyrolean sculptor Aloys Denoth (1851-93), combine humor—the fisherman's catch is escaping over his shoulder, for instance—and no little skill, but the selection is nevertheless significant: butchers, bakers and brewers are all present; but dockers, factory workers and women are not. As such, the town hall's façade reflects the political realities of a time in which an annual income of 1,200 Marks was required over a five-year period in order to qualify as a "citizen."

The interior of the Rathaus was not completed until 1907. It contains 647 rooms—six more than Buckingham Palace—and some of the largest frescoes painted anywhere in Europe since the Renaissance, most notably those in the Great Banqueting Hall by Hugo Vogel (1855-1934). Another highlight is the circular Chamber of Republics in the central tower. This temple-like chamber, with Moroccan onyx columns and gold-leafed doors, is decorated with frescoes and oil paintings on the themes of "freedom" and "the republic" by Alexander von Wagner (1838-1919). The scenes chosen by Wagner invite a comparison to be made between Hamburg and four other great city republics: Athens, Rome, Venice and Amsterdam. Another lavishly decorated room is the Emperor's Chamber, with its busts of Bismarck, General von Moltke and Kaiser Wilhelm I. Today it is often used for official dinners, although one hopes foreign guests are not offended by the huge central fresco entitled "The Triumph of the German Flag."

For the most part, however, the interiors of the building are relatively sober and restrained. There is a lot of dark wood paneling (walnut, oak and mahogany) and decorative leather wall hangings, but the town hall was built as a place of work rather than of luxurious display, and that is how it remains. It is no coincidence that the initials "SPQH"—with the H of course standing for Hamburg—recur throughout the building. Successive generations of Hamburg politicians and writers have sought to portray their city as a worthy heir to the Roman Republic, as in this piece by the novelist Alfred Andersch (1914-80):

> Strong, dignified, calm: yes, its best qualities are those of the Roman Republic. Its rationalism, the sobriety of its pale grey sky, carries a distant echo of the ancient idea of the Polis. Wandering through the streets of Hamburg, all that one misses are the great paving stones, worn down by the steps of many generations, in which the pride of the Republic is engraved in capital letters: THE SENATE AND THE PEOPLE OF HAMBURG.

Hail Caesar?

Kaiser Wilhelm II paid his first visit to the new town hall on June 19, 1895, on the occasion of the opening of the Kiel Canal. Subsequently there was much discussion about how best to commemorate his grandfather, Wilhelm I (1797-1888), the first German Emperor. The centenary of Wilhelm I's birth fell in 1897 and his grandson was anxious to elevate him to the status of "Wilhelm the Great." It was agreed that a monument should be placed opposite the town hall on the Rathausmarkt, and a design was purchased from the Dresden sculptor Johannes Schilling (1828-1910). Schilling, who had earlier designed the famous monument of Germania in the Niederwald, cast a bronze statue of Wilhelm on horseback, which was then mounted on a twenty-foot high granite plinth. In total the project cost nearly one million Marks and was not finished until 1903, when Wilhelm II returned to the city to unveil it in person.

The monument, which was damaged in the revolution of November 1918 and again in the "Hamburg Uprising" of 1923, lasted only 27 years before it was moved to a less prominent location on the city's ring road at Sievekingplatz. That is where it can be found today, minus its plinth but still accompanied by four ancillary statues representing the achievements of German unification in allegorical form: a common currency; criminal law code; system of post and telecommunications; and social welfare legislation. It is significant that during its short stay on the Rathausmarkt the equestrian statue faced towards the town hall. Usually the emperor, as father and protector of his people, looked outwards. An example of this can be seen in neighboring Altona, where Gustav Eberlein's bronze equestrian statue was erected in front of the town hall in 1898 and has not moved since. Evidently Hamburg's city fathers wanted to emphasize that while Wilhelm was a welcome guest, he found himself on republican soil.

As many as 400 monuments to Kaiser Wilhelm I were erected across Germany in the 1890s and 1900s, but such was the power of the burgeoning "Bismarck Myth" that even more were built in honor of his former chancellor, Otto von Bismarck (1815-98). These included monuments at Altona (1897) and Bergedorf (1906), and an unfinished project at Blankenese (1895). Direct comparisons between the two sets of memorials were inevitable: not only were they being built simultaneously, but the Bismarck monuments were seen as a respectably "patriotic" way of expressing concern at the direction of the empire under Wilhelm II, who had effectively sacked the "Iron Chancellor" in 1890. Following his dismissal, Bismarck had retreated to his estate at Friedrichsruh, fifteen miles west of Hamburg, and regularly used a local newspaper, the *Hamburger Nachrichten*, to vent his spleen at the headstrong young monarch. Thus while monuments to Wilhelm I were usually state-funded, most of those to Bismarck had to be financed by student associations or public donations. The latter was the case in Hamburg, where a committee of notables was established to drum up support for a monument on the elevated site of one of the city's former defensive bastions, "Casparus," between the Millerntor gate and St. Pauli. In a Senate vote, this location had won out over a setting on the Alster by a margin of thirteen to five. In just eight weeks, some 400,000 Marks were collected, including donations from German enclaves in South America, Asia and Africa.

A design competition was held in 1901 and attracted more than 200 entries. The winning effort—by the Berlin-based team of sculptor Hugo Lederer (1871-1940) and architect Emil Schaudt (1871-1957)—was built between 1902 and 1906. The granite monument is 111 feet tall, with the figure itself measuring 49 feet from head to toe, and weighing 628 tons (the real Bismarck had a weight problem too, but never went over 252 pounds). It stands on a round base, guarded by eight muscular athletes representing the tribes of Germany. A grand staircase, which was originally intended to run between the monument and the new Helgoländer Allee

(1894-8), was never built. Aesthetically the Kaiser Wilhelm I monuments in Hamburg and Altona were conventional in the extreme, but Lederer and Schaudt's Bismarck represented an attempt to find a new language for monumental statuary. The result is a rather uneasy mix of the ancient and modern, the figurative and the abstract. A stylized version of the chancellor's moustached countenance stares down the Elbe, as if on night-watchman duty. He is clad in armor, and his hands are clasped on the pommel of a mighty sword. The figure is in the medieval German tradition of "Roland" statues, which were erected in towns such as Bremen and Brandenburg as symbolic guardians of civic liberty, and which took their name from Charlemagne's loyal paladin Hruotland. In choosing to portray Bismarck in this way, the monument's backers were not only thanking him for the achievements of the 1870s, but attempting to turn him into a kind of patron saint or mythic totem, who would protect the city from its enemies at home and abroad.

Much was invested in the monument. Mark Russell (2007) has argued that it testified not only to the desire of Hamburg's patrician elite to defend their political privileges in the face of demands for democratic reform, but also to the city's awakening cultural aspirations. It failed, he suggests, on both counts. The first was always something of a lost cause. Bismarck was a hugely controversial and divisive figure in German politics, loved and hated in almost equal measure, but particularly disliked amongst the Hamburg working classes for his anti-socialist legislation, which outlawed the SPD between 1878 and 1890. For a significant section of the local population, therefore, the monument was never likely to be welcomed; nor was the growing momentum for political change likely to be halted by a ghost from Germany's past. It was, as Russell observes, no more effective in shoring up notions of community than the broadly contemporaneous decision that senators should wear costumes based on a sixteenth-century design whenever they appeared collectively in public.

On the second point, of cultural aspirations, however, the evidence is more ambiguous. At the time, the reception of the monument's aesthetic qualities was generally positive. Critics recognized that it marked a conscious departure from nineteenth-century historicism, with its obscure allegories and seemingly endless round of stylistic revivals. This was a monument for the new century: not pretty or decorative, but bold and powerful, particularly in silhouette at dawn or at dusk. The respected critic

Karl Scheffler (1869-1951) wrote that after all the "wretched naturalistic emperors and chancellors," this was at last an original contribution to German art. Meanwhile, the art historian Aby Warburg (1866-1929), who was fiercely critical of those who had wanted a more "lifelike" figure, described the monument in his diary as "simply sublime, sculptural and yet of a transcending visionary quality!" There can be no doubt that of all the many Bismarck memorials built in Germany before the First World War, it is the one that gained most attention. It is perhaps appropriate that its unveiling—it really was covered by a giant shroud, bearing an unfortunate resemblance to an oversized condom—was captured on the new medium of film. Together with the St. Pauli landing stages and the Elbe Tunnel, it contributed to the growing perception of Hamburg as a modern "world city." Significantly, one of the most popular picture postcard designs of the time purported to show a Zeppelin airship flying low over the monument and the St. Pauli townscape.

Public reactions to the monument varied widely. In 1928 the theater critic Alfred Kerr (1867-1948) recounted his first awestruck encounter:

> The first time I set eyes on Lederer's Bismarck Monument was on a
> moonlit night, between 11 and 12 o'clock. Behind me I could still hear
> the thunder of the river. Striding through a wood in the hustle and
> bustle of eveningtide, I caught sight of something huge above the tree
> tops: a Roland with Bismarck's face, growing into the night sky, ghostly,
> otherworldly, rigid and spine-chilling.

For others, however, the effect was rather more comic. In *World within World*, Stephen Spender recalled his memories of St. Pauli: "Most of these *Lokalen* were situated on either side of a broad road brightly lit with signs, opposite a park dominated by an enormous statue of Prince Bismarck, looking like a monstrous pepper-pot carved out of granite." More recently, the opera director Rolf Liebermann used the monument's 85th anniversary to call for it to be blown up as a matter of urgency; it was, he said, "hideous" and "a disgrace without compare." No doubt part of his disgust lay in the fact that when air-raid shelters were built into the catacombs at the base of the monument during the Second World War, an unknown artist had decorated them with murals containing runes, swastikas and nationalist slogans. After pictures of these mysterious relics were published in the *Bild* newspaper in the 1970s, the monument became a rallying point for neo-Nazis. The tourists stopped coming, and by the last decades of the twentieth century the only regular visitors were junkies and graffiti artists. After many years of slow decline, however, the monument was cleaned up and re-landscaped in 2006. Bismarck now basks in the permanent glow of strategically placed floodlights; a move which, if nothing else, seems fitting for a city district in which tanning salons outnumber all other commercial premises by about two to one.

Hamburg has far fewer personal monuments than former royal seats such as Munich or Dresden, and those to Bismarck and Kaiser Wilhelm are far from typical. In fact the majority commemorate bourgeois heroes such as writers, composers and artists. The city's first public monument to an individual, for instance, was dedicated to a professor at Hamburg's Johanneum grammar school, Johann Georg Büsch, in 1802. After several moves, the stone obelisk with a bronze relief ended up on parkland close to the junction of Edmund-Siemers-Allee and Rothenbaumchaussee. Other important nineteenth-century monuments include those to the writers Schiller and Lessing. Friedrich Schiller (1759-1805) had no personal connection to Hamburg but was admired by the educated middle classes throughout German-speaking Europe. The bronze statue, designed by Julius Lippelt and completed by Carl Börner, was unveiled in 1866 and was originally located in front of the Kunsthalle on Glockengiesserwall but can now be found in the small Gustav Mahler Park off Dammtor. It was followed in 1881 by the Lessing monument by Friedrich ("Fritz") Schaper, which depicts the playwright seated on an armchair, gazing out over the busy Gänsemarkt square towards the site of his short-lived National Theater. Perhaps the city's best monument to an individual, however, is Max Klinger's marble tribute to his close friend Johannes Brahms—together with his muses and listeners—which stands in the foyer of the Laeiszhalle concert hall on Johannes-Brahm-Platz (1909).

WAR MEMORIALS AND ANTI-WAR MEMORIALS

Hamburg chose to commemorate its dead of the First World War by erecting a flat marble stele or column in the very heart of the city, rising nearly seventy feet out of the water of the Little Alster. On one side is a relief by Ernst Barlach (1870-1938) depicting a grieving pregnant mother and child; and on the other, the bold inscription "Forty Thousand Sons of this City gave their Lives for you." In striking contrast, the city's main monument to the fallen of the Second World War is tucked away in a vast municipal cemetery on the outskirts of town. It is somber and anonymous, and predictably makes no such assertion. The question of how to commemorate the victims of war is, of course, a particularly difficult and sensitive one for the Germans. It periodically resurfaces in Hamburg as a consequence of one monument in particular: the 76th (Hanseatic) Infantry Regiment memorial on Dammtordamm. Before we consider that controversial structure in more detail, however, it is worth looking briefly at the city's other war memorials.

The monument to the city's Great War dead was conceived by Fritz Schumacher, designed by Claus Hoffmann and erected by the city authorities in 1930-31 as part of the reconfiguration of the Rathausmarkt that saw Kaiser Wilhelm banished to the ring road. The memorial has often been praised for its simple dignified form and steadfast refusal to glorify war. The novelist Thomas Mann, for instance, wrote at the time of its unveiling that he was "deeply moved" by the design, which stood out from the crowd of memorials "through its artistic dignity and spirituality, but also through its genuinely common touch." Yet from the beginning it was attacked by nationalists and veterans' groups, who felt it failed to acknowledge the heroism and sacrifice of the city's fighting men. Much of the criticism centered on the Barlach relief, which was not part of the original design and had only been added after complaints that the side facing the Alster Arcades was too plain. Despite his figurative approach and willingness to conform to the regime, Barlach's work was deemed "degenerate" in the Third Reich, and the relief was removed in 1938. It was replaced by a rising phoenix-cum-eagle motif by Hans Martin Ruwoldt. A copy of Barlach's relief was, however, restored in 1949.

The most striking contrast between this monument and the "memorial hall" built in 1953 to commemorate Hamburg's fallen soldiers in the Second World War lies in its location: it stands shrouded by tall trees in Ohlsdorf cemetery, about six miles north of the city center. Conceived by Gustav Oelsner, with the assistance of Robert Tischler and J. Meinert, the memorial hall takes the form of a round temple, and stands on the site of a former anti-aircraft battery. Its eight granite columns have neither bases nor capitals, and surround a brick core with two entrances. The only architectural detail is provided by two reliefs inside the building by Franz Mikorey: one depicting grieving wives and children, and the other showing comrades in mourning. As we shall see, separate monuments were also built at Ohlsdorf to commemorate the "victims of Fascism," members of the resistance, and those who perished in the bombing of the city.

Hamburg's most controversial war memorial, however, stands close to the center on Dammtordamm. It was initiated by a veterans' group anxious for a more "worthy" tribute to the heroism and sacrifice of the soldiers of the 76th Infantry Regiment than Hoffmann and Barlach's stele. A design competition, open only to "Aryan" German artists, was held in 1934. Despite being placed third, the respected sculptor Richard Kuöhl (1880-1961) was chosen to design the memorial. Kuöhl had worked on many of the city's biggest building projects of the 1920s and was particularly prolific in the field of monuments, designing some fifty different war memorials between 1915 and 1960. The Dammtor structure takes the form of a rectangular limestone monolith, with a relief of the Hamburg coat of arms, surrounded by serried ranks of marching soldiers, significantly wearing the uniform of the 1930s rather than that of 1914-18. There are also a number of inscriptions in Gothic script. The regiment's past battles are referred to as "great feats of history" and "bridges to the future," while a line from *A Soldier's Farewell* (1914), by the "worker-poet" Heinrich Lersch (1889-1936), is also quoted: "Germany must live, even if we must die!" The memorial was unveiled on March 15, 1936, with a march-past by units of the SA, SS, Hitler Youth and veterans' associations. The only civilian speaker, Senator Ahrens, told the assembled crowd that the memorial "should act as a permanent challenge to us all to be like these soldiers in stone; to march united behind the Führer's flag, every hour of the working day."

The ideological and aesthetic convergence between Kuöhl's memorial and the National Socialist regime has proved uncomfortable for the city since 1945. Many regard it as a piece of fascist propaganda that has no place in a democratic and multicultural city; others argue that it commemorates the sacrifice of conscripts in a conflict that had nothing to do with Hitler. They also point out that the democratically-elected Senate had already approved a war memorial for the 76th Regiment on the Dammtor site several months before the Nazi "seizure of power" in 1933. The debate has prompted thoughtful arguments on both sides, but also various forms of direct action. The monument is frequently targeted by graffiti artists and paint bombers. When German troops were sent by the SPD-Green coalition government to Kosovo in 1999, for instance, the boots of the soldiers were daubed in red and green paint. More constructively, the monument has also stimulated creative engagement of various kinds. The punk band Slime, for instance, recorded a song with a clever reversal of Lersch's line: "Germany must die, so we can live!"

In the early 1980s a commission set up by the Hamburg authorities came to the conclusion that the 1936 memorial glorified war and should only stay if a *Gegendenkmal* ("counter-monument") was erected nearby. A design competition in 1982 attracted 107 entries, but none was deemed worthy of first prize. Instead, a member of the prize jury, the Viennese sculptor Alfred Hrdlicka (born 1928), was himself invited to design a counter-monument which would enter into dialogue with the militaristic monolith. Hrdlicka, a Marxist who later became known for his "Warning against War and Fascism" on the Albertinaplatz in Vienna (1988-91), delivered a plan for an open and fragmented piece of public art, in striking contrast to Kuöhl's dense block. It was originally intended to consist of four elements, all derived from a broken swastika: the Hamburg Firestorm;

Persecution and Resistance; the Soldier's Death; and Women under Fascism. In some respects, however, Hrdlicka's work proved to be as controversial as Kuöhl's, and his working relationship with the city authorities soon broke down. Despite receiving 874,500 Marks of taxpayers' money for labor, materials and transport costs, Hrdlicka only completed two elements of the project: the "Hamburg Firestorm" (1985) and "The Sinking of the Concentration Camp Prisoners" (1986). The latter referred to the British bombing of two ships, the *Cap Arcona* and the *Thielbek*, which were tragically sunk off Lübeck while carrying more than 6,000 prisoners from the Neuengamme concentration camp on May 3, 1945.

OHLSDORF CEMETERY

Municipal cemeteries are seldom great tourist attractions, but Hamburg is rightly proud of Ohlsdorf: by area the biggest park cemetery in Europe and the second largest in the world, after New York's Calverton National Cemetery. While Ohlsdorf only opened in 1877, six Bronze Age burial mounds have been found on the site, adding a reassuring sense of permanence to this oasis of peace in an otherwise bustling and fast-changing city. The future Nobel Prize winner Samuel Beckett (1906-89), who spent nine weeks in Hamburg in 1936, visited the cemetery twice, and later referred to it in his short story "First Love" (1946). The narrator of the story compares the setting of his father's grave to Hamburg's necropolis:

> I infinitely preferred Ohlsdorf, particularly the Linne section, on Prussian soil, with its nine hundred acres of corpses packed tight, though I knew no one there, except by reputation the wild animal collector Hagenbeck. A lion, if I remember right, is carved on his monument, death must have had for Hagenbeck the countenance of a lion. Coaches ply to and fro, crammed with widows, widowers, orphans and the like. Groves, grottoes, artificial lakes with swans, offer consolation to the inconsolable. It was December, I had never felt so cold, the eel soup lay heavy on my stomach, I was afraid I'd die. I turned aside to vomit. I envied them.

Few things illustrate the secularization of society in the nineteenth century more clearly than the transfer of responsibility for the dead from the Church to the State. Hamburg's parish graveyards, which dated back to medieval times, had become too small to cope with the rapidly growing population. They were all situated outside the city walls, but following the dismantling of the defenses much of this land was needed for railways, roads or other developments. In 1874 Hamburg purchased a large area of land east of the Fuhlsbütteler Strasse for the purpose of laying out a new main cemetery, which would accommodate all citizens regardless of religion or nationality. It was not to be an additional cemetery, but a replacement for all existing graveyards: thousands of graves were to be dug up and reinterred at the new site. From the beginning, therefore, Ohlsdorf was a mammoth undertaking, although it only acquired its present size— the area of 566 soccer fields—through several further stages of expansion.

The initial plan for the cemetery was laid out by Hamburg's long-serving City Engineer, Franz Andreas Meyer (1837-1901). Meyer was assisted by an architect who would effectively run the cemetery for forty years: Johann Wilhelm Cordes (1840-1917). Cordes unveiled a revised general plan for Ohlsdorf in 1881. Despite his background, Cordes' vision for Ohlsdorf was as a *Friedhofspark* ("park cemetery"), with the character of an English garden. The natural undulations in the land were to be respected, and care was taken to create picturesque vistas with hillocks, lakes, trees, shrubs and flowers. He was particularly fond of roses and rhododendrons: today many visitors come especially to see the rhododendrons when they bloom in May. Cordes, who officially became Cemetery Director in 1898, was rewarded for his efforts with a "*grand prix*" at the Paris World's Fair of 1900 and a steady rise in the number of visitors, especially after Ohlsdorf was connected to the electric tram network in 1895 and the suburban railway in 1907. The first tourist map of Ohlsdorf was published in 1892, guide book in 1897, and picture postcards around 1900.

After his death in 1917 Cordes was succeeded by Otto Linne (1869-1937), who had been working as the city's landscape architect since 1914, and had recently helped to design the 365-acre Hamburg Stadtpark (City Park) in Winterhude (see Chapter Five). Linne's reputation as a garden reformer preceded his appointment as Cemetery Director, and he moved quickly to break with the main tenets of the Cordes approach. As the cemetery expanded to the east, onto the "Prussian soil" referred to by Beckett, the new director gave it a very different character: away from the romantic, "natural" landscape, and towards a more geometric, functional style. The change was also apparent in the cemetery architecture: from the neo-Gothic and neo-Baroque of the Cordes era to the dark clinker-brick modernism of the 1920s (the Cemetery Director was a close ally of Fritz Schumacher, who designed Ohlsdorf's main crematorium in 1930-32). To this day, the two halves of the cemetery each retain their distinctive character, and the cemetery's admirers tend to favor one or the other.

As one would expect, the cemetery contains Hamburg's great and the good (and a few of the bad too). Many are buried in a special section known as the Old Hamburg Memorial Cemetery, which includes both individual and collective graves for groups such as mayors, senators, judges, diplomats, merchants, architects, artists and musicians. Beyond this section, which was first laid out in the 1920s, most of the tombs are modest and understated. Carl Hagenbeck's bronze lion, mentioned by Beckett, is the exception rather than the rule, and is in any case less ostentatious than it sounds. There are some grand mausoleums—the oldest, by Martin Haller, dates back to 1887—and grottoes, although compared to other great park cemeteries, such as Graceland in Chicago, the citizens of Hamburg seem to have been remarkably restrained in the art of death. Some of the Ohlsdorf mausoleums are late nineteenth- or early twentieth-century reconstructions of family tombs from the city's old parish cemeteries, such as the Jenisch mausoleum of 1908 which had previously been situated in St. Katherine's graveyard. In the main, however, only a small minority of the city's wealthy merchant families opted for grandiose neoclassical temples or Romanesque chapels; those that did tended to be representatives of "new" money, such as Wilhelm Riedemann (1832-1920), a Catholic who made his fortune in the oil business: his company, German-American Petroleum Co. Ltd, was a precursor of Esso. Many of the individuals mentioned in this book also found their last resting place in Ohlsdorf. One of them is Wolfgang Borchert, who expressed his affection for the place in an essay written shortly before his death at the age of 26:

> This is no meagre cannon-fodder cemetery, where the dead are lined up in formation, forced into line by privet hedges, decorated with "medals" of primrose and rose, keeping an eye on the living… they can't enjoy their death! In Ohlsdorf the immortal dead can have a chinwag about everlasting life! For the dead don't forget life, and they can't forget the city—their city!

Along with around 320,000 graves, 25,000 trees, twelve chapels and seven species of bat, Ohlsdorf also houses a number of important memorials. Schumacher's Memorial for the Victims of the Years of Revolution 1918-20, unveiled in 1920, stands on the cemetery's Bergstrasse. It is a rustic, almost primitive looking stone structure, with two oval columns engraved with wreaths and torches, topped by an entablature. Its subject matter led to two attempts to blow it up in 1922 and its rapid demolition in 1933. Cemetery staff carefully hid the pieces, however, and it was rebuilt again after 1945. Opposite Schumacher's main crematorium stands Hamburg's Monument for the Victims of Fascism. A competition was held in 1946 with the intention of building the monument in a city center location, but no agreement could be reached on either a design or a site. Heinz-Jürgen Ruscheweyh was chosen to build the memorial at Ohlsdorf, which was completed in 1949, but the breakdown of relations between the wartime Allies and the onset of the Cold War resulted in separate opening ceremonies.

The memorial consists of a curved concrete tower with fifteen shelves. Each shelf supports seven red granite urns, containing soil from 25 different concentration and death camps across German-occupied Europe. On the bottom shelf the central urn contains the ashes of an unknown prisoner from the Neungamme camp. The city had hoped that this memorial would be all-embracing, but it is clear that many groups found it insufficient. Although it is a striking piece of design, it offers no explanation to the identity of the "victims," or the nature of their suffering. Consequently, representatives of persecuted groups began to articulate demands for their own specific memorials, beginning with those groups who could muster a strong lobby in post-war society: socialists and other political opponents of the regime; Jews; and citizens of other nations. Later, there would also be campaigns for memorials to be erected in Hamburg on behalf of the "forgotten" victims of the Third Reich: homosexuals; gypsies (Roma and Sinti); "euthanasia" victims and the handicapped.

The lobbying for a specific memorial dedicated to the heroes of the Hamburg resistance began almost immediately after hostilities ceased in 1945. It was not until 1966, however, that the Hamburg Resistance Fighters' Grove of Honor was created at Ohlsdorf. It consists of 55 flat gravestones, each inscribed with the name and dates of a murdered socialist or

Marcks' haunting memorial to the victims of war

communist resister, and an upside down triangle (the former symbol of a concentration camp inmate). The Grove of Honor, which is located on an actual burial ground for political opponents of the regime, is completed with a small sculpture, "The Speaker" by Richard Steffen, and a wall bearing a quote from the Czech resistance fighter Julius Fucik. The first memorial specifically for Hamburg's murdered Jews was erected at Ohlsdorf in 1951. Trees surround a paved area, in the center of which is a small urn containing ashes from Auschwitz. It is shielded by a low wall, bearing an inscription from Jeremiah, chapter 9, verse 1: "Oh that my head were waters, and mine eyes a fountain of tears, that I might weep day and night for the slain of the daughter of my people."

A year later, a large memorial was erected for the thousands who perished in bombing raids on the city; 36,918 of whom are buried at Ohlsdorf in mass graves dug by concentration camp inmates. The memorial, which sits at the center of a cross-shaped graveyard, was designed by one of the leading German sculptors of the twentieth century, Gerhard Marcks (1889-1981). Marcks' memorial is steeped in classical mythology. In a niche on the south side of a windowless and roofless limestone building are seven stylized figures standing in a boat: Charon the ferryman and six passengers en route to Hades. Marcks portrays Charon as the personification of modern mass murder: a cold emotionless figure, responsible for snaring his innocent passengers, who include a loving couple, a mother and child, and a man on his haunches with his head in his hands. By deliberately eschewing all Christian symbolism, and any of the usual comforting words, Marcks' bold and uncompromising memorial received a mixed reception in the 1950s, but it is undoubtedly an important work of art. For a time in 1951, Mayor Max Brauer considered erecting Marcks' memorial in the bombed out shell of St. Nicholas' Church in the city center, but in the end the blackened tower of the ruined church was left as a memorial in its own right, later adorned by an important mosaic ("Ecce Homo," 1977) by the Austrian artist Oskar Kokoschka (1886-1980).

Finally, Ohlsdorf also contains discrete cemeteries for the British war dead from both world wars, laid out in line with Commonwealth War Graves Commission regulations. The First World War cemetery dates from 1923 and contains 683 soldiers' graves, most of whom were prisoners of war who died in captivity, together with 25 sailors who perished in combat off the island of Heligoland. The Second World War cemetery contains 1,443 soldiers' graves—fighting reached the outskirts of the city—along with 67 members of the Royal Air Force and Royal Navy; its entrance is flanked by two small neoclassical pavilions, one of which contains a register and a visitors' book.

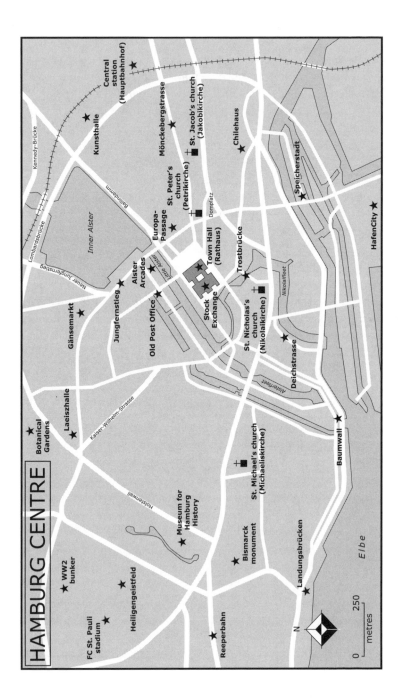

Chapter Three
A City on Water

It is a popular misconception that Hamburg is a coastal city. In fact, despite possessing Europe's second-busiest port (and the eighth-busiest worldwide), this "amphibious city" lies some 65 miles from the North Sea. The two are connected by the broad stream of the River Elbe, which rises in the mountainous northwest of the Czech Republic and flows nearly 700 miles to its mouth at Cuxhaven. At Hamburg the river briefly separates into two channels, the northern (Norderelbe) and southern (Süderelbe). The latter was originally the wider and deeper channel, but from the thirteenth century onwards the city fathers undertook a variety of measures to ensure that more water—and hence more shipping—took their northerly route, rather than the southern arm which would have bypassed the city. It would therefore be a mistake to regard Hamburg simply as the beneficiary of nature's providence. Fritz Schumacher may well have been right when he suggested that Hamburg "perhaps more than any other city, is the product of the technical energies of its inhabitants."

Between the two arms of the Elbe are a series of islands, originally marshland, covering some twenty square miles. The islands' natural outlines have been obliterated by centuries of human intervention. Most of Hamburg's dockland is located here, along with oil refineries, classification yards, allotments and the densely populated working-class districts of Wilhelmsburg and Veddel. The best view of this flat but curiously compelling landscape is obtained from the Köhlbrandbrücke: a graceful suspension bridge built in the 1970s to carry a four-lane highway over the Köhlbrand, the channel which reunites the southern and northern arms of the Elbe. The bridge, which hangs from two 440-foot pylons, has a central span of 1,700 feet and is the second longest in Germany. Unfortunately it is closed to pedestrians and cyclists, but it is worth taking the no. 151 bus which traverses it. The Köhlbrandbrücke is the icon of a city boasting more bridges than anywhere else in the world, crossing not only the Elbe, Alster and Bille rivers, but also countless canals and lakes. Hamburg is by no

means the only city to claim the title of "Venice of the North," of course, but its total of nearly 2,500 bridges is more than that of Venice and Amsterdam combined.

Serene though it might appear from the lofty heights of the Köhlbrandbrücke, the tidal lower Elbe has for centuries been prone to serious flooding. The fluvial plain on which the city stands has been inundated on countless occasions. In the eighteenth and nineteenth centuries in particular, the flood warning bell became a familiar sound to all Hamburgers, who were bound by law to offer emergency accommodation—although usually only for one night—to the thousands who lived in the city's cellars. More recently, many in Hamburg still recall the disaster which occurred on the night of February 16-17, 1962, when hurricane force northwesterly winds in the North Sea combined with an unusually high tide to cause the river to burst its banks in nearly fifty places. The sleeping city was poorly prepared: one-sixth of the urban area was submerged; 317 people lost their lives; and 60,000 people were made homeless. Subsequently the height of the flood protection barriers along the river was raised from 18 feet to almost 23 feet, and in 1976 an even worse flood was successfully averted, but in an era of projected climate change further serious incursions cannot be ruled out. The potential impact of a renewed deepening of the Elbe has provoked fierce debate in recent years. Such a step would allow larger container vessels to reach the port, but would cost more than 300 million Euros and might increase the likelihood of serious flooding in the future.

The three vast container terminals on the southern Elbe—Waltershof, Tollerort and Altenwerder—are now where most of the city's maritime trade occurs. Altenwerder, in particular, is a state-of-the-art facility operated by just a handful of staff. Visitors are not usually welcome in this highly automated world, but a bus tour runs at weekends and it is occasionally possible to take a special excursion on the freight-only harbor railway. The single carriage unit trundles slowly along tracks used by 180 container trains every day. All around are towering stacks of the ubiquitous forty-foot containers, with their distinctive orange, blue, green or gray liveries. Most arrive by ship from the Far East, before traveling on to destinations throughout Eastern Europe and Scandinavia. In 2007, ten million such containers passed through Hamburg; by 2015 the figure is expected to reach 18 million. Hamburg is already Europe's second largest container destination, and it is no coincidence that the city is twinned with Shanghai, the world's busiest container port.

The huge but strangely silent container ships, usually registered in the Liberian port of Monrovia, have become such a familiar sight that blasé Hamburgers lying on the sandy beaches at Övelgönne or Blankenese barely seem to notice these elongated sea monsters, as expert pilots guide them through the Elbe's treacherous sandbanks. While it is possible to spend many an hour watching container ships and other cargo vessels come and go, you will not see many passenger liners dock in Hamburg. Ocean-going cruise ships call in at the purpose-built Hamburg Cruise Centre no more than once or twice a week, while others are refitted at the Blohm & Voss yards, but the only regular passenger services still running on the Elbe are harbor tours and local ferries. Before the advent of plane travel, however, nearly all foreign visitors obtained their first impressions of Hamburg from the water. For Coleridge in 1798, the Elbe came as a welcome sight:

> I felt the striking contrast between the silence of this majestic stream, whose banks are populous with men and women and children, and flocks and herds—between the silence by night of this peopled river, and the ceaseless noise, and uproar, and loud agitations of the desolate solitude of the ocean.

Another British traveler to arrive by boat was John Strang (1795-1863), a future City Chamberlain of Glasgow, who wrote in 1831 that the clarity and beauty of the Hamburg townscape when viewed from the Elbe was something he had yet to find in any English or Scottish port. "If only," he lamented, "I possessed the talent of a Canaletto, to convey an impression of it." German visitors sometimes arrived by boat too. The Romantic poet Joseph von Eichendorff (1788-1857) approached the city from Harburg in 1805. He came by boat because there were no bridges over the Elbe until the second half of the nineteenth century:

> With beating heart we caught our first sight of Hamburg. At last she lay before us, this stony world of palaces and towers. The location of the harbour was indicated by a forest of soaring masts, thousand upon thousand, like some kind of woodland windbreak. As we came closer

we were surprised by the ever more immense skeletons of ships, which were being repaired on the riverbank. At last we came into the harbour. This strange spectacle, unique in the world, made an indescribable impact on us. With astonished delight we plunged into the thunderous chaos, the enormous nautical palaces surrounded us as if we were in some alien world. There were carpenters here, rowers there, sailors climbing up masts, or hovering between sky and water on the rigging; and underneath it all the muffled hum of a thousand voices in a hundred languages.

Not everyone is quite so impressed. Bill Bryson, for instance, commented:

There wasn't much to see upon arrival, just cranes and dockyards and the broad, sluggish estuary of the Elbe. Konrad Adenauer used to say: "You can smell Prussia when you get to the Elbe." I could only smell dead fish, or at least I assumed it was dead fish. Maybe it was Prussians.

In 1908 the writer Gustav Falke (1853-1916) observed that, unlike some cities, the character of Hamburg could not be captured in a single definitive view. It had two, each quite different, but both best enjoyed from the water. From the Elbe, or its banks, one could see the "working and making" Hamburg, a metropolis always in motion. From the Alster, in contrast, one saw the "resting and enjoying" Hamburg, with its almost idyllic charms. For all the dramatic changes that have occurred in the twentieth century, Falke's observation still holds true. This chapter therefore falls into two parts: the first follows the Elbe from the heart of the old dockland to the St. Pauli landing stages and beyond; while the second takes a circuitous route around the Alster and explores some of the residential districts which border its shores.

ALONG THE ELBE

Unlike London or Glasgow, Hamburg still retains the feel of a major port. A waterborne tour of the harbor, old and new, remains high on most visitors' itinerary, but at least some maritime sights and smells can also be experienced from the safety and comfort of dry land. Hamburg's first harbor on the Elbe, which dates back to medieval times, was situated at the point where a canalized section of the Alster, known as the Nikolaifleet, enters the tidal stream. This harbor, which is often referred to as the Binnenhafen ("inland harbor"), lives on in street names such as Baumwall ("Tree Wall," as the harbor could be closed by giant tree trunks), Kajen ("Quays") and Bei dem neuen Krahn ("Next to the New Crane"). A crane has operated on this site since 1352. The present crane dates back to 1570 and once required eight men to operate it manually, although it has been modernized many times since. It remained in working order until 1974. Away from the strong currents of the Elbe, there were also medieval quays on the Reichenstrassenfleet (filled in since 1877) and on the Nikolaifleet itself, where the heavily restored half-timbered houses on Deichstrasse convey some impression of how Hamburg's Altstadt once looked. They are best viewed from the Hohe Brücke, a bridge dating back to 1260.

The great expansion of Hamburg in the nineteenth century saw the port spread steadily southward, and nothing was allowed to stand in its way. "The harbor is the lord of the city," observed Alfred Lichtwark in 1897. Nowhere was this more evident than in the fate of a community sandwiched between the Binnenhafen and the city's first entirely man-made dock, the Sandtorhafen of 1862-6. Some 17,000 people lived on the Brookinsel ("Brook Island")—it was separated from the city by a narrow channel called the Dovenfleet—in streets crammed with picturesque, if unhygienic, houses dating back to the seventeenth century. The island housed two distinct communities: the working-class Kehrwieder district and the more respectable Windrahm, where the philosopher Arthur Schopenhauer (1788-1860) grew up. All were forced to move in the 1880s to make way for the new free port, along with more than 6,000 other people from the island village of Steinwerder. A total of 1,884 buildings were demolished, to be replaced by the Speicherstadt or "warehouse city." This red-brick *Gesamtkunstwerk* of more than 600 warehouses is now considered one of Hamburg's most important architectural ensembles.

As Karin Maak (1985) has shown, such a bold and brutal approach was shaped by Hamburg's comparatively recent experience of the Great Fire of 1842 and the town-planning opportunities offered in its aftermath. Yet the creation of the new free port zone, which was agreed in 1881 and came into force when the city-state joined the German Customs Union in 1888, was highly controversial at the time. Many Hamburg patriots, including some in the Senate, resented the loss of the city-wide privileges which had benefited all its citizens for centuries, and those who were forced

The Speicherstadt, c. 1890

into relocating had their advocates too, but the so-called "Annexationists" included 32 of the city's most influential businessmen.

The Senate ultimately accepted the free port compromise as the best deal Hamburg was likely to get: Bismarck was anxious that the Hanseatic cities should no longer remain semi-detached members of the Reich, and offered to pay forty million Marks towards the free port's building costs. Even with this backing, the project represented something of a financial gamble for the city, which could not be sure that such a huge capacity of warehouse space was really required. As things turned out, however, Bismarck's belated conversion to colonialism in the 1880s gave the port an unexpected boost, and the Speicherstadt—the term was already in use at the time of construction—needed to be expanded several times before the new century was even a decade old.

As part of the scheme, the Dovenfleet was renamed the Zollkanal and widened to become a free port bypass. A number of new bridges were built across it, connecting the Speicherstadt to the city. These included the Kornhausbrücke, the Brooksbrücke and the Oberbaumbrücke. Until 2001 each of these bridges was still manned by uniformed officials, checking traffic emanating from the free port zone. The customs men have now gone, following the relocation of the free port a few miles to the south, but while the Speicherstadt may have been stripped of its original function, it has not yet become a mere theme park. Vast quantities of spices, fruit and tobacco are no longer stored there, but a few import-export businesses do still remain (particularly those specializing in coffee, tea and Persian rugs), and thankfully none of the warehouses has been converted into apartments.

The original design of the warehouses was supervised by the City Engineer Franz Andreas Meyer, who ensured that the six- and seven-story structures benefited from the latest technology, including hydraulic winches, central heating and electric lighting. The ground-floor doorways and ceilings were particularly high to allow fully laden horse-drawn carts to come and go. Unfortunately their wrought-iron frames proved to be something of a fire hazard in the early years of the development. The neo-Gothic styling of the façades was largely a legacy of Meyer's education at the polytechnic in Hanover, where his favorite professor Conrad Wilhelm Hase (1818-1902) had developed his own distinctive brand of neo-Gothic architecture known as the "Hanover School" (sometimes vulgarized as "Hasik").

Hase emphasized the importance of honesty in construction, the use of local materials and the particular qualities of North German brick architecture. The latter was significant, because from the outset the Speicherstadt had a symbolic aspect too. The visual impact of the ensemble, whose copper-covered winch bays, glazed bricks and golden lettering glisten in the sun, was carefully calculated to impress. An indication of its importance was the fact that four of the seven architects engaged on the building of Hamburg's new town hall in the 1880s also designed warehouses for the free port. The city-state may have lost much of its independence by becoming part of the German Empire, but it could still express its particular identity through architecture, especially when the buildings in question were considered vital for its continued prosperity.

Appropriately, the elaborate opening ceremony for the Speicherstadt on October 29, 1888—attended by Kaiser Wilhelm II in one of his first acts as emperor—included the creation of two monumental female statues to flank the northern (city) end of the Brooksbrücke: one representing Germania and the other Hammonia. In a piece of Hamburg wishful thinking, the two patron saints stood on an equal footing, reaching out to each other as if partners in a joint enterprise. The original statues by Aloys Denoth were destroyed in the Second World War but have since been replaced by four bronze figures (representing Hammonia, Europa, Friedrich Barbarossa and St. Ansgar) by a local sculptor, Jörg Plickat. The ceremonial final stone laid by the Kaiser in 1888 can still be seen, with its inscribed toast "To the honour of God, to the Empire's best, to Hamburg's good fortune!" The Kornhausbrücke, meanwhile, has been guarded on its north side since 1903 by red sandstone statues of the explorers Columbus and Vasco da Gama (the equivalent statues on the south side, of Cook and Magellan, were lost in the war).

As befits "a city in place of the city" (Karin Maak), the Speicherstadt even had its own post office, fire station and "town hall." The latter, actually the former seat of the free port administration at St. Annen 1, is still immediately recognizable by its decorative gables and imposing copper-plated towers. It was built in 1902-3 in the style of the German Renaissance, just as were many "real" town halls in the Wilhelmine era. Opposite, at St. Annenufer 2, is the Speicherstadt Museum, offering old photographs and displays on how the warehouses used to function, together with explanations of the distinctive vocabulary used by the *Quartiersleute* ("warehouse agents"). One trade which made its home here was the import and export of spices, such as pepper from the Far East, and this is commemorated by the world's only Spice Museum at Sandtorkai 32. To this day, fat-cat businessmen in Germany are sometimes referred to as *Pfeffersäcke* ("pepper sacks").

The Sandtorkai is now part of the ambitious HafenCity development which is taking shape south of the Speicherstadt (see Epilogue). Other tourist destinations have moved into the warehouses in recent years, including an Afghan Museum (also at Sandtorkai 32), the German Customs Museum (Alter Wandrahm 15-16) and, less appropriately, the Hamburg Dungeon (Kehrwieder 2). The real delights of the Speicherstadt, however, lie in the play of light on its beautiful brickwork, and the ever-changing reflections of its towering gables in dark water (producing the optical il-

lusion that the warehouses are double their actual height).

Leaving the Speicherstadt by the Niederbaumbrücke, some sense of Hamburg's maritime history is conveyed by the museum ships permanently moored on the Elbe: the three-masted bark *Rickmer Rickmers* (1896), which won the Tall Ships' Race in 1958; and the elegant 1960s freighter *Cap San Diego*, dubbed the "white swan of the South Atlantic." From Baumwall it is possible to follow the north bank of the Elbe for many miles (the south bank is largely inaccessible to the public). Although one's gaze naturally gravitates towards the lively river scene, it is worth taking a brief look at the elevated electric railway built between 1906 and 1912, and the distinctly nautical looking building looming behind it. This gray steel and glass structure, with its portholes and deck rails, is the headquarters of Gruner & Jahr, Europe's largest publishing house, whose titles include *Stern* and *Financial Times Deutschland*. At the time of its construction in the late 1980s, Otto Steidle and Uwe Kiessler's building was regarded as a controversial break from the Hanseatic tradition of red-brick architecture, especially as the architects came from Bavaria. Since then, however, the building has gained respect for its environmental credentials and has grown into its surroundings.

Shortly after the start of the 2,230-foot-long pontoon known as the Landungsbrücken (landing stages) one enters the suburb of St. Pauli. Although only a couple of miles from Hamburg city center, St. Pauli lay outside the city wall, sandwiched into a narrow strip of land between the Millerntor gate and the Altona border. It only gained its ecclesiastical name in the 1830s, having previously been known as Hamburger Berg. The name came from the parish church of St. Paul's, which was built in 1682, destroyed by the French in 1814 and rebuilt to designs by Carl Ludwig Wimmel in 1819-20. Until the twentieth century the vast majority of the district's inhabitants relied directly or indirectly on the sea for their living: fishing, net-mending, sail- and rope-making; but also on the breweries, bars and brothels which catered for sailors while on dry land (see Chapter Six).

Robert Muller, who came to Britain on a *Kindertransport* in 1938, recalled the St. Pauli quayside in his autobiographical novel *The World that Summer*:

> The outlines of the wharves and warehouses were blurred, but the tall cranes stood out clearly. Hannes thought of them as steel giraffes, dwarfing the men who laboured beneath them. In some places the sun cut through the haze, scattering flashes of light over steel and water. Small tugs chugged past the landing stages, dodging the green-and-white painted ferries. Rainbow-tinted grease flecked the water. A smell of fish, petrol and hops hung in the air.

Few cranes now remain, although the Blohm & Voss shipyards are clearly visible on the opposite bank of the river. Although much scaled down, the yards are still an impressive sight. Thomas Mann evoked the scene perfectly in *The Magic Mountain*:

> … the confusion of the yards, the mammoth bodies of great ships, Asiatic and African liners, lying in dry-dock, keel and propeller bare, supported by props as thick as tree trunks, lying there in monstrous helplessness, swarmed over by troops of men like dwarfs, scouring, whitewashing, hammering; there were the roofed-over ways, wrapped in

wreaths of smoke-like mist, holding the towering frames of rising ships, among which moved the engineers, blue-print and loading scale in hand, directing the work-people. All these were familiar sights to Hans Castorp from his youth upwards, awaking in him only the agreeable, homely sensations of "belonging," which were the prerogative of his years.

The popularity of harbor tours ensures that the landing stages continue to be thronged with people, even on cloudy days. The first landing stages were opened in 1839, but their current appearance dates from the 1900s, when the first pontoon—linked to the shore by movable bridges—was erected. Great transatlantic liners departed from here until 1897, when Hamburg opened a new purpose-built facility near Cuxhaven at the mouth of the Elbe. The landing stages were badly damaged in the Second World War but rebuilt in the 1950s. The sandstone reception building, with its much photographed clock tower, dates from 1906-10. It was designed by Ludwig Raabe and Otto Wöhlecke, who were also partly responsible for the adjacent building with the large copper-plate dome: the Old Elbe Tunnel.

A tunnel under the Elbe had been first proposed by an engineer, Georg Westendarp, in 1882. In fact it was not until 1907 that tunneling began, but it was still the first of its kind anywhere on the continent. Five workers were killed and 174 injured during its construction, which was completed in 1911. The eleven million-Mark project was undertaken by the City Engineer's department primarily to enable thousands of dock workers to reach their workplaces at Steinwerder, on the south bank of the river. Those jobs have long gone, and the 1,400-foot tunnel now serves little purpose, especially since a much larger motorway tunnel, running between Othmarschen and Waltershof, was opened in 1975. Yet the old tunnel, with its Art Nouveau mosaics, ceramic tiles and maritime reliefs, is well worth a visit. The showy exterior, with sculptures by Hermann Perl, might bear a passing resemblance to the Pantheon in Rome, but the real achievements lie underground. The tunnel has no ramps: unlike modern road tunnels, cars and trucks have to take the elevator too.

When the future Nobel Laureate Samuel Beckett walked through the tunnel on November 4, 1936, he wrote in his diary: "Impressive & nightmarish, especially the Fahrschächten [elevator shafts], pits of steel with 6 lifts each & German expressionist film screw stairs. Whole things [sic]

somehow kinematic." Together with the Landungsbrücken suburban railway station (1910-12)—which was designed by the architect of the Bismarck Monument, Emil Schaudt, and originally had an impressive tower of its own—the tunnel and the landing stages formed a remarkable transport interchange. Even in its reduced state it remains an impressive testament to the wealth and self-confidence of the city before the Great War.

Gazing down on the landing stages from the glacial ridge known as the Stintfang is another ensemble of St. Pauli institutions, each with nautical connections: the red-brick Seemannshaus (1858-63), a hostel for sailors now converted into a hotel; the Harbor Hospital (1900); the School of Navigation (1903-5), which now belongs to the German Meteorological Office; and the Institute for Tropical Diseases (1910-14). Since the early 1950s, Hamburg's main youth hostel has also been located on the Stintfang. These venerable institutions have become overshadowed in recent years by a number of new office buildings which have been erected on the site of the former Bavaria Brewery. As a result, St. Pauli's iconic "harbor crown" skyline has been somewhat disfigured, although in truth it was already scarred by the effects of the Second World War.

Running westward from the landing stages is the Hafenstrasse, which was first laid out in the late 1850s but only acquired a dubious fame during the 1980s, when militant squatters occupied a row of condemned houses and refused to leave. Their long-running battle with the Hamburg authorities eventually ended in 1997, following a peaceful compromise brokered by the millionaire benefactor Jan Philipp Reemtsma. The houses, which date back to the 1860s, were saved from demolition, but the former squatters now pay rent to a housing association. Three sets of steps run between the Hafenstrasse and the Bernhard-Nocht-Strasse: the middle one, the Balduintreppe, becomes a lively outdoor drinking area after dark.

The next landmark to be reached on the north bank of the Elbe is the fish market. The fiercely competitive relationship between Hamburg and Altona—which first developed when the latter was under Danish jurisdiction but did not disappear after it became Prussian in 1866—was typified by the "fish market war" of the late nineteenth century. Hamburg's fish market was traditionally held in the city center, close to the old Cathedral, whereas Altona's fish market took place on the banks of the Elbe, just west of St. Pauli. In 1703 the successful Altona market was even given permission to open on Sundays, provided that it closed before 8.30 a.m. so as not to affect church attendance. By the 1870s, and despite its distance from the sea, Altona had become the largest fishing port in the whole German Empire. It was then that Hamburg decided to open its own fish market on the Elbe. Its first attempt proved inauspicious—docking steamers kept showering the produce with soot—but in 1876 Hamburg opened a new fish market hall on the St. Pauli quayside, just a hundred yards from the Altona market.

For the next six decades the two markets competed side by side, matching each other step for step: when Hamburg introduced high-volume fish auctions in May 1887, Altona followed just one month later; when Altona built a modern Fish Auction Hall with an impressive glass dome in 1895, Hamburg built an even more imposing structure in 1898. In 1900 the city of Altona commemorated its long struggle for supremacy in the fishing business with a monumental fountain, the Stuhlmann-brunnen, in front of its main railway station, but after the First World War pressure for a merger grew. Hamburg and Altona's fish markets were finally combined in 1934, three years before Altona was itself swallowed up by its larger neighbor under the Greater Hamburg Law.

Today no trawlers deposit their catch anywhere in Hamburg: instead, giant refrigerated trucks bring frozen fish from Esbjerg in Denmark to Altona's fish harbor, where it is sold, processed and distributed in industrial quantities. Although there was ultimately no winner in the "fish market war" of the late nineteenth century, one could say that Altona has had the last laugh. For while Hamburg's market buildings were demolished in 1971, the early Sunday morning market centered on Altona's Fish Auction Hall has become an unlikely tourist attraction. With much more than just fish for sale, and with live music and cooked breakfasts on offer in the Auction Hall, it has become especially popular with Saturday night revelers, who regard it as an unmissable part of the St. Pauli experience. Some of the market traders are skilled performers in their own right, offering stand-up comedy along with the smoked eels and rollmops.

Continuing along the Grosse Elbstrasse one comes across a number of former industrial buildings with new uses, such as the malt factory which now retails contemporary interior design under the name Stilwerk (Grosse Elbstrasse 66-8). A short distance later on the right-hand side is the Köhlbrandtreppe, an ornamental set of steps built in neo-Gothic style in 1887 to allow dockers and fish-processing workers easier access to Altona's residential districts. The steps incorporate a fountain—to offer a symbolic "cleansing" of the workers after their daily toil—and a relief showing the crests of Altona and Prussia, with representations of Mercury (trade) and Neptune (seafaring). On the left is the former terminal of the Hamburg-Harwich ferry, whose tortuous 22-hour crossings remain the one negative memory of my student days in the city in the 1980s. The futuristic steel and glass terminal by Alsop and Lyall was only completed in 1993, but was left to decay when the Danish-owned ferry service became a casualty of the low budget airlines. Now the site is being converted to become a second cruise ship terminal, with a 1,000-foot dock capable of accommodating ships the size of the *Queen Mary II*.

Despite this and other eye-catching developments, such as the parallelogram-shaped "Dockland" office building modeled on Capri's Villa Casa Malaparte by the fashionable architect Hadi Teherani (2006), the area around the former wood and fish harbor is still a little rough around the edges. You may prefer to turn inland on Elbberg and head for the Altonaer Balkon ("Altona Balcony"), a park with a spectacular view over the river towards the Harburg hills. From here there are four options: one can leave the Elbe altogether and walk into Altona town center; return to the quayside and follow the Neumühlen road, where a chain of new office buildings obscures the river for the next half mile or so; follow the elevated Schopenhauerweg through a series of attractive parks before rejoining the Elbe promenade; or take a look at the busy Elbchaussee, once described by the poet Detlev von Liliencron (1844-1909) as "the most beautiful street in the world."

The Elbchaussee runs parallel to the river for about five miles between Altona and Blankenese. Today it is blighted by frequent traffic jams (and twelve sets of traffic lights), but the grand nineteenth-century villas, many designed by the "Danish Palladio" Christian Frederick Hansen (1756-1845), testify to its former glory. Residents still enjoy panoramic views across the Elbe, but the distant vistas are now of the container port and the Airbus factory rather than the apple orchards of the Altes Land. Heine's millionaire Uncle Salomon had a mansion here: it was demolished in 1880 but his small garden house remains at Elbchaussee 31. In recent years it has been restored to accommodate a gallery and a small Heine exhibition. A more recent and highly eccentric villa can be seen at Elbchaussee 96. This postmodern curiosity is the work of the architect Heinrich Stöter. It is part house, part design studio and part advertisement. The five-story multicolored building only received planning permission at the fifth attempt, and one can see why.

Film fans may want to walk on to Elbchaussee 186, the so-called Säulenhaus ("column house") which provided the setting for much of Wim Wenders' 1976 film, *The American Friend*. The white neoclassical house, with a large rotunda, was built in 1817 for the businessman Wilhelm Brandt (1778-1832). Brandt had made his fortune in Russia and modeled the house on a palace he had seen overlooking the Black Sea in the Crimea. The architect was C. F. Hansen's nephew Matthias. Otherwise rejoin the Elbe promenade by taking the steps directly opposite the Stöterhaus. They lead to the former fishing and whaling village of Övelgönne, which is entirely car-free and boasts a sandy beach, attractive cottages and some very pricey restaurants. If you visit on a weekend in the summer you will soon realize that the Elbe is not only vital to Hamburg's economy, but also to the leisure and recreation of its citizens. Little yachts bob up and down; the beaches are packed with sunbathers; and the tempting aromas of barbecues waft through the trees.

To the west of Övelgönne, the Elbe promenade (Elbuferweg) passes the wealthy suburb of Othmarschen, home to Hamburg's first golf course (1906), Germany's oldest polo club (1898) and an equestrian center which hosts Germany's equivalent of the Badminton Horse Trials. One of Othmarschen's most prominent nineteenth-century residents was the banker and Senator Martin Jenisch (1793-1857), whose pearly white neoclassical country house (1831-4), adapted from plans by the great Prussian architect Karl Friedrich Schinkel, today accommodates a fine museum of furniture and interior design. The extensive grounds of the Jenisch house run right down to the Elbe. They were originally laid out by the enlightened merchant Caspar Voght (1752-1839) in the manner of a British "ornamented farm," that is to say as a landscape garden with a practical agricultural use. Voght, who reformed the Hamburg welfare system and prison service and gained the unofficial title of "Father of the Poor," was inspired by the example of poet William Shenstone's estate "Leasowes," which he had visited on a business trip to Birmingham. He was assisted in the planning of the estate by the Scottish forester James Booth. It was farmed successfully for many years before money problems forced Voght to sell it to Jenisch in 1828. Unfortunately it is Jenisch, rather than Vogt, who has given his name to the park, which was selected in 1962 as the location for a museum dedicated to the poet, painter and sculptor Ernst Barlach. The Ernst-Barlach-Haus, at the north end of the park, was a posthumous gift to the city from the cigarette manufacturer Hermann Reemtsma (1892-1961). Reemtsma had assembled a private collection of 120 sculptures and more than 300 drawings by the controversial Wedelborn artist, best remembered in Hamburg for his relief on the Rathausmarkt war memorial.

At the foot of the Jenisch Park is a small marina and ferry stop known as Teufelsbrück (literally "Devil's Bridge"). The bridge in question does not cross the Elbe, but a small stream called the Flottbek. Incidentally, there is nothing demonic about it: it once belonged to a farmer called Düwel. The Flottbek itself provides the water for the ornamental lakes of Hamburg's New Botanical Gardens (opened 1979), about a mile to the north, and served by its own railway station at Klein-Flottbek. Teufelsbrück has one other claim to fame: in the play *The Condemned of Altona*

(1959) by the Nobel Laureate Jean-Paul Sartre (1905-80), a father and son whose shipbuilding company collaborated with the Nazis commit suicide by driving a Porsche over the Teufelsbrück jetty and into the deep waters of the Elbe.

The next village on the north bank of the Elbe is Nienstedten. Originally the Danish Nygenstede, the village possesses an attractive eighteenth-century half-timbered church (particularly popular with wedding parties) and Hamburg's most venerable hotel and restaurant, the Louis C. Jacob. The "Jacob" was opened in 1791 by a refugee from the French Revolution, Daniel Louis Jacques, who was a landscape gardener by trade. In fact the garden has always been a major part of the hotel's appeal: its terrace of lime trees, with a spectacular view over the Elbe, was immortalized on canvas in two paintings by the German Impressionist painter Max Liebermann (1847-1935). One hangs in the Hamburg Kunsthalle, the other in the hotel itself, which enjoyed particular fame in the 1950s when regular guests included Maria Callas and Henry Miller. Today it is best known for its Michelin-starred restaurant. It can be reached from the riverside by climbing the steps known inevitably as "Jacob's Ladder."

Resisting temptation and continuing on the Elbuferweg, one skirts two public parks formerly owned by wealthy businessmen: the Hirschpark ("Deer Park") and Baurs Park. The former was laid out for Johan César Godeffroy IV (1742-1818) in the late eighteenth century, though it was his grandson Johan César Godeffroy VI who was the passionate huntsman. It contains an attractive avenue of lime trees, hundreds of rhododendron bushes and some real live deer. There is also a white neoclassical house overlooking the Elbe (Elbchaussee 499, 1789-92) by C. F. Hansen. The Godeffroys, who were of Huguenot extraction, became one of Hamburg's richest families thanks to an extensive trading empire in the Pacific (see Chapter Seven), but this collapsed in spectacular fashion in 1879 after misguided investments in the Silesian coalfields. Although it is hard to feel much sympathy with the "King of the South Seas," Johan César Godeffroy VI was something of a tragic figure by the time his company went bust: he was almost blind and had been deserted by all his former friends and associates. Under the terms of the liquidation he was allowed to remain in his house for a further ten years, so his death in 1885 at least spared him the ignominy of losing his home.

Baurs Park was laid out in the Romantic style for the Altona merchant Georg Friedrich Baur (1768-1865) between 1817 and 1832. It originally boasted grottoes, temples, a Gothic tower and a five-story pagoda. None of these structures now remains, although an eye-catching modern lighthouse has been built on the site of the pagoda. Baur, who lived to the age of 96 and had seven children, 34 grandchildren and 22 great-grand-children, was a true eccentric: whenever one of his company's ships passed on the Elbe, he would salute it by firing a cannon. Baur's tradition lives on at Schulau, near Wedel, where every passing ship of more than 500 tons is greeted by a loudspeaker message and a taped rendition of the appropriate national anthem. The Hamburg flag is then raised and lowered on a 130-foot mast.

Our final former fishing village on the north bank of the Elbe is Blankenese, which lies about nine miles from the center of Hamburg. The name means "pale nose" in Low German, referring to a sandy spit of land which disappeared centuries ago. Coleridge described it as "a most interesting village scattered amid scattered trees, over three hills in three divi-

sions. Each of the three hills stares upon the river, with faces of bare sand, with which the boats with their bare poles, standing in files along the banks, made a sort of fantastic harmony... It is inhabited by fishermen and boat-makers, the Blankaness [sic] boats being in great request through the whole navigation of the Elbe."

A long time has passed, however, since any fishermen could afford to live here. Blankenese has been one of Hamburg's most desirable suburbs for more than a century. On a sunny day it is just about possible to understand the frequent comparisons with Monte Carlo, Biarritz or Beverly Hills: the combination of woods, beaches and water is a seductive one. Add in hills—so rare in Hamburg—such as the Süllberg (250 feet) and the Baurs Berg (300 feet), and it is easy to see why the nineteenth-century bourgeoisie built their villas here in such profusion. The most interesting part of the village, the Treppenviertel ("Step Quarter"), is a hillside labyrinth with 58 sets of steps (4,864 steps in total), whitewashed walls and thatched or red-tiled roofs.

Prominent residents among the rhododendron bushes and antique shops have included the fashion designer Karl Lagerfeld, the madcap comedian Otto Waalkes, the historian Golo Mann (1909-94), the graphic artist Horst Janssen (1929-95) and the poet Richard Dehmel (1863-1920). The latter's works have long since fallen from favor, but he was once highly regarded: both Richard Strauss and Arnold Schoenberg put his poems to music. Dehmel had been living in Blankenese since 1901, but in 1911 he was presented with a new house in the village, as a 50th birthday present from his friends and admirers (Richard-Dehmel-Strasse 1). The strikingly simple structure, reminiscent of Goethe's "garden house" at Weimar, was designed by Walter Baedecker and contained interiors in the Arts and Crafts style, based on ideas developed by Dehmel with the designer Peter Behrens at the turn of the century. On Dehmel's death in 1920 the house became a mausoleum as well as a museum, since the poet's ashes are kept there in an urn designed by his friend Richard Luksch.

From Blankenese there are several different ways of returning to the city. So varied and interesting is the no. 36 bus route that you can purchase a dedicated guidebook by Rainer Elwers (2000) to accompany you on the 38-minute journey back to the town hall or main railway station. As a cheap way of seeing the city's sights, the "36er" certainly takes some beating. There is a fast and frequent suburban rail service too, but in the summer months the best option must surely be to catch a ferryboat to the St. Pauli landing stages. The Elbe might not be as romantic as the Rhine, or as blue as the Danube, but it remains Hamburg's main artery, the beating heart of the city at work, rest and play.

AROUND THE ALSTER

The Alster, described by Bill Bryson as "one of the most arresting city sights I have ever seen," is undoubtedly Hamburg's most striking natural feature; except it is not natural. The Alster is actually a river, a minor tributary of the Elbe, which was first dammed nearly 800 years ago to provide water for the medieval city's mills. While it is no longer a mill pond, the Alster continues to perform a vital function, offering numerous opportunities for leisure and recreation, as well as some classic views of the city. Its tree-lined shores (particularly attractive in autumn, with a mix of elm, lime, horse chestnut and weeping willow), its vintage steam-powered ferries, yachts, and above all its swans (protected by the city since 1674), have been the subject of poetry, paintings and even, in 1721, an overture by the Baroque composer Telemann. Today, no visit to Hamburg is complete without a boat trip on the Alster, but the five-mile ramble around the lake is well worth the effort too, especially as there are plenty of waterside cafés along the way. It is the sort of walk that is rewarding at any time of year, and on any day of the week, although if you go on a Sunday it may feel as if half of Hamburg is walking, jogging and cycling with you (or towards you, if you choose to travel in an counterclockwise direction).

The River Alster rises near the village of Rhen in Schleswig-Holstein. The poet von Liliencron said that "everyone born in Hamburg should be obliged to go there at least once in their life... to bow down before the holy spring, which the Republic has to thank for its most beautiful jewel." Although the source is only about twenty miles north of the city, the river meanders for nearly forty miles before it enters the lake at its northern end, under Fritz Schumacher's Krugkoppelbrücke (1927). In fact, the lake—which is divided into the square Inner Alster and rounded Outer Alster—is just the most visible part of a complex network of waterways, all of which are navigable by boat.

The division into an Inner and Outer Alster dates back to the seventeenth century, when the city's defensive fortifications were expanded: the new city wall incorporated a small section of the Alster, while the larger part remained outside. Today the two are separated not by fortifications but by a railway and two road bridges: the first of these, the Lombards-brücke, dates back to 1688 and was originally a toll bridge; the second, the Kennedybrücke, was built in 1953. The view of the Inner Alster and the Jungfernstieg from the Lombardsbrücke is one of Hamburg's most pho-tographed vistas. Samuel Beckett walked around the Alster on October 8, 1936 and stopped on the bridge. He noted in his diary, "Lovely skyline, esp. Petrikirche." A third, often overlooked, part of the Alster is the short stretch from the Inner Alster to the town hall: this is known as the Little Alster. The canalized river (Alsterfleet) then continues its journey through the heart of the old town, joining the northern arm of the River Elbe near the Speicherstadt.

The Outer Alster covers an area of nearly 400 acres. Until the nine-teenth century it was surrounded by open meadows, but today its waters lap against the city's smartest residential districts: Rotherbaum and Har-vestehude to the west; Winterhude and Uhlenhorst to the east. While any property with an Alster view is a very desirable piece of real estate, it is the western side that has traditionally been regarded as the smartest address in town. Those fortunate enough to own houses or apartments here owe much to an American, John Fontenay (1769-1835), who in 1800 boldly contradicted the demographic tendencies of his age by emigrating from the New World to Europe. Settling in Hamburg, Fontenay became an im-portant figure in shipping circles and invested much of his wealth in land. The fields to the west of the Alster had once belonged to a Cistercian convent (pulled down at the height of the Reformation in 1530), but were considered cheap grazing land before Fontenay began to speculate. He built a number of villas on and around Mittelweg, including one for himself (Mittelweg 185). To live outside the city gates was considered something of a risk, and only to be contemplated for the summer months, but Fontenay's gamble paid off. He is commemorated by both a street name and a small memorial (corner of Fontenay and Alsterufer).

One other little piece of America is close by: just south of Fontenay on Alsterufer 27-28 is the American Consulate. Hamburg became one of the very first cities to possess a US consulate in 1790. The present consulate occupies two nineteenth-century mansions, both designed by Martin Haller, which were brought together to serve as the Nazi Party's regional headquarters during the Third Reich. A new neoclassical portico modeled on the White House in Washington was added when the Americans moved in during 1951.

Some of Hamburg's wealthiest shipping families quickly followed Fontenay in moving out of the walled city. For instance, in 1848—a year of revolutions across Europe—the Slomans commissioned a Gothic fortress, complete with battlements, at Harvestehuder Weg 5-7. The house, designed by Jean David Jolaste, was the first villa outside the city gates to be occupied all year round, even though it was not connected to the mains water supply until 1853. By 1897, no fewer than 13 of the 18 members of the Hamburg Senate lived in the new district. Robert Muller recalled his memories of this part of the city in *The World that Summer*:

> Along the west side of the Alster, the city's merchants had built their villas half a century ago as monuments to optimism. The houses, reflecting their owners' rich taste, their awe of culture, had erupted in a boastful hotchpotch of styles: Hellenic porticos, ivy-clad façades, arched windows, Spanish balconies. Roofs culminated in Gothic towers or turrets with copper steeples which in time turned into green witches' hats. "English" lawns, with sundials, statuettes of Pan and fountains with marble mermaids, sloped down to the Alster. Some of Rolf's mythical plutocrats still inhabited these palaces. Others had long ago abandoned them to speculators who converted them into offices and apartment houses.

The large house at Harvestehuder Weg 12—which has been part of Hamburg's College of Music and Theater since 1959—was designed and built in 1883-4 by Martin Haller for another shipping magnate, Ivan Gans. In 1900 he sold the house to a Jewish American businessman, Henry Budge, who extended it to accommodate fifty bedrooms, twenty bathrooms and a Versailles-style Hall of Mirrors (today one of the most popular exhibits in Hamburg's Museum of Arts and Crafts). The vicissitudes of twentieth-century German history are well reflected in the house's subsequent history: following the deaths of Budge (1928) and his wife Emma (1937), it was seized by the Nazi authorities, who auctioned off the contents and handed it over to Karl Kaufmann, the party *Gauleiter* and *Reichsstatthalter* (regional governor) for Hamburg, who had an underground bunker built in the courtyard. At the end of the Second World

War it became a military hospital and then a British officers' mess until 1955. The house's private park—which once extended to the Alster shore—was opened to the public in 1953 and is now crossed by hundreds of walkers and joggers every day.

The official entrance to the College of Music and Theater is on Milchstrasse, a narrow street which runs from Harvestehuder Weg to Mittelweg. Despite its unassuming appearance, Milchstrasse is a familiar name to anyone who reads the society columns or fashion pages of the German press. Indeed, the Milchstrasse publishing house is one of Germany's leading publishers of lifestyle magazines. It all began in the late 1950s when a young antique dealer, Eduard Brinkama, bought up some semi-derelict cottages and stables, restoring them to a high standard. In 1968 the German clothes designer Jill Sander opened a shop on the street, and she was joined in the 1970s by a host of other chic boutiques, interior design workshops and expensive restaurants. Although part of Harvestehude, the immediate vicinity of Milchstrasse regards itself as a separate, and exclusive, village: Pöseldorf. Today Sander's shop is long gone, but Milchstrasse continues to be clogged with Porsches and expensive 4x4s.

Even around Pöseldorf, however, few of the grand nineteenth-century villas remain in private hands (and most of those that do have been divided into apartments). Many of the detached houses on Harvestehuder Weg have become offices, architects' studios or overseas consulates: number 8, for instance, was built for the shipping magnate's wife Sophie Laeisz in 1906-7, but for fifty years after the Second World War it was occupied by the British Consulate. The consulate was closed in 2005 (despite a petition signed by the Mayor of Hamburg and Kevin Keegan, among others) but the Anglo-German club, which was founded in 1948 to foster closer relations between the two countries, is still based at Harvestehuder Weg 44. A large oil painting of the Queen hangs in the dining room. Opposite, at Harvestehuder Weg 42, is the extensive headquarters of the Hoffmann and Campe publishing house. The location is appropriate, because Campe's most celebrated client was Heinrich Heine, author of the line "Hamburg is the best republic: its customs are English and its food is heavenly" (*seine Sitten sind Englisch und sein Essen ist himmlisch*).

HEINRICH HEINE

Heine first came to Hamburg as an eighteen-year old in 1816. In total he was to spend some six years in the city (1816-19; 1826-27; 1829-31), where his uncle Salomon—a rather boorish banker who was reputed to be Hamburg's "richest Jew"—vainly hoped to turn him into a businessman. At first Heine found the city a gloomy and philistine place compared to his native Düsseldorf, dubbing it "that damned Hamburg," a miserable hole inhabited by "rotten shellfish souls, human refuse." Hamburg was "a great counting-house by day and a great brothel by night," he wrote to a friend. By the mid-1820s, however, he began to show more affection for "the place I detest and love the most." While he continued to mock the city's mercantile ethos, he was enthusiastic about its cuisine. Incidentally, Hamburg has remained a gourmet heaven, with no fewer than nine of its restaurants currently holding a coveted Michelin star.

In Heine's day Hamburg was famous for its smoked beef—the "Hamburger" would later conquer the world, of course—but also for its seafood. One stanza of Heine's most famous work, *Germany—A Winter's Tale* (1844), observes:

> The Republic of Hamburg was never as great
> as Venice, or as Florence;
> but it has better oysters, the best can be had
> at the excellent Keller "Bei Lorenz."

Another poem, later famously set to music by Robert Schumann (1810-56), well captures Heine's ambivalent attitude to a city he was continually leaving, but to which he usually returned (if only to borrow money from his uncle). It begins:

> Fair cradle of my sorrows,
> fair gravestone of my peace,
> fair city, we must part,
> farewell! I call to you.

Heine's most important friend in the city was the publisher and bookshop owner Julius Campe (1792-1867). It suited the young writer to have a Hamburg-based publisher because censorship was less severe there than in other German states during the Metternich era. One of the book projects he considered at this time was a collection of "Letters from Hamburg." The tone was to be erudite but mischievous, as in this description of the city's people:

> [The ladies] I found not exactly thin; indeed, for the most part plump, but for all that charmingly pretty and, in general with a certain comfortable sensuality which did not displease me. If they do not seem to be altogether extravagant in romantic love, and give little hint of the great passions of the heart, it is not their fault, but that of the little god Cupid, who often puts the sharpest of love's arrows to his bow but from naughtiness or clumsiness shoots too low, hitting the women of Hamburg not in the heart but in the stomach. As for the men, I saw for the most part stunted figures, clever cold eyes, low foreheads, pendulous red cheeks, the jaws particularly well developed, hats that seemed to be nailed on to their heads, and both hands in their trouser-pockets like someone about to say: "How much must I pay?"

The book was never finished. Heine left for Paris in 1831, inspired by the July Revolution of the previous year, which had seen the reactionary Charles X replaced by the "Citizen King," Louis-Philippe. In 1830 Hamburg had also been in revolt, but in September an ugly anti-Jewish riot (the *Judenkrawall*) left Uncle Salomon with broken windows. Heine, who had witnessed the disturbances, was understandably shocked by "the heathen savagery of the unleashed masses," and frustrated by the lack of political progress in his homeland. Hamburg may have been more liberal than Prussia—where Heine's writings were banned in 1833—but its freedoms remained largely rhetorical. Heine wrote with characteristic sarcasm: "Hamburg is the best republic. It is a free state and the greatest political freedom exists in it. The citizens can do as they will; and the noble and wise Senate likewise does as it will."

Even though his widowed mother Betty now lived in the city (Neuer Wall 28), Heine returned on just two further occasions, in 1843 and 1844. He had to travel by boat, because a warrant out for his arrest made overland travel through Prussia too risky. Despite his long absence, Heine was genuinely shocked and saddened by the Great Fire of 1842, which burned down his mother's house and one of his favorite old haunts, the Swiss

Pavilion on the Jungfernstieg, and narrowly missed his beloved sister Charlotte's house (Esplanade 39). His mother moved to the Dammtorstrasse, and when Heine visited in 1843-4 he was able to observe the after-effects of the conflagration at first hand. It is a nostalgic, post-fire view of Hamburg which runs through *Germany—A Winter's Tale* (see Chapter Four). Apart from Heine, Campe published the work of other radical writers from the so-called "Young Germany" group, such as Karl Gutzkow (1811-78) and Ludwig Börne (1786-1837). Hoffmann von Fallersleben's *Song of the Germans*, with its opening line "Deutschland, Deutschland über alles," was also published for the first time by Campe in 1841. More recent "HoCa" authors have included Siegfried Lenz, Wolf Biermann and Marion Gräfin Dönhoff.

In the Hoffmann and Campe company grounds there is a monument to Heine, the main part of which—a bronze panel with a garlanded relief of the poet's head by Caesar Heinemann—was hidden during the Third Reich to prevent it suffering the same fate as Hamburg's main Heine monument, which was unveiled in the Stadtpark in 1926 but removed in 1933 and melted down a decade later. A copy by Waldemar Otto (1982) now stands on the edge of the Rathausmarkt, in front of the town hall.

Another Heine monument which once resided in Hamburg has an even more checkered past. It was commissioned in 1879 by Austria's Empress Elisabeth ("Sisi") and sculpted by the Dane Ludvig Hasselriis, who also designed Heine's gravestone in Paris. It was first erected in Elisabeth's summer palace on Corfu, the Achilleion. Following her tragic death the palace was acquired by Germany's Kaiser Wilhelm II, who had little regard for Heine's subversive poetry and swiftly sold the marble monument to Heinrich Julius Campe, son of Heine's original publisher. Campe donated it to the city and it was exhibited for a time in the Barkhof office building on the Mönckebergstrasse, and then in Altona's Donnerspark, but its presence outraged nationalists and anti-Semites who regarded the poet as a treacherous figure. It was dismantled in 1933 and taken to France in 1939, where it now resides in the botanical gardens of the city of Toulon. There are periodic calls for it to be returned, but one may feel that Hamburg has forfeited all its rights in the matter.

Winterhude and St. Georg: Contrasting Suburbs

From the Krugkoppelbrücke at the north end of the Outer Alster, it is worth making a short detour to see Hamburg's millionaires' row, the Leinpfad, which runs along the river bank as far as Hudtwalckerstrasse. Every other car might be a Porsche or a Mercedes, but there is a huge variety in architectural styles to admire. If you return to the Outer Alster on the other side of the river, along Heilwigstrasse, you will see an interesting clinker-brick building with the initials KBW (Kulturwissenschaftliche Bibliothek Warburg) at Heilwigstrasse 116. This is the Warburg-Haus, built in 1925-6 by the architect Gerhard Langmaack as a library for the independent scholar Aby Warburg.

Warburg was one of the most interesting and gifted figures in Hamburg's cultural life in the late nineteenth and early twentieth centuries. Born into a leading Jewish banking family at Mittelweg 17 in Harvestehude, Warburg was allegedly only thirteen years old when he made the famous deal with his younger brother Max to relinquish his rights in his father's business, provided that Max would buy him any book he wanted. Max (1867-1946) went on to become one of Wilhelmine Germany's leading bankers, a close confidant of the Kaiser himself, while Aby became an innovative art historian, who rejected purely stylistic interpretations in favor of a very modern interdisciplinary approach. He had a particular interest in the Renaissance period and once described himself as "a Jew by birth, a Hamburger at heart, and a Florentine of the spirit."

Aby Warburg became a professor at the newly founded University of Hamburg in 1919, though he rarely taught due to bouts of depression. He had moved to Heilwigstrasse 114 in 1909, but there was little room for his collection of books, which by the 1920s consisted of some 46,000 volumes. The library, which he had built next door, was designed to include an oval reading room in homage to the famous reading room at the British Museum. Warburg died in 1929, and in 1933—under threat from the Nazis—the whole collection was shipped to Britain, where it today forms the basis of the University of London's Warburg Institute. The Warburg-Haus was restored about a decade ago and is now a research library and venue attached to the University of Hamburg.

If residents of the Alster's west bank owe much to John Fontenay, then a similar debt is owed in the north and east to the goldsmith Adolph Sierich (1826-89). In 1861 he purchased a large, marshy plot of land, which was considered of little use even for agriculture. Once a canal had been built to drain the land, however, he was able to lay out a network of wide, tree-lined streets which formed the basis of the new suburb of Winterhude. Not only does Sierich's name live on in one of the area's main thoroughfares and underground stations, but the canny jeweler ensured that he was forever accompanied by his family and friends too: his mother (Dorothea), first wife (Maria Louise), second wife (Klärchen), sister-in-law (Agnes), eldest son (Willi), best friend (Andreas) and the executor of his will (Wentzel) are all commemorated in local street names. Sierichstrasse has one other claim to fame: in 1952 it became the first road in the world to operate a variable one-way system, by which its two lanes are open for inbound traffic only between 4 a.m. and midday, and outbound traffic only between midday and 4 a.m.

Canals and ponds may have been needed to drain the marshy land to the east of the Alster, but they also contribute to the attractiveness of Winterhude as a residential location. They ensure that many properties away from the Alster still enjoy a waterside view, and some even have their own private landing stages. Hamburg's main yachting and canoeing clubs are based on this side of the Alster, in the district of Uhlenhorst. This area is also home to the oldest and most attractive of the more than forty mosques that serve the 1,300-strong Iranian Shiite community in the city; Imam Ali

Mosque (1960) has a turquoise-green dome flanked by two minarets, and blends in surprisingly well with its surroundings on the Alster shoreline (Schöne Aussicht 36).

Further south, but still in Uhlenhorst, is Hamburg's Literature House (Schwanenwik 38). Occupying part of a nineteenth-century terrace which looks as though it might have been transported from the seafront at Brighton or Eastbourne, the Literaturhaus has been the venue for regular readings by authors from home and abroad since 1989. Coincidentally, one of the great names of contemporary German literature, Günter Grass, lived for a time in this street in the 1980s (Schwanenwik 31), and two brothers who both enjoyed some success as novelists in the USA—Edgar and Joachim Maass—were born at Schwanenwik 33. Edgar Maass (1896-1964), author of numerous historical novels, is the better known of the two; while his brother Joachim (1901-72) was highlighted by Hermann Hesse as one of the most talented young novelists of his generation. A much less highbrow, but no less interesting venue stands almost directly opposite the Literaturhaus: the Alsterperle ("Alster Pearl") is a former public convenience now converted into a café.

In 1988 Stephen Spender published a short prose work called *The Temple*, which he had first written in 1930 and dedicated to Christopher Isherwood, but withheld from publication on the advice of Virginia Woolf. Clearly based on Spender's own experiences as a visitor to Hamburg in the late 1920s, much of the novel takes place on and around the banks of the Outer Alster:

> Paul could hear the rustling of the boats through the water, a throbbing base under the splash of paddles and the laughing and shouting of the canoers. One canoe was very close to where they stood. It had penetrated right under the willow boughs which barred off the lake from the Stockmann property. Seeing Ernst and Paul, and with a decent sense perhaps that they were trespassing, two boys plunged the blades of their paddles into the water and moved away powerfully, the lifted shining varnished side of their canoe resembling the swishing side of a dolphin sheering away from a ship's prow. The stooping willow boughs, the scent of lime trees, the browns and pinks of flesh, the summer clothes, the murmuring laughter, the distant sails further out on the lake, and beyond them the lights of the city, rectangles and

triangles of walls and towers reflected, gave Paul the strongest sense of young foreign life.

The southeastern corner of the Outer Alster borders on the grittier districts of Hohenfelde and St. Georg. The latter is now an inner-city district, but it originally developed in medieval times as one of Hamburg's first suburbs. Its location outside the medieval city walls meant it became home to some of the less reputable trades and to immigrants who had not yet acquired the right of residence in the city. St. Georg obtained its name from a leprosy hospital established on open fields here in around 1200. It was located outside the walls to reduce the danger of disease spreading through the city itself. St. Georg was also the location of the city's cemeteries and gallows. Public executions remained a popular spectacle here until as late as 1818, when the beheading of Conrad Lorenz drew a crowd of 40,000.

A new general hospital opened in the early 1820s. Designed by Carl Ludwig Wimmel, it was claimed to be the largest and most modern in Europe at the time. It has been rebuilt many times since. In the 1820s St. Georg also became the site of the city's Tivoli pleasure gardens, whose principal attraction was a 550-foot slide, which snaked its way down from the second floor of a pub. Amusements, hospitals, immigrants and prostitutes all remain, although on-street prostitution—which used to be a serious problem around Steindamm and Hansaplatz—has largely been removed, and the only plague scourging the community today is drugs. If that sounds a little bleak, it should be stressed that St. Georg is one of Hamburg's most colorful, varied and interesting districts, with a strong sense of identity and an active local history workshop. It is also the center of the city's gay community.

It is certainly worth turning off the Alster path to walk down the Lange Reihe: one of St. Georg's oldest streets, with a host of independent shops and restaurants. Its name ("Long Row") comes from the fact that for many years only one side of the street was built on. It was in a house on this street (no. 71) that the legendary German film star and singer of the 1930s, 1940s and 1950s, Hans Albers (1891-1960), was born. As someone who never emigrated to Hollywood, Albers is far less known in the English-speaking world than Marlene Dietrich or Peter Lorre, but he remains a household name in Germany. A propos Marlene, the man who wrote the lyrics for the song "Lili Marleen," Hans Leip (1893-1983), was also born in Lange Reihe at no. 91, before moving on to more prestigious Hamburg addresses. Although written while Leip was on sentry duty at a barracks in Berlin in April 1915, it was not until the Second World War that Lale Andersen's interpretation of the song became a hit on both sides of the lines.

St. Georg has an important place in the history of the German labor movement too. It was the home of Carl Legien (1861-1920), the man who led the free trade unions following the lifting of the German Empire's repressive anti-socialist laws in 1890; and of Ernst Thälmann (1886-1944), who used to work as a drayman on Lange Reihe before rising to become head of the German Communist Party in the Weimar Republic. More importantly, when the Hamburg trade union federation built a grand new headquarters in 1905, they chose to do so in St. Georg (Besenbinderhof, on the south side of Kurt-Schumacher-Allee). The building, which was designed by Heinrich Krug and extended in 1913, still serves the labor movement today, although it was badly damaged in the Second World War and much of its original character has been lost. This is a pity because, by adopting the monumental neo-Baroque style often used by the imperial German state, the union building laid down a symbolic challenge to Hamburg's city fathers, whose neo-Renaissance town hall made much of the city's Hanseatic heritage. The majority of workers in Hamburg by this time were migrants, with no particular loyalty to the city or its traditions, so it is understandable that they should feel little obligation to adopt its architectural style or symbols: for them, Hamburg meant an undemocratic franchise and a concentration of power in the hands of a patrician elite.

St. Georg is also home to Germany's newest cathedral. In 1995 the Catholic Church created a new diocese, uniting Hamburg and Schleswig-Holstein with the former East German region of Mecklenburg, and the late nineteenth-century Marienkirche (St. Mary's Church) was upgraded to a cathedral as a result. It was built in the 1890s, and was the first new Catholic place of worship to open in the city since the Reformation. Architecturally, however, it is an unremarkable example of the neo-Romanesque style that was often employed for ecclesiastical buildings (of both confessions) in the Wilhelmine period. It can be found in the Danzigerstrasse.

A short distance away is one of Hamburg's most venerable and re-

spected hotels, the Atlantic (An der Alster 72-79), which is where Adolf
Hitler always stayed on his visits to the city, and which has subsequently
accommodated Michael Jackson and Madonna, among others. With its
freshly whitewashed walls, mighty caryatids and giant illuminated globe,
the late Wilhelmine structure (built 1907-9) might resemble "an ocean
liner made out of cement," according to the French writer Henri Béraud,
but it is hard to imagine the Alster shoreline without it. If it looks vaguely
familiar, you may have seen it in the 1997 James Bond film *Tomorrow
Never Dies*, where Pierce Brosnan escapes from captivity in one of the
hotel's suites. However, its grandeur is not just a celluloid fantasy: its
restaurant boasts a highly-coveted Michelin star. St. Georg's proximity to
the main railway station means that the district has more than its fair share
of hotels. One of them, the Reichshof Hotel Maritim on the corner of
Kirchenallee and Lange Reihe, claimed to be the largest hotel in the whole
of Germany when it opened in 1909, and was famous for its giant chan-
deliers, but today many of the area's hotels have a down-at-heel feel, re-
flecting a reliance on coach parties and backpackers rather than the more
discerning traveler.

For a time in the late 1960s it looked as if the whole of St. Georg
might be flattened to make way for a colossal "Alster Center," consisting
of offices, retail space and a series of pyramid-like apartment blocks, with
some sixty stories soaring into the sky. Hans Konwiarz's plan, scheduled for
completion in 1973, was predicated on the belief that the existing central
business district was too confined to remain competitive. In its unashamed
conviction that commerce comes first, it was a classic Hamburg solution:
its boldness and brutality reminiscent of the decision to build the new free
port in the 1880s. For once, however, a mixture of local opposition and financial shortfalls meant that this particular "city of the imagination," unofficially dubbed Alster Manhattan, did not make it beyond the
drawing-board. In hindsight this was a blessing: for all its problems, St.
Georg is a quirky and attractive neighborhood. The undoubted need for
more commercial office space was instead addressed by the City Nord development (near the airport) in the 1980s, and currently by the huge
HafenCity docklands project (see Epilogue).

The most famous of all Hamburg's town planners, Fritz Schumacher,
was himself a St. Georg resident for many years, living at the prestigious
address of An der Alster 39 until forced out by Allied bombing in 1942.

Turn-of-the-century view of the Jungfernstieg

While he was by no means afraid of bold plans, it is hard to believe that Schumacher would have approved of the Alster Center scheme. The key to his success as both an architect and a planner was his sensitivity to scale, and his ability to strike a balance between preservation and development. For an illustration one need look no further than the Inner Alster townscape. Individually, the buildings on Ballindamm, Jungfernstieg and Neuer Jungfernstieg—erected at different times and for different purposes—are unremarkable. As an ensemble, however, they form one of the iconic images of Hamburg. This townscape was not arrived at by happy accident, but by a piece of planning legislation, the 1912 *Baupflegegesetz* ("Law for the Preservation and Care of Buildings") which was one of Schumacher's most important early achievements in the city.

The Jungfernstieg (the Maidens' or Virgins' Walk) has long been Hamburg's best-known street: a wide boulevard beloved by serious shoppers and *flâneurs* alike. Coleridge, who found Hamburg a "filthy town," acknowledged that the "Jungfer Stieg... made an exception. It was a walk or promenade planted with treble rows of elm trees, which, being yearly pruned and cropped, remain slim and dwarf-like. This walk occupies one side of a square piece of water, with many swans on it perfectly tame." It was first laid out in 1665, when an avenue of lime trees was planted on top of the Alster dam. At that time it was known as the Palmaille, but its present name derives from the respectable young ladies who liked to promenade there. Houses, shops and hotels followed—including Streit's Hotel (1837), whose name lives on in an attractively old-fashioned cinema specializing in English-language films—but most fell victim to the Great Fire of 1842. A decade and a half earlier, Heinrich Heine had sat on the Jungfernstieg, watching the girls and the swans go by:

"She's an angel!" cried a sea-captain, so loudly that both girls turned around and then looked jealously at each other. I never said anything myself, just thought my sweetest nothings, and looked at the girls and the pleasant gentle sky, and the tall tower of St. Peter's with its slender waist, and the calm blue Alster, on which the swans swam, so proud, and beautiful, and secure. The swans! I could look at them for hours— these lovely creatures with their soft, long necks, as they so voluptuously cradled themselves on the soft waters, diving up and down, and proudly splashing till the heavens grew dark and the golden stars came out, yearningly, promisingly, wondrously tender and transfigured.

Heine's wealthy Uncle Salomon lived at Jungfernstieg 34, but today the promenade consists mostly of shops. The largest is the Alsterhaus department store (Jungfernstieg 16-20), which opened in 1912 and is regarded as a bona fide Hamburg institution, despite frequent changes in ownership. Its 75th anniversary in 1997 was even marked by a visit from Prince Charles and Lady Diana. A plaque on the Alsterhaus commemorates the poet and publisher Matthias Claudius (1746-1815), who died in a house on the site. Although only a minor poet himself—best known for the hymn "We plough the fields and scatter" (1782)—Claudius edited a heavyweight literary journal, the *Wandsbecker Boten*, which boasted a stellar cast of contributors: Goethe, Herder, Klopstock and Lessing, to name but four. At the western end of the Jungfernstieg, on the other side of the road, is a bookshop (Jungfernstieg 50). The cellar of this bookshop was the secret meeting place of the Hamburg branch of the White Rose resistance group in Nazi Germany. Thirty members of the group were arrested by the Gestapo in 1942 and executed, including its leader Reinhold Meyer.

The Alster Pavilion, at the western corner of the Inner Alster, is the latest in a long line of similar structures on the site. The first was built in wood in 1799 and rebuilt in stone in 1841. Early in the nineteenth century a second wooden structure was erected at the opposite end of the Jungfernstieg: this "Swiss Pavilion"—Heine's favorite coffee house—was destroyed by the 1842 fire. The original Alster Pavilion was replaced by bigger and more ostentatious structures in 1875 and 1900. In the 1920s a modernist "Temple of Swing" in glass and concrete did a roaring trade. Since the Second World War several further versions of the Alster Pavilion have stood at the water's edge, all offering over-priced food and drinks in return for a classic Hamburg view of boats, swans, and the sun glinting off copper-plate roofs.

If you stop for a coffee or to admire the view, one thing you will not see is an island in the Alster. Imagine then the panic in the Senate when, as part of the preparations for a royal visit to mark the opening of the Kiel Canal in June 1895, Kaiser Wilhelm II expressed a wish for the reception to take place on the "Alster Island." For all the city's republican traditions, no one felt brave enough to point out the ruler's error. So, just in time for the celebrations, a wood and canvas "island" was built on pontoons and floated out into the middle of the Inner Alster. The island, bedecked in colorful electric lights, was large enough to accommodate a marquee and an impressive lighthouse. Heavy rain led to the cancellation of a planned firework display, but otherwise the reception went without a hitch, and without the Kaiser appearing to notice the deception.

On the western bank of the Inner Alster, the Neuer Jungfernstieg survived the 1842 fire. A rare example of a middle-class townhouse dating from 1833 can be seen at Neuer Jungfernstieg 19, built for the banker Gottlob Jenisch, but now home to one of the city's most elite clubs, the Übersee-Club. The club was founded in 1922 by the banker Max Warburg, to represent the interests of the city's business community. It disbanded in 1934 but was re-established in 1948. The most prominent building on this side of the Inner Alster, however, is the Vier Jahreszeiten ("Four Seasons"), which was purchased by Friedrich Haerlin in 1897 and is today the city's most prestigious hotel. If you look closely at its apparently uniform façade you can see how it expanded by buying up neighboring properties and incorporating them within the building's structure. Regular guests have included Aristotle Onassis, Maria Callas, Sophia Loren and Luciano Pavarotti.

The eastern side of the Inner Alster, known since 1947 as Ballindamm (after the Hamburg shipping magnate Albert Ballin), was not laid out until the mid-nineteenth century, when debris from the 1842 fire was used to build up its embankment. The head office of Ballin's company HAPAG, which was founded in 1847 and became the largest shipping company in the world, was built here in 1901-3. The monolithic neoclassical building was designed by Martin Haller and extended by Fritz Höger in 1913/22. It was here that the workers' and soldiers' council was based during the revolution of November 1918. The entrance to Hamburg's newest and largest shopping mall is also located at the southern end of Ballindamm. A 1908 office building, the Europahaus, was controversially demolished to make way for the Europa-Passage (2004-6), which offers 110 shops on five levels, and a great free view.

Chapter Four

A CITY ON FIRE

"Most great cities", observed Herr Footh…, "owe their aspect to the interplay of water and fire. All of them have been thoroughly burnt out some time."

Arnold Zweig, *The Axe of Wandsbek*

In the modern era alone, Hamburg has been "thoroughly burnt out" on two occasions. The Great Fire of May 1842 and the firestorm of July 1943 may have had quite different causes, but both had a profound impact on the city's appearance. Areas of bomb-damaged wasteland—a common sight in the early 1960s—may no longer be visible, but the traumatic impact of the two events can still be seen if one knows where to look. Their significance, however, goes beyond issues of architecture and town-planning: the way Hamburgers live and work changed forever in the aftermath of 1842; while 1943 remains central to ongoing debates about Allied "war crimes" and the so-called "Germans as victims" discourse. Good reason, then, to dedicate a chapter to the conflagrations, their consequences and their lasting legacies for the city.

FIRE! FIRE IN THE DEICHSTRASSE!

In the mythology of Hamburg's Great Fire, the cigar-maker Cohen's property in the Deichstrasse has the equivalent status of Thomas Farriner's bakery in London's Pudding Lane. The fire broke out in Cohen's tobacco warehouse at the rear of Deichstrasse 42 in the early hours of May 5, 1842. The precise cause was never established: some have even suggested arson, but this remains conjecture. Certainly the fire spread quickly, and it was not long before no. 25, on the opposite side of the street, was also ablaze. Hamburg did not have a permanent fire brigade until 1872, but its volunteer force had been around since 1676 under the aegis of the city's fire insurance association (the "Cassa"), and had a good reputation. Known in the local dialect as the *Wittkittel* ("white smocks"), they were organized into teams of four officers and sixteen men to each pump cart. The pumps had

to be operated by hand. A typically Hanseatic method was employed to ensure their rapid deployment: a financial premium was paid to the first team to arrive on the scene. In other respects, however, Hamburg's fire-fighting procedures were little different from those employed in London in 1666. The night watchmen who patrolled the city's streets until 1876 carried fire horns, while the main churches were manned by so-called *Türmer* or tower watchmen, equipped with red flags by day and lanterns by night. If a fire was spotted, the church bells would toll, with the seriousness of the blaze and its location identified by the number of rings: an even number in the parish where the fire was located; an odd number elsewhere.

The fire in the Deichstrasse was spotted quickly, but the tightly packed wooden-framed houses allowed it to spread at an alarming rate. The traditional Hamburg merchant's house was not just a dwelling, but a warehouse and workshop as well, and many of the properties around the Deichstrasse contained large quantities of commodities such as rubber and shellac, which further fueled the flames. Add an unusually dry spell of weather and a strong but changeable wind—which made it hard to predict the fire's course—and Hamburg's fate was more or less sealed. By daybreak much of the Altstadt was alight and a dark pall of smoke hung over the city.

Drawn by a steady rain of ash, the writer and charity worker Elise Averdieck (1808-1907) traveled from her home in the suburb of St. Georg to witness the event. She described the atmosphere in the city as a curious mixture: "here solemn earnestness and desperate worry, there ridicule and gawping curiosity." While some were fleeing with their belongings hastily piled on to handcarts, others were still turning up at the theater expecting an evening's entertainment. Sustained by copious quantities of alcohol, hundreds of firemen—including some from as far away as Lübeck and Kiel—and other volunteers fought for hours to stop the fire spreading to key buildings such as St. Nicholas' Church, but its landmark wooden spire began to lean at an increasingly precarious angle above the sea of flames. It eventually collapsed, hissing and wailing, into the sea of flames at 4 o'clock in the afternoon on May 5, just hours after holding its traditional Ascension Day service.

The fire continued for three days and three nights, destroying approximately one-third of the built-up area. To make matters worse, many abandoned shops and warehouses were plundered, and the citizens' militia—which had been helping to fight the fire—had to take up arms against the looters. In total the fire cost 51 lives, 1,700 homes and more than 100 warehouses. A number of important public buildings were lost to the flames as well, including seven churches, sixty schools, the Bank of Hamburg, and the old town hall. After hours of fatal hesitation, and the removal of 18 cartloads of historic records, it was blown up by the city authorities in a belated attempt to create a fire break. The detonation was only partly successful, however, and the sacrifice was in vain. In the end only a change in wind direction, and the wide arc of the city's former wall, enabled the fire to be brought under control. The final flames were extinguished at 7 o'clock on the morning of May 8, close to the present site of the main railway station. The spot is marked by the street name Brandsende, or Fire's End.

The poet and dramatist Friedrich Hebbel (1813-63) witnessed the event. He recorded its aftermath in his diary:

> The burning Hamburg became a burnt-down Hamburg; the fiery dragon crawled back into the glowing embers from whence it came; and the flame red sky once more became gloomy and grey... In the cold light of day one saw with a shudder the horrific sight of a city's corpse.

Public interest in the fire extended far beyond the German lands. In the absence of 24-hour rolling news bulletins, it was left to weekly journals like the *Illustrated London News*—which published wood engravings of the fire in one of its earliest numbers—to provide the first pictorial images of the event. For those prepared to wait a little longer, the city's plight was depicted in several full color dioramas which went on show across Europe later that year. These panoramic paintings included objects placed in the foreground to create a "3-D" effect, and offered "before, during and after" views of the devastated city. Amazingly, there are also photographs showing the immediate aftermath of the blaze. Hermann Biow (1804-50), a German pioneer of the daguerreotype process, climbed onto the roof of one of the few buildings to survive, the new Stock Exchange, and used a camera obscura to take the very first photographs of the city. Indeed, some photographic historians consider these grainy images of Hamburg's smoldering ruins to be the world's first example of photo-journalism, even if they were not published until many years later.

REBUILDING HAMBURG

With the cost of conflagration estimated at around one billion Euros in today's currency, the collapse of the city's fire insurance association was inevitable: there were simply too many claimants and insufficient funds for the "Cassa" to pay out. However, an international appeal raised nearly seven million Marks for victims of the blaze, with Tsar Nicholas of Russia and King Louis-Philippe of France heading the list of contributors. Special commemorative medals and certificates were produced by the city authorities for the most generous donors. In October, Adalbert Harnisch (1815-89) published a fund-raising *Hansa-Album*, with special poems donated by sixty leading writers, as a "gift from Germany's writers to the burnt-out poor of Hamburg." It was, Harnisch suggested, a "worthy monument to the fire and its consequences." A lively market in souvenirs also developed, with melted glass and coins becoming collectors' items.

All this was of little comfort to Heinrich Heine, by now living in Paris, who wrote in a letter of May 20, 1842:

> My poor Hamburg lies in ruins, and the places which are so well known to me, so profoundly bound up with all my youthful memories, are just a smoking pile of rubble! Above all I mourn the loss of St. Peter's, which towered over the meanness of its surroundings! No doubt the city will be quickly rebuilt, with a rigid grid of straight streets and neat houses, but it won't be my wonky, slithery old Hamburg!

Heine had a chance to see the rebuilding work himself when he visited the city for the last time in 1844, staying at Esplanade 19. His most famous work, *Germany—A Winter's Tale*, was published in the same year. It contains the following verses:

> They're slowly rebuilding Hamburg—one half
> was burnt in the fire disaster.
> The town's now like a half-shorn dog,
> looking sadly up at his master.

> I'm sorry certain streets have gone,
> there are places that one misses –

where is the house where my very first love
inspired my very first kisses?

Or the firm where my "Travel Sketches" saw print,
my first work, witty and boisterous?
Or that splendid oyster-cellar where
I swallowed my very first oysters?

And Dirtwall, where is Dirtwall gone?
It isn't much use my looking.
Where's the Pavilion where they did
such marvellous pastry-cooking?

Where's the Town Hall where the Senate sat
and the Burgher Assembly debated?
It seems the most sacred things weren't spared,
that too was incinerated.

Later in the poem Heine observes: "I found the people of Hamburg changed/even more than the city/like walking ruins they go about/poor broken objects of pity." This statement cannot be said to apply to Heine's Uncle Salomon, however, who features prominently in both the history and mythology of the 1842 blaze. When news of the fire reached his country house, he not only gave permission for his Jungfernstieg home to be blown up as a firebreak, but he is also supposed to have enquired "Has the River Elbe burnt down too?" When that question was answered in the negative, his response quickly entered the city's folklore: "Well so long as we have the Elbe, nothing can harm us." In the immediate aftermath of the fire, moreover, it was Salomon Heine who persuaded Hamburg's merchants not to proceed with a proposed moratorium on payments, fearing that any such move would have serious consequences for the city's credit-worthiness and prosperity. He insisted on meeting all his obligations, and the rest of the city's business community followed suit.

Prior to the Great Fire, private initiative and charity provided what little infrastructure Hamburg possessed. As we saw in Chapter One, this included neither a main water supply nor a sewage system. Although there were several small privately-owned waterworks, many people had to buy their water by the bucket load from water-carriers like Johann Wilhelm Bentz (1787-1854), who lived in the Grosse Drehbahn and became an unlikely icon of the city. Bentz, a cheery soul with a shambling gait and a tuneless song permanently on his lips, was a familiar sight on the streets of the Neustadt. He gained the nickname "Hummel" ("bumble-bee") from children's taunts. The greeting "Hummel Hummel," and its Low German response "Mors, Mors" (short for "kiss my arse") now unites Hamburgers around the world, but the figure of the water-carrier which adorns countless Hamburg souvenirs was essentially a symbol of the city's backwardness. A folksy statue of Hummel by the sculptor Richard Kuöhl stands at the corner of Rademachergang and Breiter Gang. It was erected in 1938 as part of the National Socialist regime's attempts to "clean up" the last of the Neustadt alley quarters, which was not only a communist stronghold but had a large population of Jews and gypsies.

One of the beneficial consequences of the 1842 conflagration was therefore to highlight the woeful nature of Hamburg's infrastructure. Admittedly, many of the reforms were a long time in coming, but the city fathers did at least establish a Technical Commission to advise on such matters. The central figure was to be a British civil engineer, William Lindley (1808-1900), who was appointed as a consultant in the autumn of 1842 and spent the next two decades working in the city. In fact, Lindley had already begun to design a water supply and sewage system for the city before the fire broke out. The events of May 1842 made his task more pressing, but in some ways more straightforward too, since much of the city center had been cleared by the fire.

Lindley had first come to Hamburg in 1838, with the personal recommendation of Isambard Kingdom Brunel, for whom he had worked on the Thames Tunnel project. Lindley was entrusted with the planning and building of northern Germany's first railway: the modest 12-mile stretch between Hamburg and Bergedorf was due to open on May 7, 1842, but the fire forced a change in plan. Rather than carrying VIP guests, the first train brought teams of firemen and firefighting equipment to the city, and returned to Bergedorf with some of the 20,000 people made homeless by the blaze. All the stations on the line were designed by Alexis de Chateauneuf (1799-1853), the Hamburg-born son of French aristocrats who had fled the 1789 revolution. The original ticket office and waiting room of Bergedorf station were restored in the early 1990s and can be found at Neuer Weg 54 in the town.

Lindley was a controversial figure on the Elbe. At the height of the fire, he had pleaded with the authorities to take the unpopular decision to blow up buildings in an effort to create fire breaks. Subsequently, he and his compatriot George Giles had been attacked by an angry mob, as rumors began to spread that "the English" had started the blaze. Other more respectable figures predictably objected to Lindley's reforms on the grounds of cost. Yet the success of the railway boosted the Englishman's credibility, and in 1843 he traveled to London for consultations with the sanitary reformer Edwin Chadwick, whose report on *The Sanitary Condition of the Labouring Population* had just been published. In the autumn of that year most of Lindley's plans were finally adopted: "dirty" Hamburg was to build the first underground sewage system on the continent.

In 1848 a large and architecturally imposing waterworks was opened at Rothenburgsort, two miles upstream of the city center. By 1860 there were thirty miles of oval-shaped brick tunnels under Hamburg's streets; by 1913, 345 miles. Some of the widest tunnels could be navigated by boat and became a most unlikely tourist attraction; the Prussian Crown Prince was among the visitors. By 1850 more than one-third of houses in the city were connected to the mains supply, and a few decades later the majority of homes had water on tap. However, what might appear to be a triumphant story of nineteenth-century progress has a rather sorry postscript. Against Lindley's advice, the parsimonious city fathers decided against installing a proper sand filtration system at Rothenburgsort, so water drawn directly from the Elbe was pumped more or less directly into people's homes. All kinds of creatures, both living and dead, were known to come out of Hamburg's taps. Evans (1987) quotes an anonymously written poem published in a local newspaper:

> Of beasts in Hamburg's waterpipes
> There can be found some sixteen types:
> The lamprey, eel, and stickleback,
> Of worms—three kinds—there is no lack,
> Mussels three, slow snails the same
> With jolly woodlice frisk and game.
> A sponge, some algae, and a polyp,
> Through the sieve they jump and frolic.
> As corpses in the pipes are found

The mouse, the cat, also the hound;
Unfortunately lacking yet –
The engineer and architect!

In 1892, when the cholera bacillus entered the city's water supply, it was the centralized and efficient main supply system that spread it with such devastating effects. The city fathers' smug confidence that the water supply was not to blame—most continued to uphold the outdated "miasmatic" theory that the disease was airborne—contributed to the unusual severity of the outbreak.

Lindley's post-fire plans for Hamburg also included the introduction of gas lighting, for which a modern gasworks was opened in 1846 on the Grasbrook, formerly the city's place of execution, where pirates' skulls were once displayed on pikes, and where the HafenCity development is now rising (see Epilogue). By 1870 the city boasted a 150-mile-long gas network, powering more than 9,000 streetlights. The largest gasometer in Europe would later be erected at the Grasbrook site. Yet the Englishman not only dealt with the city's technical infrastructure: he played a central role in reconstructing the city above ground too. The new town hall may have taken another fifty years to build, but its location was decided in 1842, after much discussion between the Technical Commission and the Altona-born architect Gottfried Semper (1803-79), who had put forward his own rival proposals. Despite the protracted gestation of the town hall project, much of the post-fire reconstruction of the city center was actually carried out with remarkable speed.

Hamburg has long been synonymous with brick architecture (see Chapter Five), but the dominant vision at the time of its rebuilding was of a classical "white city." This was not entirely without local historical precedent—the Danish neoclassical architect C. F. Hansen had built extensively in and around Altona in the late eighteenth century—but its mid-nineteenth-century revival was to prove relatively short-lived. Its most obvious legacy was what Fritz Schumacher referred to as the "artwork Hamburg": that area around the Little Alster, with the wide piazza of the Rathausmarkt on one side and the round-arched, flat-roofed Alster Arcades (1843-6) on the other. The latter, with their striking white plaster façades, were designed by de Chateauneuf, who chaired the Technical Commission for most of its 121 sittings. The same prolific architect was also behind the Old Post Office in Poststrasse, with its elegant tower in the style of a Florentine palazzo (1845-7). What might now appear as a rather whimsical piece of architecture was actually a building at the cutting edge of information technology in the 1840s: the tower housed a signal station for an optical telegraph network linking Hamburg to the coast at Cuxhaven. The system could not function at night or in bad weather, so lasted only a few years before it was made obsolete by the introduction of electrical telegraphy.

Arguably, however, the most lasting change brought about by the Great Fire had nothing to do with either Lindley or the Technical Commission. Until 1842 Hamburg merchants had tended to live, work and store their goods all under the same roof. These three functions had been combined for centuries on the city's thin but deep building plots, which offered both a street and a canal or river frontage, and can still be glimpsed in streets such as the Deichstrasse or Admiralitätsstrasse. The half-timbered houses, often with a richly decorated brick façade and a stepped or curved gable, faced on to the street; while at the rear, goods could be winched directly to or from the water. In between, away from the noise of both the street and the water, were the sleeping quarters. The most characteristic internal feature was the large open hall or parlor known as the *Diele*, which often extended over the whole ground floor and could—as in a preserved house at Deichstrasse 37—be two storys in height. It was used for the temporary storage or exchange of goods, but also to entertain and impress clients, and for important family events such as weddings and funerals. The merchant's office or *Comptoir* was usually situated to one side of this *Diele*. In 1939 there were still around 2,000 such houses in Hamburg, but very few now remain *in situ*. Nevertheless, carved beams, doors, ceiling panels and other architectural details, including a complete reconstruction of a seventeenth-century *Diele*, can be viewed in the Museum of Hamburg History.

The lesson the city's business community drew from the fire disaster was that it was unwise to keep all one's eggs—or any other commodity—in one basket. Change did not occur overnight, but increasingly goods would be stored in purpose-built warehouses close to the docks; merchants would move to the new suburbs on the banks of the Alster or the Elbe; and their businesses would be run from offices in a new type of flexible office building, known in Hamburg as the *Kontorhaus*. While architectural his-

Deichstrasse, 1884 by Johann Theobald Riefesell (1836-95)

torians generally look to late nineteenth-century Chicago for the birth-place of the modern office environment, Hamburg was undoubtedly at the forefront of such developments in Europe. More than a hundred *Kontorhäuser* were built in the city before the end of the century, and several hundred more followed in the first decades of the twentieth.

The first *Kontorhaus* was the Dovenhof, built in the southern Altstadt in 1885 but sadly demolished in 1967 to make way for the headquarters of *Der Spiegel* news magazine. Its patron was Heinrich von Ohlendorff (1836-1928), a nouveau riche guano importer who also published the conservative *Norddeutsche Zeitung* newspaper (mouthpiece of Otto von Bismarck) and was reputed to be Hamburg's richest man. Although the French Renaissance façade by Martin Haller was conventional in style, the building was remarkably modern inside. Like many of the warehouses in the Speicherstadt, it was an iron-framed construction without load-bearing internal walls. This meant that the private firms which rented the sixty or so available offices could change the internal arrangements to suit their needs. Individual offices could be made larger or smaller, or indeed removed altogether. Some of the very first "open plan" offices would later be found in Hamburg. All the offices, moreover, had their own telephone connection and were let on a fully serviced basis, with a charge for cleaning, electric lighting and heating included in the rent.

The building also boasted a pneumatic tube postal system and one of the first "paternoster" elevators, for which Hamburg would later become famous. These open elevators, which operated on a continuous loop and whose nickname derives from the string of rosary beads they resembled, were not admittedly invented on the Elbe. An Englishman, J. E. Hall, owned the patent and installed the first "cyclic elevator" in the City of London, but they lasted longer in Hamburg than almost anywhere else in Europe. Sadly most have been closed on safety grounds in recent years, but for anyone curious to find out what happens when you fail to disembark on the top or bottom floor, there are still half a dozen in operation—including one in the HAPAG-Lloyd headquarters at Ballindamm 25, and another in the Axel Springer offices at Kaiser-Wilhelm-Strasse 16.

The Dovenhof features in *Die rote Stadt* (The Red City, 2003), a novel by the Hamburg-based crime writer Boris Meyn (born 1961). It is based at the time of the building's opening in 1886, and actually begins with the discovery of a dead body in the paternoster. Meyn's half dozen

Hamburg novels still await an English translation; while they are not great works of literature they do have a strong sense of place, in some ways comparable to Ian Rankin's Edinburgh. Meyn's version of Rebus is Commissar Hendrik Bischop, but by the time of the events in *Die rote Stadt*—the title refers to the Speicherstadt rather than the city's politics—the commissar has retired, and the murder becomes a case for his lawyer son Sören instead. Meyn describes Sören's bafflement as he notices the paternoster for the first time:

> He couldn't believe what he was seeing. In a recess in the wall, part of the building was moving slowly upwards, seeming to disappear into the ceiling of the floor above, only to emerge almost immediately from the floor below. Alongside it, another part of the building was sinking to the ground at the very same speed, before repeating the trick and reappearing from the ceiling on its side too. Sören at first thought he was dreaming, but it continued even after he had rubbed his eyes several times...

Most of Hamburg's early *Kontorhäuser* were built to the south of the city center, in the area located between the town hall and the River Elbe. Several examples can be seen from the Trostbrücke: the much-photographed Globushof at Trostbrücke 2 (1907), with model ships and a Neptune balancing on its neo-Baroque gables; and the Laeiszhof, home of the Ferdinand Laeisz shipping line, at Trostbrücke 1 (1897-8). Other early examples include the Sloman-Haus on the corner of Baumwall and Steinhöft (1908-9) and its neighbor the Elbhof, with *Jugendstil* detailing, at Steinhöft 9 (1904-5). The most famous *Kontorhaus* of all, however, is the Chilehaus, designed by Fritz Höger and completed in 1924, which ushered in a second wave of office building between Steinstrasse and the Speicherstadt (see Chapter Five).

None of these buildings was erected on green-field sites: many were in fact the result of slum clearance projects in the wake of the 1892 cholera epidemic. Hamburg's slum districts, a warren of picturesque but overcrowded alleyways known as *Gängeviertel* (alley quarters), were among the very worst in Europe. Indeed, the celebrated bacteriologist Robert Koch (1843-1910), who traveled from Berlin to see at first hand the effects of the 1892 epidemic, commented: "I have encountered nothing worse than the workers' accommodation in the alley quarters, neither in the Jewish

District in Prague nor in Italy. In no other city have I come across such unhealthy dwellings, such plague-spots, such breeding places of infection." He then added a remark that Evans claims was "to do more than any other single statement to discredit the government of Hamburg, its social policy, and the political system on which it rested": "Gentlemen, I forget that I am in Europe."

The Slum Clearance Commission, established by the city authorities after the epidemic, identified three inner-city districts in need of demolition. In the first area to be tackled, the southern Neustadt, the authorities proceeded with some caution, removing buildings which were identified as a threat to health, but leaving others standing. A total of 4,577 dwellings, housing 21,094 people, were removed in 1900. When the commission came to tackle the alley quarters of the northern Neustadt and the Altstadt in 1906, however, it was decided to raze each district to the ground and begin from scratch: a combined total of 41,151 dwellings and 17,027 people were removed. The only ensemble of half-timbered houses to survive the slum clearances and the Second World War can be seen at Bäckerbreitergang in the Neustadt: nos. 49-50 date from 1780; 51 and 58 from around 1820. Of course, isolated from their original context, and without the appropriate sounds and smells, they convey only the vaguest impression of life in the alley quarters.

Initial assurances that new housing would be provided in the cleared areas were quickly forgotten, as the city fathers began to recognize the commercial opportunities presented by the development sites. So, while the slums were cleared, the underlying problem of a lack of affordable housing remained: it was simply relocated further out of the city. Working-class Hamburgers would now have to travel by train — particularly by the new electric *Hochbahn* or elevated railway, which also had underground sections (1906-12)—to reach their dockland workplaces. The centerpiece of the Neustadt redevelopment was the Kaiser-Wilhelm-Strasse. Its equivalent in the Altstadt was to be an even wider thoroughfare of offices and shops, below which an underground railway would run, linking the central railway station with the town hall square. This new transport artery, laid out between 1905 and 1908, was named after the long-serving chairman of the Slum Clearance Commission, Johann Georg Mönckeberg (1839-1908). Today, of course, the Mönckebergstrasse is Hamburg's principal shopping street (see Chapter Five). Meanwhile the displaced slum-dwellers were moved to districts several miles to the east of the city center, such as Barmbek, Borgfelde, Hamm, Hammerbrook and Rothenburgsort. In a particularly cruel twist of fate, it was these densely populated working-class districts which suffered most from the Allied bombing of Hamburg in 1943.

OPERATION GOMORRAH

In 2002 the respected military historian Jörg Friedrich published a study of the Allied bombing of Germany under the title *Der Brand* ("The Fire"), which prompted great controversy at home and abroad. It was less the factual content of Friedrich's book which sparked debate than the words he chose to describe the effects of the bombs: the air war was a *Vernichtungskrieg* ("war of extermination"), in which Germany's air-raid shelters became *Krematoria*; its cities became *Hinrichtungsstätten* ("places of execution"); and its libraries suffered *Bücherverbrennungen* ("the burning of books"). Although the author was no right-wing revisionist, his use of terms more usually associated with the crimes of the Nazis was provocative to say the least. While it would be unfair to suggest he portrayed the bombing solely from a German perspective—he took care to explain why the British saw "area bombing" as their only available means of striking back at the aggressor—he nevertheless reached the conclusion that by unleashing terror on the German civilian population, both Winston Churchill and the Chief of the Air Staff, Sir Arthur Harris, could be said to have committed war crimes. Friedrich maintained, however, that he was less concerned with the question of guilt than with the pain and suffering of ordinary men, women and children.

One reason why Friedrich's book received so many column inches in the German media was that it seemed to be part of a wider trend within the Federal Republic: one which no longer saw the Germans solely as perpetrators, but also as victims, of the Second World War. The Germans, it was suggested, had long preferred to ignore the "open wound" of their own suffering because of the difficulty of reconciling it with their collective guilt. They may have come to terms with the crimes of the Nazis, but not with the cruelty of the treatment meted out to them by the Allies. It was, W. G. Sebald (2003) wrote, "a kind of taboo" for the Germans, "like a shameful family secret, a secret that perhaps could not even be privately acknowledged."

Many of the thorny moral issues discussed in Friedrich's book had in fact already been raised by Sebald in an essay published in German in 1999. Subsequently Friedrich's emotive book has been published in English (2006), and the first scholarly studies of what has become known as the "Germans as victims" discourse have appeared too (see Niven, 2006). In 2007 they were joined by Keith Lowe's more sober and balanced study of the bombing of Hamburg. For our purposes, therefore, a brief outline of the campaign should suffice. The remainder of the chapter then takes the form of a walk through those parts of the city that suffered most in 1943: the area which chillingly became known as the "dead zone."

In the course of the first three years of the war there were 112 bombing raids on Hamburg, which left a total of 751 dead. In 1944-5 there were a further 65 attacks, which killed 5,390 on the ground. These numbers pale into insignificance, however, against the 40,000 or so who perished during the last week of July 1943. Five main raids took place during that week: three at night, by the Royal Air Force; and two during daylight hours, by the United States Air Force. During the night of July 24-25, 791 RAF bombers crossed the North Sea from airfields in East Anglia. They dropped some 2,300 tons of bombs on Hamburg, including a total of 350,412 individual incendiary bombs. Both figures were unprecedented at the time. Most of the bombs fell in the northwest and western districts of the city: Hoheluft, Eimsbüttel, Harvestehude, Altona and St. Pauli. Later that day, more than 1,200 American bombers set off with two specific targets in their sights: the Blohm & Voss shipyards, a center of U-boat production; and the Klöckner aero-engine factory. On July 26, in another daytime raid, the Americans targeted the Neuhof power station, the MAN diesel engine factory and the Howaldtswerke shipyard.

By far the most deadly chapter in the destruction of Hamburg came on the night of July 27-28. This time 722 British aircraft bombed the city from a north-easterly direction, with most of the bombs landing on the city's east end. It was this attack which produced the infamous firestorm. On July 29 the British hit the northern and eastern suburbs again, with Barmbek particularly affected. A fourth attack, on the city's southern districts, was cut short on August 3 due to heavy cloud. Even so, as Lowe observes, "Over the course of their four raids on the city the RAF attacked in turn from the northwest, the northeast, the north and the south. Effectively they were destroying the city a segment at a time." The city center, however, was barely touched by the 1943 raids. It was not until June 18, 1944 that the town hall was hit, and only then because the American crews aiming for the Blohm & Voss shipyards delayed the release of their bombs by a few seconds.

Before we consider the firestorm in more detail, it is worth pointing out that if this one raid is excluded from the statistics, the Allied attacks succeeded in killing only 0.31 percent of the pre-war population of Hamburg. Friedrich argues that "in view of the 1.7 million bombs dropped on the city"—equivalent to one for every resident—Hamburg's defenders could claim a victory of sorts. Certainly, the initial failure of the RAF to strike a meaningful blow against Hamburg was a testament not only to the city's military defenses—there was a ring of flak batteries around the outskirts of the city and four formidable gun towers close to the center—but also to the efficiency of German civil defense preparations. In most cities this had involved strengthening cellars for use as air-raid shelters, but the high water-table in Hamburg meant that cellars were a comparative rarity. This led to an accelerated program of public air-raid shelter construction, with 549 completed by April 1940 and 1,700 a year later. At the same time, people were ordered to remove all flammable material from the attics of their houses and tenements, and fire wardens were appointed in each apartment block. In the spring of 1941 a fake plasterboard island, complete with painted roads and buildings, was again laid out on the Inner Alster. This time it was not to satisfy the whim of a monarch, but to confuse enemy bombers. It did not work. Pictures of it were published in the British press that July. In any case, it assumed a degree of accuracy which the RAF could only dream of: half the attacks made on Hamburg up to 1940 were actually intended to strike Kiel or Lübeck.

The relative failure of the RAF's bombing campaigns in the first years of the war led to a change in strategy, drawing on the realization that, as Friedrich puts it, "a city was easier to burn down than to blow up." Ironically it was a German who had first outlined the theory in print. Friedrich quotes Wilhelm Siegert, an air force officer during the First World War, who wrote in 1927: "If it is possible to start numerous sources of fire in a city such that the existing fire departments cannot extinguish all of them at once, the seeds of catastrophe are sown. The individual fires merge into a major blaze. The superheated air shoots upward like a giant chimney.

The air that rushes in along the ground creates the 'firestorm', which in turn causes the smaller fires to unfurl completely." Since the start of 1943, researchers at the Air Ministry in London had been working not only on the precise combination of high-explosive bombs and incendiaries needed to create the "giant chimney," but also on the kind of cities where this effect might take hold. Hamburg was not one of them: as we have seen, many of its old wooden-framed buildings had been lost in 1842, and its urban area was sprawling and dispersed compared to many German towns.

There were also other reasons why Hamburg was not an obvious target. Lowe quotes the British radar pioneer Sir Henry Tizard, who wrote to Churchill with his misgivings: "Hamburg is anti-Russian, anti-Prussian and anti-Nazi. It may well be soon, if not already, anti-war. Apart from submarine construction and shipping, generally it is not industrially important… It is a very important port and might therefore be much more useful to us alive than dead." Yet Tizard's arguments were quickly dismissed. Hamburg was the second city of the Reich and less well defended than Berlin. It was just a few hours' flying time from East Anglia and relatively easy to locate, thanks to the broad stream of the Elbe and the wide expanse of the Outer Alster. Above all, Harris was convinced that the eradication of a major German city would be such a crippling blow to morale that it would serve as a "knock-out blow," which could end the war within weeks.

With hindsight we can see that this was an illusion. Although morale was damaged by the shock of the first bombs getting through, the accumulation of experiences tended to dull the effect. As Friedrich puts it, "The soul did not rebel; it shrivelled. Apathy and depression predominated. People felt an overwhelming need for sleep and none at all to overthrow Hitler." In fact, it is dangerous to generalize about the response of ordinary Hamburgers to the attacks. For some Christians the air raids seemed like the inevitable retribution for Germany's sins. For others, such as the left-wing novelist Hans Erich Nossack (1901-77), there was a sense of relief and even elation at the sight of British bombers overhead. In his classic eyewitness account of the bombing of Hamburg, *Der Untergang* ("The End," 1948), he wrote:

> I jumped out of bed and ran barefoot out of the house into this sound
> that hovered like an oppressive weight between the clear constellations

and the dark earth, not here and not there but everywhere in space… One didn't dare take a breath for fear of inhaling it. It was the sound of 1800 aeroplanes [sic] approaching Hamburg from the south at an unimaginable height. We had already experienced two hundred or even more air raids, some of them very heavy, but this was something completely new. And yet there was an immediate recognition: this was what everyone had been waiting for, what had hung for months like a shadow over everything we did, making us weary. It was the end.

While the firestorm was carefully planned, its devastating effects were caused as much by luck as judgement. As in May 1842, Hamburg had been enjoying unusually warm, dry weather. On July 27-28, 1943, temperatures ranged from 70 to 85 degrees Fahrenheit. According to Friedrich, it was the "combination of the climate, the incendiary ratio, the collapsed defenses, and the structure of the city blocks [that] created what Harris's codename 'Gomorrah' predicted." Although it took the RAF just 43 minutes to drop their payload, the firestorm raged for some six hours. Wolf Biermann, who later became a prominent singer-songwriter and dissident in East Germany, was a small child at the time:

The firestorm was so strong that it converted streets into jets. Schwabenstrasse, where we lived, was in a good position, aslant to the suction of the fire. But once you got into a street which was part of the suction, people started to burn like tinder and they had no chance. So we ran close to the walls to escape the storm. I saw how roofs were flying through the air; it was like in the movies, like science fiction, but real.

In an area of about 4.5 square miles, temperatures rose to more than 1,000 degrees Fahrenheit. Hurricane-force winds devoured everything in their wake. Oxygen was sucked out of cellars and shelters, creating the "giant chimney" described by Siegert in 1927. The effect reminded Professor Franz Termer, Director of Hamburg's Museum of Ethnology, of a volcanic eruption:

Because of the hot air, which rose and then cooled and condensed in the upper atmosphere, a downpour fell over Hamburg from the 2,000-

3,000-metre high cloud of smoke… the rain mixed with the ash and created a thick black mud, as we know of volcanic eruptions—a mixture that covered everything, distorted people's faces and matted their hair.

Rescue crews had to wait ten days for the rubble to cool down. While they found some bodies incinerated beyond recognition, many others appeared almost untouched: between 70 and 80 percent of the July 27-28 casualties were from asphyxiation. The shelters that had proved so resilient against high explosives offered much less protection against the firestorm. In the basement shelter of the Karstadt department store in Barmbek, for instance, 370 bodies were found poisoned by the fire's gases.

The July 1943 raids made 900,000 Hamburgers homeless and belatedly prompted one of the biggest mass evacuations in history. In total more than a million people left the city: 786,000 were transported on 625 special trains; 50,000 departed by boat on the Elbe; and many thousands more left on foot. The destination for the special trains was the Bavarian town of Bayreuth, many hundreds of miles to the south, which was accustomed to the more genteel invasion of opera lovers for the annual Wagner festival. The Nazi hierarchy was undoubtedly shocked by the ferocity of the attacks. Despite pleas from the *Gauleiter* Karl Kaufmann, Hitler refused to see the scene for himself. Goebbels wrote in his diary: "A city of a million inhabitants has been destroyed in a manner unparalleled in history. We are faced with problems that are almost impossible of solution."

For some, this was itself sufficient justification for the raids. The Nazi regime had to divert effort and resources into dealing with Hamburg's plight, which could otherwise have supported their frontline troops. Lowe notes that, after the war, "the Americans estimated that Hamburg lost 1.8 months of its entire industrial production as a direct result of the raids, about half of which was intended for the armed forces. This meant that fewer supplies were sent to the Russian Front, fewer aircraft took to the skies, and fewer U-boats were launched to attack British shipping in the north Atlantic." On the other hand, as he acknowledges, it only amounted to a temporary setback for the Nazi war machine. Contrary to "Bomber" Harris's expectations, the Germans fought on for another two years.

In total, Friedrich suggests, Hamburg accounted for 56 million of the 523 million cubic yards of rubble that the Allied bombs left behind in

Germany. Around 275,000 apartments, or 61 percent of the city's accommodation, were either completely obliterated or rendered uninhabitable. The poet Stephen Spender, no stranger to the city, returned in August 1945:

> At the side of a lake there is a city which in the gloom suggests a vast construction of many forms, all shaped like gallows. Buildings, some of which are only blackened façades with broken windows, rise from its shores. An outline of the town's centre still exists, with churches, offices and hotels. Indeed, some of the buildings are remarkably unscathed, just as in a corpse some flesh seems perfect and even flushed with life. But that astonishing and total change, that incalculable shift from a soaring to a sinking motion which distinguishes a dead body, has taken place in Hamburg.

Nowhere was this more apparent than in that sector of the city which was still roped off when Spender passed through in the summer of 1945: the "dead zone." In other parts of the city it had been possible to clear roads and debris relatively quickly, but in the districts of Hamm, Hammerbrook and Rothenburgsort there seemed little point. Such was the devastation it seemed inconceivable that life would ever return.

A Walk through the "Dead Zone"

The epicenter of the firestorm was located on Ausschläger Weg, between the Mittelkanal and the Südkanal in Hammerbrook. This walk, however, starts at Berliner Tor, which was once one of three gates into Hamburg's oldest suburb, St. Georg, and the main entrance into the city from the east. The gate itself was removed in around 1820. Directly opposite the exit of Berliner Tor railway station, and next to the high-rise BTC office development by Jan Störmer and Partners (2004), is the fire headquarters from where the response to the firestorm was coordinated. The red-brick building with the tall mansard roof was the first of a number of Hamburg fire stations designed by Fritz Schumacher and reflects his early style developed in Dresden. The planning phase lasted from 1909 to 1914, but the outbreak of the First World War meant that it was not finished until 1922. The building, which originally included apartments for fire officers, was itself damaged by wartime bombing, but has been restored several times

since. The bridge that carries Borgfelder Strasse over the busy Hei-
denkampsweg marks the border between St. Georg and Borgfelde. Below
the bridge, on the far embankment, is a tile mosaic dating from the 1970s,
designed to remind passersby of the divided nature of Germany's former
capital city: the word BER/LIN is split in two.

Looking south from the bridge one can also see two very different
generations of Hamburg *Kontorhäuser*. On the right is the Leder-Schüler
building, in dark clinker brick with green transom windows (Hei-
denkampsweg 34). It was designed by the architect of the Chilehaus, Fritz
Höger, and built between 1927 and 1929. Its basement has housed a
number of legendary Hamburg nightclubs, including the Cotton Club
(1965), Danny's Pan (from 1966), Front (where I danced in the 1980s)
and Chocolate City (from 1997). Today it goes by the name of Shake! A
listed building, it typifies Höger's more sober and less Expressionist style
of the late 1920s and early 1930s. Facing it across the six-lane highway is
the elegant 120-foot steel parabola of the prizewinning Berliner-Bogen
development, designed by the fashionable BRT practice, and built between
1998 and 2001 (Anckelmannsplatz 1). The solar-powered building offers
a winter garden with its own microclimate and more than 320,000 square
feet of flexible office space. It is used by more than a dozen firms, employing some 1,200 people in total.

As you proceed eastwards along Borgfelder Strasse, which was once
the main road to Bergedorf and on to Berlin, you will notice in a small
park to the right the familiar shape of a Second World War round tower
bunker, albeit with the addition of windows, and now converted into
apartments. In the early months of the war the Germans concentrated on
building underground shelters, but then switched to tower bunkers that
proved equally sturdy and more economical. Bunkers of this sort had a
capacity of between 500 and 1,000, and were built all over Hamburg. One
located near Baumwall station, which now houses a Portuguese restaurant,
still bears the relief of a very martial looking Nazi eagle (although with the
Swastika removed from its talons). Compared to a mega-bunker like that
on the Heiligengeistfeld, which also served as a flak tower and could accommodate many thousands, these bunkers were modest in size, but even
the smaller shelters could quickly became unpleasant environments. Keith
Lowe quotes one survivor of the raids on Hamburg:

Hochhaus 1: the mega-bunker on the Heiligengeistfeld (1942)

Imagine around a thousand people crammed into the small rooms, a real heat inside, sweat running down our bodies, the bunker full of smoke from outside, not a drop of water to drink, no food and no light. The electricity went straight away. Torches were all flat; the few tallow candles were soon finished. And the whole time there was such an atmosphere; outside the bombs roared, often so close that the bunker shook. Can you imagine this with women and babies?

Despite a vast program of bunker building, there was still only room for around a quarter of the city's population by 1943. In a desperate effort to increase shelter capacity, the authorities began laying concrete pipes in the ground, six feet below street level. The pipes had a circumference of about six feet and were between sixty and 260 feet long. They could, Friedrich observes, "protect against shrapnel and falling rubble but little else." In wet weather they quickly took on the character of the sewers they so closely resembled. There were 370 such pipe shelters in Hamburg, with room for around 60,000 people.

At the next junction, turn right into Ausschläger Weg. This road, which links Borgfelde to Hammerbrook and Rothenburgsort, was first mentioned in print in 1525. Its name comes from the Low German word *Utslag*, which refers to marshy land used as pasture in summer, but allowed to flood in winter. It was the ubiquitous William Lindley who in 1840 first identified the area to the southeast of St. Georg as potentially suitable for settlement. Before a geometric, American-style grid of streets was laid out in the second half of the nineteenth century, a network of canals was dug, also to a strict grid pattern. These waterways were intended partly for irrigation, but also to provide easy transport access to the Bille and Elbe rivers. You will cross two of these canals—the Mittelkanal (Central Canal) and the Südkanal (South Canal)—in quick succession. A third, the Nordkanal (North Canal), was filled in during the 1950s, but lives on in the street name Nordkanalstrasse. The embankments were built up with debris from the Great Fire, and the first people to settle here—albeit on a temporary basis—were some of those made homeless in 1842.

As warehouses, factories and tenements sprang up on the banks of the canals in the second half of the nineteenth century, Hammerbrook became a byword for the worst excesses of speculative development and poor housing. With depressing predictability, many of those displaced by both the Speicherstadt in the 1880s and the slum clearance programs of the early 1900s found their way to the district nicknamed *Jammerbrook* ("wailing brook"). In 1901 the district elected Otto Stolten (1853-1928) of the SPD to the Citizens' Assembly: he was the first socialist to sit in Hamburg's parliament. By 1910 Hammerbrook's population had reached 60,000, and its overcrowded and insanitary streets were identified as one of Hamburg's most pressing town-planning problems. Little was done, however, until the problem was "solved" in the most brutal fashion in July 1943: 36 percent of Hammerbrook's residents perished in the Allied attacks. Significantly, there was no clamor from survivors to return to this unloved part of the city after 1945. It has remained a kind of "dead zone" of garages, industrial units, offices and warehouses ever since, with only 600 permanent residents. It is particularly quiet at night, and, unsurprisingly, there is also no plaque or monument to mark the epicenter of the firestorm.

Continue to the end of Ausschläger Weg, then cross the River Bille on the so-called Green Bridge. A left turn brings you onto Bullenhuser

Damm. What might seem like another anonymous industrial street holds a particularly dark secret. The large red-brick building with the pitched roof on the right-hand side of the street is one of the city's former elementary schools, built in 1908-10 to a design by Albert Erbe. Above the front door is an attractive relief of happy children at play. During the Second World War, however, the school was used as an overspill for the Neuengamme concentration camp. During the night of April 20-21, 1945, a series of horrific murders took place in the school's basement. One of the doctors at Neuengamme, Dr. Kurt Heissmeyer (1905-67), had been using Jewish children for medical experiments, including injections of the tuberculosis bacillus. As British troops closed in on the city, an SS unit took twenty of the children, two Polish caregivers, two French doctors and 24 Soviet prisoners of war, and hanged them all in the school's cellar.

Although most of the men responsible were later brought to justice, the episode was largely forgotten until the *Stern* journalist Günther Schwarberg wrote a series of articles and a book on *Der SS-Arzt und die Kinder vom Bullenhuser Damm* ("The SS-Doctor and the Children of Bullenhuser Damm"). Behind the school, which continued in use until 1987, is a small rose garden, in which each of the victims is commemorated. There is also a collective bronze monument, in Socialist Realist style, to the 24 Soviet victims (1985).

Exit the rose garden and cross Grossmann Strasse, heading for the Ausschläger Billdeich. This road takes you across another canal, the Billekanal, and into the district of Rothenburgsort. You will notice an underground air-raid shelter, built into a traffic island and covered with soil and grass, at the junction with the Billhorner Deich. With more than 50,000 inhabitants crowded into a few square miles, Rothenburgsort was once Hamburg's most densely populated community: the 1901 census revealed that 9,287 people lived on one street alone, the Billhorner Röhrendamm. As the name implies, the Röhrendamm ("pipe causeway") was laid out in 1865 on top of the tunnel carrying Hamburg's main water supply from the Rothenburgsort waterworks to the city. Before the war it was a bustling street of shops and tenements. All that changed in July 1943, a fact commemorated in a recent piece of public art situated on the left-hand side of Billhorner Deich, shortly after its junction with Marckmannstrasse. The work, by the artist Volker Lang (born 1964), is a 1:2.5 scale reproduction of a five-story terraced tenement, typical of the sort of homes built at Rothenburgsort in the 1880s, but obliterated in the firestorm. In the white-painted interior of the slate gray house are a series of quotes and memories from local residents.

As this might suggest, there was always a strong sense of community in Rothenburgsort, which was, and is, something of an island, cut off by waterways and classification yards. In the 1920s, for instance, a local workers' soccer team, FTSV Lorbeer 06, attracted crowds of up to 20,000 and twice won the national Workers' Amateur Championship, before losing their star player Erwin Seeler—father of the legendary Uwe—to the professional ranks, and being banned by the Nazis in 1933. The district was also the location of the Hanseatenhalle, at one time the largest indoor arena in the world. More than 27,000 crammed in to watch a fight between the German Max Schmeling and the American Steve Hamas in 1935. Both Goebbels and Hitler would later address rallies in the vast hall, and yet Rothenburgsort was always a stronghold of the Left. Today it has a rather neglected and isolated feel, even though it is only a 15-minute journey from the city center. More than a quarter of its present inhabitants are immigrants.

The last stop on our walk through the "dead zone" is, appropriately enough, one of the few pre-war buildings to survive the inferno: William Lindley's waterworks of 1848 at Billhorner Deich 2. The waterworks, with its 200-foot pumping tower designed by Alexis de Chateauneuf, is now a listed monument and houses an interesting museum, the WasserForum. Even so, few tourists ever make it to Rothenburgsort, and it must be conceded that this part of Hamburg has little aesthetic charm. Yet its story, and the struggles of its people, should not be forgotten.

Chapter Five
A CITY OF BRICK

THE CHILEHAUS AND CENTRAL BUSINESS DISTRICT

In Adrian Lyne's 1993 film *Indecent Proposal*, an architect played by Woody Harrelson remarks that "a common ordinary brick wants to be something more than it is." If that is the case, then there is probably no better place for a brick to be than Hamburg. It is not just that brick has been an important building material in northern Germany for many centuries, or that Hamburg has been described as a city "held together by brick" (Manfred Sack). Since the early 1900s the "common ordinary brick" has also been invested with a host of social, political and even spiritual qualities by the city's writers and architects. One of the latter, Fritz Höger (1877-1949), put it this way: "for me, every building in brick expresses something sacred and religious if it comes from the hand of a good master-builder."

Höger, a carpenter's son from rural Holstein who preferred the artisan title of *Baumeister* (master-builder) to that of architect, set up his own practice in 1907. He particularly favored the use of clinker bricks, which are denser and heavier than regular bricks, and which develop a purplish metallic hue when fired more than once, or at particularly high temperatures. Some 4.8 million such bricks were used in the construction of his most famous building, the Chilehaus, which stands in the heart of what is now Hamburg's central business district, located between Messberg and Steinstrasse. The latter, so named because it was the first cobbled road through the medieval parish of St. Jacob's, is only five minutes' walk from the main railway station. The Chilehaus was designed at the end of the First World War, and built between 1922 and 1924 on an elongated hexagonal plot demarcated by Burchardstrasse, Pumpen, Messberg, Depenau and Niedernstrasse. It is not only Hamburg's most dramatic individual building, but also a potent symbol of its maritime heritage.

It was built for the Hull-born businessman Henry Brarens Sloman (1848-1931), who had spent his childhood in northern Germany before emigrating to South America at the age of twenty in 1868. Sloman, who

did not return to live in Hamburg until the 1900s, made his fortune trading in Chilean saltpeter, a mineral used in both fertilizer and gunpowder. According to the *Yearbook of Wealth and Income of Millionaires in Hamburg, Bremen and Lübeck* (1912), Sloman's wealth was estimated at sixty million Marks, and his annual income at three million, which made him the richest man in Hamburg by some distance. He purchased the site—actually two separate plots divided by a narrow street called Fischertwiete—in a municipal auction. Previously, 69 slum properties and numerous narrow alleyways had stood there, alongside a foul-smelling waste dump which lives on today in the street name Messberg (from *Mistberg*, or mountain of dung). Indeed, during the construction of the Chilehaus, workers had to dig through many centuries' worth of accumulated waste, which added an extra ten to fifteen feet of soil to parts of the site.

Sloman chose Höger's designs over those of two other architectural firms, even though his richly decorated façades added significantly to the cost. Höger turned what might have been a rather monotonous ten-story office building into a brick ocean liner, complete with deck-like recessed upper stories, a pointed ship's prow and even an ornamental figurehead, supposedly modeled on the HAPAG liner *Imperator*. The building was not only a bold statement on behalf of its architect and client, but also for the city itself, as it sought to recover from the crippling effects of war, revolution and hyper-inflation. Hamburg's merchant fleet may have been decimated, it seemed to say, but its entrepreneurial self-confidence remained intact. It quickly became an icon of the city, and was cited in architectural journals around the globe as a prime example of German brick Expressionism. The leading photographers of the 1920s, including Andreas Feininger and Albert Renger-Patzsch, made dramatic black-and-white images of its "pointed" eastern end; while artists such as Heinrich Vogeler and Arthur Illies recognized its potent symbolism too. The building was first depicted on tourist posters as early as 1925, and even featured on Germany's standard forty-pfennig postage stamp for many years.

Yet the Chilehaus has always polarized opinion. Shortly after its completion, the Expressionist poet Rudolf Binding (1867-1938) pompously asserted: "Whoever is not moved by this building has no idea of courage, of freedom, self-confidence, optimism, indomitability, invincibility; and nothing either of modesty, sobriety, simplicity, truthfulness or faith in one's own time." Meanwhile the architect Hermann Sörgel (1885-1952) wrote:

"Its creator should be named alongside other great evangelists of German power and invention such as Zeppelin… Einstein, Spengler or Strauss." On the other hand, some of the classic histories of twentieth-century architecture regarded it as a stylistic aberration, out of step with the pure functionalism of Gropius or Le Corbusier, and therefore difficult to place in the dominant narrative of "heroic" modernism versus reactionary historicism. Nikolaus Pevsner (1960), for instance, conceded that the building's dramatic prow was "sensational," but was nevertheless unable to warm to its decorative style, in which he heard echoes of Art Nouveau. The fact that the Chilehaus actually has a reinforced concrete frame and the brickwork is mere cladding led some to suggest that it was no more "honest" than the nineteenth-century historicist façades which Höger was so quick to condemn. Ironically, the most talked about aspect of the building—the way in which its prow seemed to become a gigantic gable, soaring up to the heavens—was something of an unintended optical illusion. It was the photographer Franz Rompel who pointed it out to the architect after taking a shot of the newly completed building from ground level at the junction of Pumpen and Burchardstrasse.

Although it was struck by bombs several times during the Second World War, the Chilehaus was never burned out and required only modest repairs after 1945. Today it is a protected monument on Hamburg's preservation register, and has also been included on the "Tentative List" of UNESCO's World Heritage Sites. Yet it remains a working office block, home to more than a hundred companies (including the television station Spiegel-TV) and 1,000 employees. While sightseers are not particularly welcome, it is possible to take a peek at the three entrance halls and stairwells. Guided tours are rare, but a stroll around the outside of the building at least conveys something of its huge proportions. It has, for instance, 2,500 windows and more than two miles of guttering. Indeed, so large is the building that no single vantage point can offer a complete view: its façades follow the irregular and asymmetrical street pattern, stopping for an existing building (a police station dating from 1906-8), and even crossing over the Fischertwiete to create an internal courtyard. The Tudor arch over the Fischertwiete not only evokes a castle gate, but quotes directly from Sloman's own home too.

There is a wealth of sculptural detail to enjoy, both in the intricate patterns woven into the brickwork and the terracotta carvings—of puffins, owls, turtles and a host of playful *putti*—which protrude from the building's arcades like gargoyles from a medieval church. They were designed by Richard Kuöhl and manufactured at the Meimersdorf ceramic workshops in the nearby suburb of Wandsbek. Many were clearly chosen for their South American connections, such as the giant Andean condor which adorns the prow.

By all accounts, both the architect and the client were prickly characters, and their working relationship proved difficult. Sloman later suggested that while he was satisfied with the design, he would have preferred to employ a different architect as project manager. He also claimed that the choice of clinker bricks was effectively made prior to Höger's appointment, when the businessman purchased a job lot of building materials at a knockdown price. It was typical of Höger, Sloman implied, that he should try to advance an aesthetic justification for a decision which had been made on purely economic grounds. Despite their disagreements, however, both men recognized that the building made a striking impression on the cityscape, and each had reason to be satisfied with the results. None of Höger's subsequent buildings ever had quite the same impact, and the Chilehaus was not followed by a fleet of other nautically-themed buildings.

If you pay a visit to the Chilehaus it is worth spending a little time looking at some of the other buildings in the area, which the city now refers to as the *Kontorhausviertel* ("office building quarter"). Across the road from the Chilehaus, facing the Messberg on the south side of Pumpen, is the Messberghof. One of the first attempts to build a skyscraper on the Elbe, it was designed by the brothers Hans and Oskar Gerson and built at the same time as the Chilehaus (1923-4). Like its more famous neighbor, it is clad in clinker brick and has some Expressionist detailing on the ground floor, but it places a greater emphasis on the vertical axis, with distant echoes of a Gothic cathedral. The sandstone sculptures are by Ludwig Kunstmann (1877-1961), who also sculpted the mythical creatures guarding the building's entrances. The most striking internal feature is an open spiral staircase, which rises some 170 feet in a hexagonal, roof-lit central stairwell. The Messberghof was originally called Ballin-Haus, but was renamed by the Nazis in 1938 because the late director of the HAPAG shipping line was Jewish. Chillingly, some of the profits made from the manufacture of Zyklon B, used in the gas chambers at Auschwitz, were administered in this building.

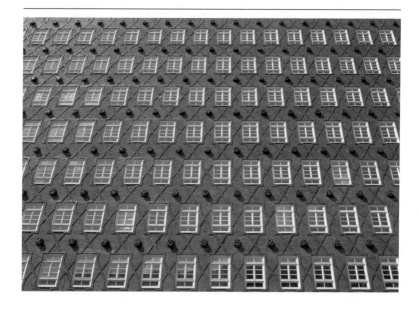

Höger and the Gerson brothers collaborated on another *Kontorhaus* project adjacent to the Chilehaus. Located at Burchardstrasse 6-14, the Sprinkenhof was built in three stages between 1927 and 1943, and is the largest building in the *Kontorhausviertel*. The original structure, erected in 1927-8, took the form of a nine-story cube. As with the Chilehaus, it was built over the Springeltwiete to create an internal courtyard. The brick façades were enlivened by a net-like grid made from gilded terracotta. The western (1930-32) and curved eastern (1939-43) wings were by Höger alone, since Hans Gerson had died in 1931 and his brother was not allowed to practice in Germany after 1933 on racial grounds.

Finally, also on Burchardstrasse, facing Burchardplatz, is another office building on the city's preservation list: the Mohlenhof. Designed by Rudolf Klophaus, August Schoch and Erich zu Putlitz in 1928, the Mohlenhof reflects the shift away from Expressionism and towards the more functional style of the *Neue Sachlichkeit* ("New Sobriety") in the later 1920s. Its façade, while still of brick, is smooth and largely unadorned. The only decoration is a stone statue of Hermes by the ubiquitous Richard Kuöhl. Elsewhere in Germany, the architecture of the New Sobriety was associated primarily with pure white concrete surfaces. Yet in Hamburg the "common ordinary brick" was invested with such powerful properties that the shift away from Expressionism was not accompanied by any significant change in materials. This gives the city's central business district a coherence and consistency in appearance which is arguably unmatched by any other ensemble of buildings dating back to the 1920s and 1930s in Germany. It also begs the question, why brick?

Brick was first used as a building material in Hamburg around the middle of the twelfth century, but initially only for the cathedral and other churches. It was regularly used for the façades of half-timbered domestic buildings from around 1300 onwards. By the eighteenth century, however, "naked" brickwork was increasingly regarded as crude and utilitarian. The fashion was for plastered façades or, for those who could afford it, stone. The first conscious revival of brick architecture began in the first half of the nineteenth century with architects like Alexis de Chateauneuf (Old Post Office, 1845-7) and Theodor Bülau (Patriotic Society, 1845-7). The latter building, which stands in much altered form at Trostbrücke 4-6 (its height was greatly increased by the addition of four further stories in 1924), was the result of a competition staged by the society in the wake of the Great Fire. The intention was to create an example of good modern architecture which could serve as a model for the city. The competition's guidelines specified that the Patriotic Society's new home should be built with "real" materials, and should be "honest" in its construction. The fashionable practice of covering buildings in plasterwork, as demonstrated by the new Alster Arcades, was condemned as "a sickly aberration." The winning architect, Bülau, went along with the brief, but privately mocked the "Progressives" who had commissioned him, and subverted their program by incorporating all manner of Romantic and reactionary neo-Gothic details.

Far from acting as a model, Bülau's building remained a one-off. Although brick was used extensively in the second half of the nineteenth century—both as a structural material, and as a cladding for iron or steel framed buildings—it was predominantly employed in industrial or functional settings: for warehouses, factories or workers' housing. A number of charitable foundations also used brick, but representative buildings such as the new town hall or the Museum of Arts and Crafts (1873-6) were built in stone, with an increasingly eclectic range of historical styles employed. In this, of course, Hamburg was no different from other European cities, but when the backlash against nineteenth-century historicism duly arrived in the years around 1900, the city's cultural leaders were particularly vitriolic in their criticism. Alfred Lichtwark, for instance, wrote:

> All the styles of the civilized world held a rendezvous in our backyard. One could call it an architectural masquerade in cement. English country house Gothic, Flanders Gothic, Berlin Hellenic, French Classical, Venetian and Munich neo-Romantic, all stand alongside the few attempts to take up the local brick Gothic, or at least... to show the local material to advantage.

For the judge and art collector Gustav Schiefler (1857-1935), the only way the city could find its way back to a "healthy" culture was to abandon the styles of other eras and regions and return to its own local traditions. He was particularly dismissive of the recently completed town hall, which he condemned as "a monument of its age," which was culturally "the bleakest era that Germany has ever lived through." Arguably the most influential architectural commentator in Hamburg at this time, however, was Paul Bröcker (1875-1948), who first made a name for himself with a series of pamphlets such as the 1908 *Hamburg in Distress!*, subtitled "an urgent cry for help, and a suggestion for how to save the architectural culture of our home town." "We squabble enough amongst ourselves about political and social things," Bröcker wrote. "Let us for once think sincerely about what unites us: our home; our home town; and the beauty of the things produced by our labour, whether we are bricklayers or businessmen; the things which make life worth living." In an article of September 1905 entitled "Old and New: In the Slum Clearance Areas," Bröcker wrote:

> Old Hamburg is passing away... After the fire and the Customs Union there now follows the slum clearance... and this is necessary too, if our descendants are not to accuse us of serious negligence. It is just a pity that the new, being erected in place of the old, is so much worse, despite all the fancy decoration.

The characteristics of old Hamburg buildings were, Bröcker argued, being lost in favor of the ostentatious and superficial. The sins of the

German Empire's founding decades, the eclectic use of historicist motifs in what Bröcker called "palace style," were still being committed thirty years on, only now motifs from English country houses and north German vernacular architecture were being appropriated too. Bröcker saw these new buildings as part of a much wider problem: "He who has tradition also has soul... Man has been alienated from the land. Even if he owns a piece of it, its only value is like that of the calf to the butcher: what did it cost? How much does it make?" There was, of course, nothing particularly original about these sentiments. What makes Bröcker interesting is the influence his ideas had. As the art historian Dörte Nicolaisen (1985) has shown, "the character and meaning of Höger's early office buildings can only be worked out if one attempts to understand them in the context of Bröcker's theories."

In his writings Bröcker paid particular attention to the *Kontorhaus*. He noted that just as the first cars had resembled horse-drawn carriages, so the first office buildings in Hamburg had looked like ordinary dwelling houses, until new building materials had opened up fresh possibilities. Bröcker was quick to praise the aesthetic potential of iron, steel and glass, but was anxious that the city should not lose its unique historical character. In an article on Hamburg's new main railway station (1903-6), for instance, he dismissed the neo-Renaissance façade and towers by the Berlin architects Reinhardt and Süssenguth, but eulogized about the great iron and glass roof, which was modeled on the Halle des Machines at the Paris World Exhibition of 1889. He recognized that an international style of steel-framed office building was developing, but he urged clients and architects not to succumb to the banal or the anonymous. Hamburg's new buildings for commerce and trade should instead combine the local with the international, the traditional with the modern. As Bröcker put it:

> The construction of the human skeleton tells us: this is a person! And the colour of the skin tells us: this is a paleface, a redhead, a Japanese! In the same way, the brick skin of an office block should tell us: this is a Hamburg building!

Bröcker saw in the brick not only a simple and functional building material, which could produce a pleasing aesthetic effect through its color and pattern, but also a symbol of continuity running from the half-timbered houses of the medieval *Hansestadt* to the multistory office blocks of the twentieth century, whose steel frames fulfilled much the same function as the wooden beams of old. Bröcker's admiration for brick architecture was by no means typical in turn-of-the-century Hamburg. One person who did share Bröcker's enthusiasm, however, was Fritz Höger. It was perhaps inevitable then that the two men should become friends and, for a time, collaborators. The main result of their cooperation was the book *The Architecture of Commercial Buildings in Hamburg* (1910), for which Bröcker supplied the theoretical ideas and Höger the practical suggestions. It was illustrated by the self-taught artist Ferdinand Sckopp (1875-1967), a childhood friend of Höger, who had made a name for himself with numerous drawings of the rapidly disappearing Altstadt and had joined Höger's studio a year earlier.

The book demonstrated a number of ways in which buildings could serve modern commercial and retail functions, whilst at the same time enhancing the Hamburg townscape and remaining in harmony with Hanseatic traditions. Höger's designs varied in the extent to which they borrowed formal motifs, like the curved Baroque gable, from Hamburg's past architecture, but all the façades emphasized load-bearing steel columns and brick infill. Some of the illustrated schemes were merely academic exercises, but others had been submitted with real sites in mind. Indeed, three of Höger's schemes were already under construction in Hamburg when the book appeared, and one of them, the Niemannhaus, was all but finished. However, as the book's subtitle—"A topical word on the development of the Mönckebergstrasse"—made clear, it was on the major new traffic artery through the Altstadt that the two men most wanted to make an impact. They did not have long to wait. Following the book's publication, Höger picked up commissions to build a series of large commercial buildings on the Mönckebergstrasse, including three—the Haus Glass, the Rappolthaus and the Klöpperhaus—which are still standing in some form today.

The Mönckebergstrasse

The Mönckebergstrasse, which opened to traffic on October 26, 1909, had been at the heart of Bröcker's concerns for several years. From the beginning, the proposed route of the new street had caused controversy. The engineers who dominated the city planning department wanted to strike a straight line, 200 feet wide, from the railway station to the town hall square. This made sense from a transport management perspective, especially as an underground railway line was to follow the course of the road. Yet for Bröcker and many local architects, this "American" solution threatened to be a scar on the face of the city. They argued for a less geometric and more picturesque approach. Bröcker was appalled that such a major project could proceed without any serious consideration of its aesthetic impact. In his pamphlet *Hamburg in Distress!* he called for the establishment of a Commission of Artists to judge major planning issues on aesthetic as well as technical grounds. He suggested such a commission should include representatives from the architects' association, the art galleries and museums, some practising artists, and possibly representatives of property owners' and tenants' groups, with a senator or civil servant as chair.

In a 1908 article for the *Hamburgischer Correspondent* newspaper, Bröcker repeated his call for a Commission of Artists but combined it with a plea for greater public involvement in planning and architectural issues, "because a true architecture is impossible without the sincere participation of the people." To this end, he suggested measures to educate and inform the population, including evening classes and easily understood pamphlets. Bröcker's own contribution to public enlightenment included a series of open lectures and a new magazine, *Der Hamburger*, which he launched as a monthly in December 1910, but which was soon appearing fortnightly. Bröcker's calls for the establishment of a commission to assess planning applications on aesthetic as well as technical grounds received widespread support, and a commission was indeed set up to vet the façades and roof lines of new buildings in the Mönckebergstrasse. It ensured that the finished street reflected an aesthetic unity sadly lacking in earlier roads through the slum clearance areas.

No visit to Hamburg is complete without a stroll down this majestic shopping street, which is now closed to traffic except for slow-moving buses and taxis. A century on from Bröcker's campaign, it is still possible to see evidence of its impact. The best way to experience the "Mö" is to begin at the main railway station and proceed in the manner of a *flâneur* to the town hall square. The first building of note, facing the southwest corner of the station at Mönckebergstrasse 3, is the Klöpperhaus. This building, which today houses the Kaufhof department store, was originally built as an office block for the wool merchant Heinrich

Adolf Klöpper. In the film *Tomorrow Never Dies* James Bond crashes into one of its shop windows, but does not stay long enough to appreciate the view.

The Klöpperhaus originally formed one half of the symbolic entrance to the new street, combining with the Südseehaus to frame a vista of two major churches: in the foreground St. Peter's, and in the distance the tower of St. Michael's. The Klöpperhaus was designed by Höger after a competition in which the client—a friend of Alfred Lichtwark and a keen supporter of Bröcker's efforts—had specified that the building should have "local character." This was expressed in the choice of red brick for the façades, Elbe sandstone for the entrance, and a steeply pitched roof. Höger's winning design had a number of stylistic features associated with the Baroque era in Hamburg, but these were toned down by the Commission of Artists before construction began. The two groups of bronze sheep and rams grazing on Lange Mühren were by August Gaul (1869-1922), a founder member of the progressive Berlin Secession.

Höger's Rappolthaus (1911-12), next to St. Jacob's church at Mönckebergstrasse 11-13, features the same dark clinker brick as the Chilehaus. It was built for the textile company Rappolt & Sons as a six-story office building with retail premises on the ground floor. It originally featured an imposing series of exaggerated neo-Baroque gables rising from a tall mansard roof. These were lost in the war, but some of the original statuary, by Richard Kuöhl and Georg Wrba (1872-1939), has survived. Rappolt & Sons was a family firm which employed more than 600 people in Hamburg during the 1920s, but Franz and Ernst Rappolt were of Jewish descent and were forced to sell their business in 1939.

Next to St. Peter's Church at the junction of Mönckebergstrasse and Bergstrasse is another early commercial building by Fritz Höger, the Haus Glass (1911). This eight-story corner property retains two neo-Baroque gables similar to those lost from the Rappolthaus. Höger's pre-1914 style, with its self-conscious evocation of Hamburg's eighteenth-century townhouses, might appear a long way from the Expressionism of the Chilehaus, but a common thread is provided by the conviction that the *genius loci* resided in the "common ordinary brick." That the young and inexperienced Höger—a country boy with no academic training—was able to tap such a rich seam of work in Hamburg owed much to Bröcker's brick evangelism, which reached a peak in the years around 1910.

Following the successful campaign to introduce an aesthetic dimension to the planning of the Mönckebergstrasse, it took a further four years before city-wide legislation was in place, but when it came the 1912 *Baupflegegesetz* ("Law for the Preservation and Care of Buildings") made a significant impact. The law introduced an aesthetic dimension to Hamburg's planning procedures for the first time. The city's existing building code, which had been drawn up in 1865 and revised in 1892, was purely technical in character, limiting the height of buildings and dealing with such issues as fire safety and hygiene. The new law established a commission of three senators and six members of the Citizens' Assembly, together with an advisory committee of 25 professionals and laymen, to vet new building plans for their impact on their surroundings and to advise on the preservation of existing buildings. The commission had the right to call in any building plans from the whole of Hamburg and ask for alterations, though it could not block projects permanently. Even so, the commission subsequently achieved an impressive record of persuading developers to adapt their plans, and the law made a considerable impact on the appearance of the city center.

The new law was only passed after much heated debate, in which such heady concepts as the freedom of art and the rights of the individual were frequently invoked. Bröcker joined in regularly via pamphlets and the pages of his journal *Der Hamburger*, but the law's most important backer was Fritz Schumacher, who had taken up the reins as *Baudirektor* (City Architect) in 1909. Indeed, Schumacher is often given sole credit for both the *Baupflegegesetz* and the successful completion of the "Mö." The very revival of brick architecture in early twentieth-century Hamburg is invariably associated with his name. This reputation is by no means undeserved: as an architect and as a town planner he had a decisive influence on the appearance of the city for a quarter of a century or more, and his red-brick municipal buildings and housing schemes are rightly admired. Even so, it is clear that the revival of brick architecture had begun before his arrival in the city. This was not only due to Bröcker, Höger and Lichtwark, but also to Schumacher's underrated predecessor as (acting) City Architect, Albert Erbe (1868-1922).

In his memoirs, Schumacher was curiously dismissive of Bröcker's influence, remarking "to the disappointment of its leaders, I kept my distance from the literary brick movement, which began around this time."

Schumacher's public library (1914): once a Burger King; now a Starbucks

He claimed that the decision to use brick as the consistent feature of his Hamburg architecture was taken while he was still a professor at the Technical University in Dresden. Yet, as we shall see, Schumacher may have been more influenced by Bröcker's agitation than he was prepared to admit. Ironically the only building on the "Mö" to be designed by Schumacher was built in stone. The small neoclassical structure built in 1914 at Barkhof 3 was originally a public library, but today it houses a Starbucks coffee bar. Schumacher designed it to provide an arresting visual feature at the mid-point of the "Mö," where its junction with Spitalerstrasse and Lilienstrasse formed what was initially little more than a triangular traffic island. He combined it with a memorial fountain (begun in 1913 but not completed until 1926) in honor of Mönckeberg, the city's former mayor. As if to emphasize a point of contrast with the large commercial premises surrounding it, the library building was small but perfectly formed. (For those offended by the thought that this Doric temple of culture should now house a Starbucks, it is at least a marginal improvement on its previous tenant: Burger King.)

Another architectural curiosity on the opposite side of the road is the Hulbehaus at Mönckebergstrasse 21. This small detached property, designed by Henry Grell, is in the style of the Dutch Renaissance (1910-11, rebuilt 1947). The gilded boat, which can be seen hovering above the stepped gable, originally contained a time capsule with documents from 1910. After a particularly heavy storm in the 1970s the documents were taken out and placed in the Museum of Arts and Crafts. Georg Hulbe (1851-1917), who lends his name to the building, was a highly successful craftsman, responsible for much of the leatherwork in Hamburg town hall and even the Berlin Reichstag. His shop's unlikely presence amongst the office blocks and department stores owed much to the desire of the Commission to find a way of mediating between the modern commercial structures and Hamburg's oldest church, St. Peter's.

The modest scale of the Hulbehaus allows the red-brick Lutheran church to be seen in all its glory. A church has stood on this site (Speersort 10) since the twelfth century, but the original building was a prominent casualty of the Great Fire of 1842. The present neo-Gothic structure, designed by Alexis de Chateauneuf, was built in 1843-9 on the original foundations, although it does contain some much older elements. The fearsome looking bronze lion's head on the left-hand door of the main entrance (on Bergstrasse), for instance, dates back to 1342. The interior also incorporates several pieces of historic statuary, including sandstone figures of the Madonna and St. Paul from the mid-fifteenth century. During the Napoleonic occupation the church was used as stables, and horse urine was produced in such quantities that its corrosive effects can still be observed on the building's foundations. The church's medieval altarpiece by Master Bertram (*c.*1380) is now on display in the Hamburg Kunsthalle.

The neighboring St. Jacob's Church (Jakobikirchhof 22), which was begun in 1340, has also been rebuilt on several occasions, although parts of the chancel are original. St. Jacob's was always the poor relation of the Altstadt churches, serving the medieval city's poorest parish. Even so, its west gallery can boast an original Baroque organ (1689-93) by Arp Schnitger. It is here that the young J. S. Bach tried unsuccessfully to secure the job of organist.

The "Mö" was built in remarkably quick time (1908-14), and a degree of aesthetic coherence was achieved which was highly unusual in laissez-faire Hamburg. By no means all the major commercial buildings were executed in brick—the Barkhof, Seeburg and Mönckeberghaus all have stone façades in the typical monumental style of the years around 1910—but contemporary critics nevertheless viewed the street as a significant *Gesamtkunstwerk*, which managed to combine Hanseatic tradition with international flair. Wartime bombing and post-war redevelopment have subsequently altered much of its original character. Yet for all the changes to individual buildings, the effectiveness of Bröcker's campaign can still be appreciated by observing the line taken by the street itself. While not exactly meandering, the street follows an indirect course, exploiting the undulations of the landscape, and taking advantage of historic landmarks (like the city churches) to create a series of picturesque vistas, very much in the spirit of the town-planning pioneer Camillo Sitte (1843-1903).

A particular thorny issue for the Commission of Artists was how best to link the new street to the town hall square, without upsetting the carefully contrived cityscape achieved in the previous century. Here it was a masterstroke to run the new street into the south-eastern corner of the square at a 45-degree angle, so that the full effect of the town hall and the expansive public space in front of it is revealed only gradually. The street's construction removed the southern flank of the square, but its integrity was restored with the commissioning of the bulky Versmannhaus at Mönckebergstrasse 29-31 (1910-12, rebuilt 1949), which spans the Knochenhauerwiete with a mighty arch. It was designed by Rambatz and Jollasse in the German Renaissance style, so as to mediate between the modern commercial architecture of the "Mö" and the town hall's historicist façade.

Arguably the biggest compliment one can pay to the planners and architects of the Mönckebergstrasse is that it is hard to imagine Hamburg without it. The street's construction represented great business for the city too: while building costs amounted to nearly forty million Marks, all but 2.7 million of this was recouped in land sales, since the prices achieved by the city far outweighed the sums paid out to former freeholders. It could be argued, of course, that all this came at the expense of the former residents of the northern Altstadt—artisans, workers, the old and infirm—who were forced to leave their homes for tenements in the outer suburbs. Schumacher, a liberal with a social conscience, was not insensitive to this fact, but it would take another decade before he could do anything about it.

Fritz Schumacher's Hamburg

Schumacher was the City Architect of Hamburg from 1909 until 1933, with a three-year hiatus between 1920 and 1923 while he developed a new urban plan for Cologne. Given his importance as both an architect and town planner, it is worth touching briefly on his biography. Friedrich Wilhelm Schumacher was born into an upper-middle-class family in Bremen, and spent part of his childhood in Bogotá and New York, where his father served as Consul General. After studying in Berlin and Munich, his architectural apprenticeship was spent with Gabriel von Seidl in Munich and Hugo Licht in Leipzig. Schumacher's appointment in Hamburg was something of a gamble for the city. He was already forty years old and had built only one substantial structure—a crematorium in Dresden (1907-8)—together with a handful of private houses.

He was not the first choice for the role, but nor was he was plucked from obscurity either: his first collection of essays had been published in 1899; his first book of architectural plates had appeared in 1900 (some of which were displayed at the 1904 World's Fair in St. Louis); and his first Chair at the Technical University in Dresden had been awarded in 1901. He had organized the Third German Arts and Crafts Exhibition in Dresden (1906), and was also the man chosen to give the keynote speech at the founding congress of the German Werkbund in 1907, when he addressed an influential audience of industrialists, politicians and designers on the theme of "The Re-conquest of a Harmonious Culture": "We must win back the joy of work, which means in effect we must increase the quality of work," he said. "In this way art is not only an aesthetic force but an ethical one too, and together these forces will eventually lead to the most important power of all, economic power."

The young Schumacher was, in other words, the sort of architect who spent more time writing and talking about building than actually doing it. He aspired to be a social reformer, a poet, a philosopher and, above all, an artist. Nowhere was this more apparent than in the illustrations of fantasy monuments to his heroes Nietzsche, Wagner and Bismarck, which he published as a young man. There has been a tendency to regard these exercises as youthful excesses, quite out of character with the schools, hospitals and housing estates which came to characterize his time in Hamburg. In fact, however, the desire to give humble municipal buildings an appropriate monumental form remained a consistent feature of his long period in

139

office. As he put it in 1916: "We are living in the age of state education, the department store, the social housing development, the factory, welfare buildings, the public park. We need to find a form of expression for the great social institutions of our time."

While few of his buildings have survived intact, many still exist in one form or another. The city's pride in them has grown steadily in recent years. He may not be regarded as a truly great architect, but he has nevertheless achieved the notable distinction of becoming synonymous with his adopted city: the phrase "Schumacher's Hamburg" appears almost as often these days as "Mackintosh's Glasgow" or even "Gaudí's Barcelona." To be sure, he did not possess the brilliant originality of those architects, but he was far more prolific, with around one hundred major buildings in the city to his name. Indeed, the length and breadth of his output are such that the opus requires dividing into four subcategories: pre-First World War public buildings; post-war public buildings; urban planning; and social housing schemes.

The first phase of Schumacher's period in office resulted in a series of showpiece buildings: the College of Visual Arts (Lerchenfeld 2, 1909-13); the Institute for Tropical Diseases (Bernhard-Nocht-Strasse 74, 1909-14); the Hamburg Education Authority (Dammtorstrasse 25, 1911-12); the Johanneum grammar school (Maria-Louisen-Strasse 114, 1912-14); the Harbour Pilot Station in Waltershof (Bubendeyweg 33, 1913-14); the Holthusen swimming baths (Goernestrasse 21, 1913-14); the Davidwache police station (Spielbudenplatz 31, 1913-14); and the Museum of Hamburg History (Holstenwall 24, 1913-22). All of these buildings reflected Schumacher's desire to restore a sense of place to the increasingly anonymous modern metropolis. As the architect later admitted, however, when he received his letter of appointment in the spring of 1909 he had only the vaguest notion of what Hamburg's sense of place really was. His "city of the imagination" owed more to sentimental childhood memories of Bremen and his own family's patrician heritage than to any real knowledge of life on the Elbe.

In fact, since he was not able to commence his employment until 1 November 1909, his first building projects for Hamburg were actually conceived in Dresden: the Institute of Tropical Medicine, the fire brigade headquarters at Berliner Tor, the restaurant in the City Park and even the Museum of Hamburg History were all drawn up without any first-hand knowledge of their locations. Schumacher was certainly quick to recognize that the use of brick would be important in his efforts to (re)create a sense of place, but it is nevertheless the case that some of these early buildings were initially planned with stone façades. This perhaps helps to explain his later eagerness to dismiss the influence of people like Bröcker and Höger. Once Schumacher's fame had come to rest on the "the magic of brick" (the title of one of his numerous essays), he was reluctant to share much of the credit, beyond acknowledging the mid-nineteenth-century achievements of Bülau and de Chateauneuf.

Schumacher was undoubtedly a progressive figure in German architectural circles before the Great War, railing against the heavy ornamentation and historical fancy-dress of recent public buildings, the nineteenth-century city's "dark inheritance" of social division and the dangers of untrammeled urban sprawl. Yet he was equally critical of those who saw the answer to everything in new technology, or those who adopted a crudely mechanical "form follows function" approach: "test-tube architecture" he would later dub it. His ideal, outlined in one of his very first Dresden lectures, was to combine tradition and innovation. As one of his successors as City Architect observed in the 1980s, his buildings were not particularly modern, nor did they define a new style or set important milestones in the history of architecture, but what they did do was to form unmistakable reference points in Hamburg's urban landscape. This was due in part to their dignity, sobriety and harmonious proportions; in part to their accessibility and functionality; but above all it was due to their consistent use of a single building material. Brick has been described by the Hamburg-born historian Maiken Umbach (2009) as the vernacular material par excellence. She argues that its use, and the employment of other vernacular motifs, helped ordinary people "to imagine the abstraction that was modernity." If so, then it was ideally suited to Schumacher's vision of a reformed city, which he liked to refer to it as "the liveable metropolis."

The Schumacher building most likely to feature on a tourist itinerary today is the Museum of Hamburg History, which is located on the site of one of the city's former defensive bastions. With its Oldenburg clinker walls, white transom windows, high mansard roof and internal courtyard, the museum not only provides a good introduction to the architect's pre-war style but also offers an interesting meditation on architecture, time

and place. This comes in part from its location on the former city wall, but also from the incorporation of numerous fragments of real Hamburg buildings within the inner and outer fabric of the museum.

The Association for Hamburg History had been diligently reclaiming doors, windows, statues and other architectural artefacts since 1839, with particularly large quantities rescued in the aftermath of the Great Fire of 1842, the Speicherstadt development in the 1880s and the slum clearances of the 1890s. Schumacher ensured that many of the best pieces became more than just exhibits in the traditional sense. These include statues from the lost seventeenth-century town hall, which were incorporated into the façade of the museum, and the south doorway of St. Peter's church from 1604, which was installed in the internal courtyard. Incidentally, while the museum might appear symmetrical from the front, it actually has a complex layout designed to allow as much natural light into the galleries as possible; it was originally intended to operate without any artificial lighting at all. The courtyard was covered by an impressive glass roof in 1989 and now houses a popular café.

If you visit the museum, two other nearby buildings are worthy of inspection. A short distance to the north, on the city side of Holstenwall, is another early example of Schumacher's work: the Chamber of Handicrafts (Holstenwall 12, 1912-23). The twin-gabled building, whose brick façade features six sandstone statues by Oskar Ulmer, each evoking a different craft, was commissioned at a difficult time for the artisan trades, increasingly squeezed between the interests of capital and labor. It would not be fanciful, therefore, to see the building as a direct response to the grand trade union headquarters, erected just a few years before in St. Georg (see Chapter Three).

In a similar vein, and only a hundred yards further north, the tall clinker-brick office block at Holstenwall 1 was the headquarters of the white-collar employee association, the DHV. It was not designed by Schumacher or Höger, but by Wilhelm Vortmann and Ferdinand Sckopp, whose friend Paul Bröcker wrote a pamphlet to celebrate its completion in 1931. At the time the fifteen-story tower was not only Hamburg's tallest building but the highest steel-framed structure anywhere in Europe. The entrance hall features the coat of arms of cities lost by the German Empire after the First World War: Metz, Tondern, Memel and Thorn. There is also some eye-catching external statuary, including six larger-than-life bronzes of naked men, who are stacked vertically on the side of the main tower. Bröcker did his best to explain the building's symbolism:

> Thousands upon thousands of bricks, each one just a tiny lump of clay hardened by fire, create something extraordinary when brought together, through organization, through union, through the concentration of forces in a single goal. The brick walls of our building prove the truth of the simple words: Unity is Strength!

In Hamburg, however, it was not the nationalist and anti-socialist DHV that held sway between 1918 and 1933, but the SPD. The establishment of democratic rule resulted in a rapid growth of the city's public sector, with particularly large numbers of new schools required, as well as social housing on a massive scale. Schumacher had little difficulty in adjusting to his new political masters, and entered the most prolific period of his professional life. Prominent post-war examples of his work include the City Treasurer's Department (Gänsemarkt 36, 1918-26); the Magistrates' Court in Bergedorf (Ernst-Mantius-Strasse 9, 1926-7); the Gorch-Foch-Hall in Finkenwerder (Focksweg 12-14, 1927–9); and the main crematorium at Ohlsdorf cemetery (1930-32). Of the many schools designed by Schumacher—he was responsible for 31 elementary schools alone—the Emil-Krause grammar school in Dulsberg (Krausestrasse 53, 1919-23) and the Winterhude comprehensive school (Meerweinstrasse 26-8, 1928-30) stand out. The latter, built to serve the Jarrestadt housing estate, is a six-story structure with a flat roof and a highly visible reinforced concrete frame. It was as close as he ever came to the kind of architecture associated with Walter Gropius and the Bauhaus, and it is still in use today.

As we have seen, Schumacher's role in Hamburg had at first been confined to designing individual buildings. To his dismay, urban planning remained largely outside his remit. This led to prolonged bureaucratic wrangling with the City Engineer, Fritz Sperber, whose department had drawn up the last city plan in 1896. One pre-war project on which the two men did collaborate successfully, however, was the design of the Stadtpark (City Park), located northeast of the city center between the middle-class suburb of Winterhude and working-class Barmbek. Developed on woodland purchased from the Sierich family in 1902, it is the largest of Hamburg's 120 parks, covering an area roughly equivalent to the principality of Monaco.

The 370-acre site had already been the subject of extensive debate—and an unsuccessful competition—before Schumacher took office. The architect and the engineer worked out a compromise plan, combining elements of two competition entries to produce "a geometric skeleton embedded in a free form body" (Schumacher). Their design rejected the nineteenth-century ideal of a pseudo-rural English garden as seen in Munich, and instead adopted a more formal layout, with a geometric pattern of tree-lined avenues and lakes partly inspired by the architect's childhood memories of New York's Central Park. Exotic varieties of plants and nonnative species of trees were to be avoided, with the emphasis instead on large lawns, flower beds, neatly trimmed hedges and an ambitious program of public art, including sculptures by August Gaul, Georg Wrba,

Ludwig Kunstmann and Arthur Bock. For better or worse, much of this architectural formality has been lost since the Second World War, and the park has effectively become another English garden.

The principal feature of the park was—and to some extent still is—a dramatic central axis, running from the southeast to the northwest corner, and covering a distance of more than a mile. In the absence of Baroque palaces, other buildings had to be constructed to act as focal points. A 125-foot brick water tower was built at the northwest end of the park in 1913-14. Its brooding monumental presence owed much to Schumacher's Dresden crematorium of 1907, although it was actually designed by another Dresden architect, Oscar Menzel (1873-1958). The tower, which has housed a planetarium since the 1930s, quickly became one of Hamburg's most iconic buildings. With a diameter of some seventy feet, its dome was one of the largest in Europe. At the opposite end of the central axis, close to the park's main gates, Schumacher planned a large symmetrical building with restaurants, bars and a terrace overlooking the lake. Its first incarnation, drawn in Dresden during the summer of 1909, was planned in sandstone. When it was finally built between 1910 and 1914, however, it was clad in brick. Paul Bröcker claimed that the decision to change materials had come as a result of his intervention, but Schumacher always denied this. Either way, the building lasted only three decades before falling victim to the bombs of 1943.

Following the park's opening in 1914, other structures were added at regular intervals: a fountain and water cascade (also made of brick, but lost in the war); a spa garden and pump room (1915); an athletics stadium (1919); a paddling pool (1921); an area for sunbathing, where nudity was permitted behind high hedges (1922); and an open-air theater (1924). As this list implies, the Stadtpark was intended to be a true People's Park, offering sunlight and fresh air to all ages and classes, with a particular emphasis on sport and active recreation. Alan Tate, in his study of *Great City Parks* (2001), describes it as "one of the first modernist parks in the world"; for Jenkins (2003) it enshrined a "liberal vision of culture and politics, of space and belonging"; while for Hipp (1992) it was intended to be a kind of "open air community center." More critically, Umbach (2009) emphasizes the authoritarian impulses which lay behind Schumacher's attempts to mobilize the alleged healing potential of nature, pointing to the "tight visual regimentation" and "idealized patterns of physical and social 'order'" which characterized such projects.

While Schumacher derived great satisfaction from planning this "city in miniature," it was no substitute for the real thing. His struggle for more influence over urban planning in Hamburg finally began to bear fruit after 1918, and particularly after his sojourn on the Rhine: he returned from Cologne to a new title, *Oberbaudirektor* (Chief City Architect), and wider responsibilities. Schumacher preferred to develop within the existing built-up area, but he also lobbied for the idea of a "Greater Hamburg" authority, and argued for a controlled expansion into the surrounding countryside. In a famous graphic from 1919 he portrayed his vision of the city as a stylized outstretched hand, with the Elbe represented by the thumb and little finger; the historic center as the palm; and the planned areas of expansion as fingers, stretching out into the countryside along suburban rail lines. In a later version, the "fingers" were portrayed as feathers or leaves, but the ultimate effect was the same: they all reflected his belief that a city is a living organism, which needs to grow organically.

The influence of this vision was to linger long after Schumacher's forced retirement in 1933, but the bulk of his work as an urban planner was more mundane, revolving around the layout and design of new housing estates, such as those at Langenhorn (1919-21), Dulsberg (1919-31), Veddel (1926-31) and Jarrestadt (1927-30). Apart from the obvious need to solve the city's serious housing shortage, Schumacher was motivated by the conviction that its residential districts—and particularly those thrown up by private developers in the decades either side of 1900—needed more green space. Districts such as Hamm, Barmbek and Eimsbüttel may not have seen the grinding poverty of Hammerbrook or Rothenburgsort, but developers had naturally sought to extract the maximum profit from their investments: the six-story tenement blocks were built with long "wings" or rear terraces stretching back from the street to create narrow rear courtyards with little natural light.

Schumacher became convinced that the only solution lay in the Hamburg authorities taking more responsibility for the provision of housing. The changed political circumstances after 1918 made this possible: new social housing was to be funded by a tax on existing properties. In total, some 65,000 new apartments were built under the city's aegis during the Weimar period. Schumacher's first estate, at Langenhorn in the north of the city, consisted of rows of small detached houses with large private gardens in the British style. As a young man, Schumacher had been an active supporter of the Garden City movement, and this was readily apparent at Langenhorn. The development proved expensive, however, and was not considered an unqualified success.

Schumacher changed tack: his aim would now be to bring the "garden" into the city. Most of the city's social housing schemes were from now on characterized by four- or five-story apartment blocks, laid out in rows with large communal gardens. The developments would be integrated into existing city districts, with good transport links, to create a mix of private and public sector housing. Jarrestadt, for instance, the estate considered by many to be Schumacher's finest achievement, is in the respectable middle-class suburb of Winterhude. The lofty aim was nothing less than the restoration of social harmony through the spatial reintegration of the working class.

Following a competition in 1926, Schumacher selected ten architectural practices to design individual blocks within the Jarrestadt development. It was hoped that this would prevent the monotony of other public housing schemes and, despite the universal use of red brick, long horizontal bands of windows and flat roofs. It paid off; today it is considered one of the great modernist housing projects of the 1920s. Two main kinds of layout were used: most of the estate follows a conventional block pattern, with the front of the apartments following the street line, allow-ing for large communal gardens to the rear. In the eastern corner, however, the blocks run at right-angles to the street, with lawns to both front and back (so-called *Laubenganghäuser*). This was part of an experiment by the National Research Association for Economy in Building and Housing to compare different building types. At the heart of the estate was a large central square (designed by Karl Schneider), with apartment blocks arranged around a formal, almost Baroque, garden. The estate's tree-lined streets and 1,800 well-appointed apartments undoubtedly proved popular, but whether the project worked as an exercise in social engineering is another matter. The subsidized rents were still too high for many working-class Hamburgers, and before long the estate was inhabited by clerks and teachers rather than dockers or factory workers.

Architecture became increasingly politicized in 1920s Germany, as opportunist politicians exploited ostensibly aesthetic debates between traditionalists and modernists. The controversy over the flat roof—which the Nazis were eager to portray as an alien (Jewish) intrusion into the German landscape—was a notorious case in point. Most of the avant-garde regarded brick with suspicion—Erich Mendelsohn famously covered his brick Einstein Tower in white plaster to give the impression it was made of concrete—but Hamburg architects demonstrated it was a material that could give modernity a human face. As a result, the "shock of the new" was less keenly felt on the Elbe than elsewhere in the Weimar Republic.

With their deliberate synthesis of the traditional and the modern, the local and the international, Hamburg's leading architects of the 1920s defy easy categorization. Things become further complicated if their own political views are taken into consideration. Fritz Höger, for instance, was a right-wing nationalist, who made no secret of his Nazi sympathies, yet his flat-roofed buildings became increasingly functionalist in the later 1920s. He continued to practice, but received few new commissions after 1933. Today he is commemorated by Hamburg's smallest monument: a bronze statue, just a few inches tall, which is embedded into the façade of the Renaissance Hamburg Hotel, on the corner of Grosse Bleichen and Heuberg in the city center. The building was designed by Höger in 1926 as the headquarters of the *Hamburger Fremdenblatt* newspaper. The statue of the architect, seated but animated, was added in 1981 when the building was converted and extended by Gerkan, Marg and Partners (GMP).

Meanwhile Schumacher, who had always styled himself as "unpolitical," was probably too closely associated with the Weimar system to survive the "national uprising," even if the precise circumstances of his departure in May 1933 have remained clouded in mystery. In public it was presented as an honorable retirement—he was 63—rather than a dismissal. Either way, he was hardly shunned by the new regime: he was elected to the Prussian Academy of Arts in 1937 and was even awarded the prestigious Goethe Medal by the *Führer* in 1939. Most of his team remained in office, and their housing estates of the later 1930s continued to be built in brick, albeit mostly with conventional red brick rather than clinker, and with pitched rather than flat roofs. Indeed, brick proved its ideological versatility by becoming the preferred material for National Socialist housing projects in Hamburg, such as the redevelopment of the former slum area around Rademachergang in the Neustadt (1934-6), or the Klein Borstel estate in Ohlsdorf, designed by the brothers Paul and Hermann Frank (1936-9).

In the immediate post-war years there was undoubtedly something of a reaction against red-brick architecture: the International Style was in vogue, and anything which appeared to evoke the "blood and soil" tradition was tainted by association. Hamburg's first major housing development after 1945, the Grindelberg tower blocks (see Chapter One), did not seek to pick up where Schumacher left off, but instead turned to Le Corbusier and the principles of the Charter of Athens. Even so, there appeared to be a tacit acknowledgment that Hamburg was not Marseille or Chicago: the towers were not clad in glass or concrete panels, but pale sandy-colored bricks. Such bricks enjoyed a brief period in vogue during the 1950s, but for the most part Hamburg architects shunned the material altogether.

A one-off in the 1970s was a brand new ensemble of red-brick neo-Baroque townhouses, built to original eighteenth-century plans, on Peterstrasse in the Neustadt. It was funded by the millionaire benefactor Alfred Toepfer, an architectural enthusiast who had already endowed a Fritz Schumacher Prize in 1949. In truth it was little more than stage-set architecture, a Potemkin village, but the Peterstrasse quickly became popular with parties of tourists, particularly those from the Far East. Today, if nothing else, the gabled houses do create an appropriate context for the Johannes Brahms Museum (Peterstrasse 35-9), which is housed in a genuine red-brick building from 1751 (although one without any connection to the composer).

It was only in the late 1970s that brick architecture enjoyed a proper comeback on the Elbe. The Norwegian Christian Norberg-Schulz published a hugely influential book on the importance of *genius loci* in architecture, attacking modernism's disregard for place and location; the fashionability of neo-vernacular architecture ensured a renewed interest in "traditional" building materials; and Postmodernism displayed a fondness for in-jokes and the playful appropriation of history. All of these factors ensured that many of Hamburg's new retail and office developments in the 1980s and 1990s made a feature of brick. GMP, the city's leading architectural firm at the time, proved highly capable of building eye-catching glass and steel structures around the world—including the impressive terminal buildings at Hamburg Airport (competition 1986, built 1989 onwards)—but chose brick for city center projects like the Hanse-Viertel shopping center on the corner of Grosse Bleichen and Poststrasse (1979-81); the Steigenberger Hotel at Heiligengeistbrücke 4 (1993); and the German-Japanese Center at Stadthausbrücke 5-7 (1995). When the respected architectural correspondent of *Die Zeit* wrote an article on the city's "New Brick Splendour" in 1994, his title was only partly ironic.

Today, of course, bricks are mass-produced in computer-controlled kilns, losing the subtle variations in color and pattern which so appealed to Fritz Höger. The "hand of a good master-builder" seldom enters the equation. Yet Hamburg still has architects capable of working creatively and sensitively with the material. One such figure is Bernhard Winking, who refers to brick as the "red gold" of building. His Fleethof in the Herrengraben sought to revive the Hamburg *Kontorhaus* tradition (1990-93), while his ultra-modern rear extension to Schumacher's Davidwache police station on the Reeperbahn is a bold, sculptural addition to a familiar building (2002-3). Winking denies that he is solely a "brick architect," pointing out that his choice of material depends on the *genius loci*, varying from project to project and place to place: "architecture and city are an integral part of each other," he says. On this, at least, Schumacher, Höger and Bröcker would all have agreed.

Chapter Six

THE NEON CITY

Wolfgang Borchert once described Hamburg as "more than just a heap of stones." The observation could apply to any city, of course, but it is no less valid for that. The previous chapters have looked at the city's bricks and mortar—literally in the case of Chapter Five—but many people's view of the city will have been shaped by more fleeting encounters: the drunken blur of a night on the Reeperbahn; the lurid neon lights of the Dom funfair; the reverberations of a rock band in a backstreet cellar. Great cities can be experienced in many different ways, and it is often a chance encounter, an unexpected sight, a memorable taste or smell, which leave the strongest mark. Curt Moreck (a pseudonym of the prolific writer Konrad Haemmerling) recognized as much in 1930:

> Big cities are indefinite promises. They are conglomerations of endless possibilities. They are labyrinths in which the most beautiful streets betray no hint of where they might lead… Every city has an official and an unofficial side, and it is superfluous to add that the latter is more interesting and more informative of the essence of a city. That which appears so clearly in the light of the arc lamps has a face more like a mask than a physiognomy. The smile it offers is more an appeal to the visitor's purse. It wears the makeup of the coquette, applied too thickly to permit the true features underneath to be recognized. Those who are looking for experiences, who long for adventure, who hope for sensations: they must go into the shadows.

This chapter "goes into the shadows" to explore Hamburg's "unofficial" side. The temporal emphasis is on the hours after dark, because cities become different places at night; and the spatial emphasis is on the district of St. Pauli—not because the city's nocturnal life stops and starts at the Millerntor gate, but because the area has more than enough places, characters and stories to fill a volume of its own. Although St. Pauli is one of Hamburg's smallest administrative districts, and is often used as a synonym

for a single street—the Reeperbahn—it is actually one of the city's most varied communities, with about one-third of its 28,000 inhabitants coming from outside Germany. It also encompasses two former working-class quarters which have developed distinct characters of their own: the Schanzenviertel and the Karolinenviertel.

St. Pauli has a proud tradition of political radicalism: in March 1848 a demonstration on the Reeperbahn was brutally dispersed by Prussian troops; on July 31-August 1, 1917, the third anniversary of the outbreak of the First World War, several thousand protesters gathered on the Heiligengeistfeld to protest "Against the War! For Freedom, Equality and Bread!"; little more than a year later, 40,000 workers and soldiers again assembled on the field before occupying key public buildings in Hamburg and Altona; and in the March 1933 general election—which took place in an atmosphere of intimidation following the Reichstag fire—the two left-wing parties (SPD and KPD) still secured 56 percent of the popular vote. More recently, the long-running (1981-97) battle between squatters and the Senate over a row of condemned houses in the Hafenstrasse (see Chapter Three) showed that the spirit of radicalism—or radical posturing—was far from dead. Yet it is for pleasure that the district is famous around the globe. In his autobiography *World within World*, Stephen Spender recalled:

> During these months in Hamburg, I discovered a terrifying mystery of cities which fascinated me in the way that one reads of people in the past being fascinated by the Eleusinian Rites. This is that a city is a kind of labyrinth within which at every moment of the day the most hidden wishes of every human being are performed by people who devote their whole existences to doing this and nothing else.

THE REEPERBAHN

In answer to the question "What is the Reeperbahn?" Ronald Gutberlet (2000) turned to statistics for an answer: "A four-lane road, 900 metres long and with a total area of 800,000 cubic metres, containing over 400 bars, 48 bordellos, 22 casinos and gaming halls, 17 sex shops, 10 striptease and live sex-shows, 5 meeting places for sadomasochists, 4 businesses selling sexy underwear and a 'Condomerie'." One could add that it is also thirty music venues, six theaters, four museums and a waxworks. But the

Reeperbahn has a history too; less well documented than other aspects of Hamburg's past, but a history nonetheless. St. Pauli's most notorious street takes its name from the rope-makers who settled there in 1625. Rope-making was a vital trade in the age of the sailing ship. It required a long straight road, 275 yards or more, so that individual strands of hemp could be stretched and wound tightly together before tarring. The process is explained in a permanent exhibit at the Museum of Hamburg History.

"Ropewalks" can still be found in many harbor towns, but the Reeperbahn was not officially known as such until 1810, and was not even laid out as a permanent road until the 1820s. It ran through what was effectively a no man's land between Hamburg and Altona. Its location outside either city's gates inevitably meant that it was populated by those on the margins of society, and its proximity to the harbor attracted a range of ancillary trades: not just rope- and sail-makers, but bar-keepers, tattooists and prostitutes. The historic border between the two cities ran across the western end of the street, close to its junction with Grosse Freiheit. The site of Altona's eastern gate, the Nobistor, is marked by a cast-iron lamp post, dating from the mid nineteenth century, which you can see by the side of the road shortly before Beatles-Platz. The post bears the Latin inscription NOBIS BENE NEMINI MALE ("what is good for us cannot be bad for anyone"). Altona's town crest, on the road side of the column, differs from Hamburg's in one significant detail: the city gate is portrayed as open, whereas Hamburg's is permanently closed. Altona's expansion was the direct result of its rulers' open-door policy, which contrasted so markedly with its bigger neighbor.

In 1611, in an effort to attract more skilled craftsmen to Holstein, the ruling Count von Schauenburg granted freedom of religion and lifted guild restrictions—on payment of an annual license fee—for any artisan who wished to settle in a new community. This new settlement, close to what was then the fishing village of Altona, was to be called Freiheit ("Freedom") and its name lives on in two streets off the Reeperbahn: Grosse Freiheit and its shorter neighbor Kleine Freiheit (which is still cobbled at its northern end). When, in 1664, Altona was raised to the status of a town under the Danish crown, these freedoms were extended to the whole borough. Large numbers of migrants, denied residency in Hamburg, chose to settle here instead. The Catholic church of St. Joseph's (Grosse Freiheit 43), built in 1718-23 by the Austrian Melchior Tatz

Spielbudenplatz, c. 1800

(rebuilt 1953-5), is one surviving document of this policy of religious tolerance: it is worth remembering that no new Catholic churches were built anywhere in Hamburg between 1529 and 1890.

A trace of the area's industrial history can be glimpsed at Grosse Freiheit 70: the tall chimney and nineteenth-century factory building used to belong to a fish processing plant and smokehouse. Looking over the fence from the factory car park, one can see a low row of original craftsmen's cottages dating back to 1842 (Grosse Freiheit 84). It is hard to believe, but the cottages were once even smaller: the upper story is a later addition. It would be a mistake, however, to think that the area was full of pious craftsmen and fishermen right up to the twentieth century. The Reeperbahn's reputation as "the most sinful mile in the world" had already begun to form more than two hundred years ago. Another contemporary street name is helpful in this regard: the southeastern corner of the Reeperbahn has been called Spielbudenplatz since 1795. In other words, traveling showmen, salesmen and charlatans had been setting up their *Spielbuden* (fairground booths or stalls) here since the eighteenth century. The booths housed all manner of wonders, from freak shows and puppet theater to the "Professor of Drumming," who played a dozen or more drums while dressed in a clown's costume. A particular favorite was Wilhelm Holter's troupe of tightrope dancers, which returned year after year. Ex-sailors, experienced in climbing rigging and with no fear of heights, were particularly gifted tightrope performers. The Swiss writer Jeremias Gotthelf described his impressions of the street in 1821: "Here all kinds of pickpockets, wild animals, tightrope walkers etc. have found their place. It's so lively, I didn't know where to look, or who I should avoid."

In 1833, when the suburb of Hamburger Berg was officially renamed St. Pauli and its residents became eligible—in theory, if seldom in practice—to become citizens of Hamburg, its population was around 10,000. Fifteen years later, in the "Year of Revolutions," there were 158 registered prostitutes (and 19 legal brothels) among a total population of around 16,000. Increasingly, however, St. Pauli's traditionally "rough" character was tempered by growing numbers of "respectable" citizens, who came from the city for a coffee or a game of billiards in one of the earliest permanent buildings on Spielbudenplatz, a wooden pavilion called the Trichter or "Funnel" (1805). The pavilion, which took its name from the shape of its roof and which lives on in the street name Beim Trichter, was rebuilt in stone in 1820 and survived until 1958.

There were also an increasing number of theaters appealing to a broad audience: the Circus Gymnasticus, a 3,000-seat hippodrome, was a particular attraction. It went bankrupt in 1864 but continued under a succession of other names. One of them, the Centralhalle, even pioneered "non-smoking evenings" a century ahead of its time. Visits to St. Pauli could be an expensive pleasure, however, since anyone returning to the city at night had to pay a toll at the Millerntor gate: four Schillings after sunset; eight Schillings after 10 p.m.; 12 Schillings after 11 p.m.; and 16 Schillings after midnight.

The removal of Hamburg's city gates in 1860 therefore gave a huge boost to the St. Pauli economy. People could now come and go at any time of the day or night, and the district's population shot up to around 70,000 by the turn of the century, all crowded into an area of just a few square miles. Most of the new residents were neither sailors nor craftsmen, but factory workers: the last rope-makers were forced to leave the street in 1883. The incomers were accommodated in rental tenements to the north of the Reeperbahn. To make maximum use of their plots, developers built *Terrassen* (terraces) behind the main street frontage: running at a right angle to the road, these three-story rows could only be accessed via rear courtyards or side alleys. As a result they received little natural light. Surviving examples can still be seen at Wohlwillstrasse 20-28 (the so-called Jäger-Passagen, in one of whose doorways John Lennon was famously photographed) and Talstrasse 67.

The contrast between the superficial glitz and glamour of the Reeperbahn and the poverty of the streets behind it grew starker as the nineteenth century progressed. It was exacerbated in particular by electrification: it became a standard trope of Reeperbahn reportage to compare the illuminated glamour of the street at night with its dowdy appearance in the cold light of day. Two descriptions, exactly a century apart, illustrate the point. Writing in 1891, Johannes Meyer was clearly impressed with what he saw: "Coming from the city at nightfall, St. Pauli appears like a magical fairy kingdom. As you approach the former Millerntor gate, electric suns shine high overhead, as countless arc lamps cast a blinding brightness over the fresh green leaves of the tall trees." A century later, Bill Bryson made the mistake of viewing the same street by day. It looked, he said, "disappointingly unlusty... Almost the only thing that told you this was a neighbourhood of dim repute was the hard look on the people's faces. They all had that gaunt, washed-out look of people who run funfair stalls."

For Stephen Spender, meanwhile, the contrast provided a useful device for comparing his two trips to the city in 1929 and 1932: he "came back with a memory of Sankt Pauli not as the brilliantly lit pleasure garden of his nights out with Joachim, Willy and Ernst, but as a desolate area of grey, wet streets and quaysides where young men who had absolutely nothing to do stood aground staring at dismantled docks" Other Britons to visit the Reeperbahn in 1932 included a well-heeled pair of brothers: a playboy called Edward and his shy sibling George. They would both go on to become king. The two princes were staying at the Atlantic Hotel, but when the Prince of Wales saw that his planned schedule for the evening included a theater visit, he was visibly disappointed. He told the hotel manager, Oscar Geyer, that he and his brother had hoped for something "more Hamburg," which Geyer took to mean a visit to St. Pauli. So it was that the three men—without aides or security guards—set off for the Reeperbahn. Geyer feared that the royals would seek out a house of ill-repute, but instead they made straight for the Zillertal, a mock Tyrolean beer hall with hard wooden chairs, *Lederhosen* and a live brass band. They stayed until the early hours, and the Prince of Wales enjoyed himself so much that he grabbed the baton to conduct the band himself. This curious episode would seem to indicate that even Germanophile Britons with strong family connections to Germany could be remarkably ignorant of the differences between the north and south of the country.

The princes may not have been typical visitors, but the Reeperbahn's clientele was certainly more varied than its image suggested. While sailors still came in large numbers, the impression conveyed in the three famous St. Pauli films starring Hans Albers—of bars full of shanty-singing, accordion-playing, pipe-chewing sailors—already owed more to myth than reality. The first, *Grosse Freiheit Nr. 7* (1944) was a piece of wartime escapism intended to take the German public's minds off air raids and food shortages. Directed by Helmut Käutner, it tells the story of Hannes Kröger, "the singing sailor," whose life has become becalmed in a hippodrome on the Grosse Freiheit. He is torn between the dream of settling down to marriage or returning to the high seas; the film ends with him predictably taking the latter option. Filming started in 1943, but the bomb damage in St. Pauli was so severe that it had to be finished in Prague. It received its premiere in that city in December 1944, but Goebbels prevented its release in the rest of the Reich because it "denigrated the German seaman."

Grosse Freiheit Nr. 7 was followed by *Auf der Reeperbahn nachts um halb eins* ("On the Reeperbahn at half-past Midnight") in 1954, which took its name from a song which had already featured in the earlier film and is often referred to as St. Pauli's unofficial anthem. It was first performed as part of the 1912 Wolf Brothers' review *Rund um die Alster* ("Around the Alster"), and was written by two outsiders: Alfred Müller-Förster from Silesia, who wrote the lyrics, and Ralph Arthur Roberts (actually Robert Schönherr, 1884-1940) from Saxony, who was responsible for the melody. The last of the trilogy, *Das Herz von St. Pauli* ("The Heart of St. Pauli," 1957), tried to repeat the popular formula but looked tired and dated. As the film itself acknowledged, most Reeperbahn venues had long since turned to more commercial "American" entertainments: dance bands, musicals and glittery revue shows.

The Salon Alcazar at Reeperbahn 108-14 was typical. It opened in 1925 and advertised "a sensation every 15 minutes, and in the breaks—no breaks!" There were dance routines and costumes borrowed from the Moulin Rouge; many American jazz musicians performed there, and so did the legendary naked dancers Anita Berber and Josephine Baker. At the time of the Spanish Civil War, when heavy fighting around the Alcazar in

Toledo led to a defeat for General Franco, the Nazis insisted that the venue be renamed the Allotria. "Nigger music" was dropped from the program, and the audiences dwindled too. It reverted to the name Alkazar (with a "k") after 1945, but finally closed in 1958, unable to compete with the new challenge of television. A Bavarian beer-hall, Bayrisch Zell, then took over the building, offering a diet of Löwenbräu, sausages and oompah music to Scandinavian and British tourists. Today it is home to a branch of Penny-Markt, a budget supermarket chain. Like all Reeperbahn addresses, then, it is a palimpsest whose historic layers are occasionally revealed before disappearing again in another refurbishment.

Spielbudenplatz 19-20 is another case in point. It now houses the rock and dance music venue Docks, but spent much of its life as Hamburg's first cinema, Knopf's Lichtspielhaus (founded 1900), and prior to that was one of the early venues of zoo pioneer Carl Hagenbeck's live animal shows (see Chapter Seven). On the opposite side of the road, the Café Keese at Reeperbahn 19-21 now operates as a comedy club, but when it opened in 1953 it was a dancehall famous for staging "Paradox Balls"; the paradox being that here, in the crazy mixed-up world of the Reepberbahn, the woman asked the man for a dance. Telephones were positioned on every table so that women could dial their prospective partner, and the man was forced to oblige; anyone who declined soon found himself back on the street.

As for Albers, a square on the south side of the Reeperbahn was renamed in his honor in 1964. The St. Georg-born actor and singer had first trod the boards at Hamburg's Thalia Theater before the First World War. He was one of the first actors to play Mack the Knife in Brecht and Weill's *Threepenny Opera*, and had featured in over a hundred silent films before his handsome looks and rugged charm made him a major star in the 1930s. Despite his left-wing views and half-Jewish wife, his fame protected him in the Third Reich. He died in 1960, but he remained a familiar figure in Germany thanks to countless television repeats. His admirers were delighted when it was announced in the mid-1980s that a ten-foot bronze statue was to become the square's centerpiece. The sculpture was to be the work of the controversial contemporary artist Jörg Immendorf (1945-2007), who also owned a nearby bar at the time. The bar, La Paloma, was a popular haunt for bohemian intellectuals, but when the monument was unveiled in 1986 it proved too challenging for many of Albers' fans.

It portrays "the blonde Hans" giving a seaman's salute while standing on a flying seagull, with his accordion at his side. The style could perhaps best be described as naive, or folk-art. The public, or at least a section of it, demanded a more conventional statue. Taken aback by the criticisms and angered by what he perceived to be the square's decline, Immendorf eventually removed his work and re-erected it in Düsseldorf. For a while it looked as if the city's "celebrated philistinism" would secure another victory, but a combination of financial donations from wealthy individuals and apologetic pleading from the Hamburg authorities persuaded the artist to produce a second cast of the sculpture, which was restored to the square in 1999.

If nothing else, it provides a useful meeting point in a square which can become very crowded after dark. Most of the bars surrounding the square and in its southern extension, Gerhardstrasse, are regular pubs, and there is sufficient variety to suit most tastes, although the proliferation of so-called "99 cent" bars has led to a rise in teenage binge drinking and violence. Certainly you are unlikely to hear an accordion or catch a whiff of fish from the St. Pauli docks; today pizza and spilled beer set the tone here. As a result, British visitors have sometimes been heard to describe it as "Blackpool without the beach." Looking around at the neon-lit, drunken chaos of Hans-Albers-Platz, it would be churlish to deny they have a point, but in one sense the analogy no longer holds true: a perfect white sandy beach, complete with potted palm trees and a small pool, is now laid out every summer just five minutes' walk away at Hafenstrasse 89. The beach goes by the punning title of StrandPauli (*Strand* being the German word for "beach").

The area between Davidstrasse and Hans-Albers-Platz is the main location for prostitution on the Reeperbahn. The history of the city's attempts to regulate and control "the world's oldest profession" is fascinating but complex, and only its broad outline can be sketched here. Prostitution on the Hamburger Berg was first banned in 1732, but the ban was lifted in 1807. Thereafter, like many German states, Hamburg attempted to maintain a register of legal brothels and prostitutes, although the restrictions (including degrading medical inspections) and social stigma attached to being on the register meant that many more women worked the streets illegally, usually on an occasional basis. Following German unification in 1871, the Imperial Criminal Code allowed for regulated prostitution within certain specifically defined areas, but anything which facilitated prostitution—such as pimping and procurement—was declared illegal. As Julia Bruggemann (2005) has pointed out, "this legal ambiguity created problems for local governments and police forces, since the prostitution trade was dependent on pimps and procurers." In 1883 the Hamburg Senate purchased much of the land at the eastern end of the Reeperbahn. This was parceled up and then leased or sold to the private sector. The vast majority of businesses to take up the offer were public houses (or "Viennese cafés") operating simultaneously as bars and brothels. This led to criticisms not just from the churches, temperance groups and morality campaigners, but also from some concerned with the welfare of sailors and dockers.

The Senate's half-hearted response to such criticisms was to introduce a law which forced premises to decide whether they were bars or brothels: in theory, bar owners could no longer rent rooms, and those found guilty of accommodating prostitutes would lose their liquor license. The unintended consequence, however, was to spread street prostitution and to strengthen the power of illegal pimps. By the end of the nineteenth century there were an estimated 700 unregulated street prostitutes working on the Reeperbahn. The *Hamburger Abendblatt* newspaper of 20 December 1892 described the scene: "Throngs of women pounced upon male passers-by trying to drag them into their houses until the vice squad was sighted. Then things suddenly became quiet until the police disappeared, and the 'Witches' Sabbath' began again."

In response to complaints from the street's "respectable" businesses, and in an effort to curb the excesses of pimps, the Senate sought to move prostitution from the Reeperbahn to the Heinrichstrasse: a short alleyway running parallel to the Reeperbahn between Davidstrasse and Gerhardstrasse. The street, which dated back to 1797, opened for business in 1900 and gained its present name, Herbertstrasse, in 1922. The intention was to allow prostitutes to work in a controlled and pimp-free environment, and to spare "respectable" citizens from being hassled by streetwalkers. The barriers at either end of the Herbertstrasse were installed during the Third Reich in an effort to prevent the "corruption" of minors. Today around 200 women work on the street, or more precisely in the windows of the street, even though regulated street prostitution is now permitted on some of the surrounding roads as well, between the hours of 8 p.m. and 6 a.m. The prostitutes have to pay tax on their earnings. Incidentally it is part of St. Pauli lore that if curious women dare to venture through the Herbertstrasse they are liable to be on the receiving end of a bucket of cold water, or at the very least some colorful invective from those who work there.

No measure has ever managed to rid the area of pimps. Unofficially police acknowledge that there are around six or seven main operators on the Reeperbahn, controlling around 400 girls and a business worth an estimated thirty million Euros per annum. Arguably St. Pauli's biggest pimp of all time was Willi Bartels (1915-2007), a local butcher's son who became known as the "King of St. Pauli." Bartels had taken control of a venue called the Jungmühle in 1937, where he offered lavish Busby Berkeley-style entertainment to regular parties of guests from the Nazis' "Strength through Joy" cruises. Scantily clad nymphs swam with swans in a real pool, and the hall was illuminated by more than 60,000 colored lights. After the war, Bartels became a major beneficiary of West Germany's "economic miracle," accumulating a portfolio of bars and nightclubs. His most rewarding venture was the infamous Eros Center, which opened in 1967 and revolutionized the world of the brothel.

A cross between a multistory car park and a student hall of residence, the Eros Center initially offered 136 bedrooms, but at its peak in the 1970s it grew to a staggering 700 beds on six floors. Each was rented out on a monthly basis. The project was supported by the city authorities in the hope that it would solve the perennial problem of street prostitution, but it was no more successful in this regard than the Herbertstrasse had been sixty years earlier. Although it soon gained a copy-cat competitor in the Palais d'Amour, the Eros Center remained a hugely profitable venture for a decade or more. The rise of the container ship, with its skeleton crew and rapid turnaround times, may have meant fewer sailors coming to St. Pauli, but they had not been a significant business factor for some time anyway. It was really only with the onset of the AIDS crisis in the early 1980s that business entered a period of rapid decline. The Eros Center eventually closed in 1988.

As in the East End of London, there has been an unfortunate tendency to romanticize the individuals who controlled organized crime in St. Pauli after the Second World War. While Bartels stayed more or less "legit," the former docker and banana packer Wilfrid Schulz, who became known as the "Godfather of St. Pauli," did not. From his headquarters in the Hotel Austria (Talstrasse 4), Schulz cultivated friendships with top policemen and politicians. His power was based on the ever-present threat of blackmail and violence. In many ways a caricature of a crime boss—he was rarely seen without a big Havana cigar—his fabled vanity meant that he was known to his close friends as "Frida." On 23 separate occasions the police tried and failed to pin charges on him, and when he was finally jailed in 1983 it was for the relatively minor crime of tax evasion. He then briefly became something of a television personality in Germany, before his death in 1992.

The AIDS crisis was followed by a series of gangland killings and shootings, which badly affected trade in the street's bars and clubs. The rise of internet pornography in the 1990s led many to predict that the Reeperbahn's decline would be terminal. Such stories have refused to go away, and in 2008 the closure of one of St. Pauli's oldest brothels, the Hotel Luxor, prompted new headlines on "the death of the Reeperbahn." Yet in many re-

spects the street has enjoyed a renaissance in recent years. Even the Eros Center has re-opened in a scaled down form. One is reminded of the old song which proclaims "St. Pauli will always be St. Pauli," but Stefan Becker is probably closer to the mark when he observes that "every generation gets the Reeperbahn it deserves, that it needs. That is a law of nature here: this sensitive organism is continually reinventing itself."

Today around 40,000 visitors of all ages make their way to the street every night, drawn by a wide range of entertainments. For instance, while the days when there were sixty theaters in St. Pauli will never return, the variety scene has boomed in recent years. The revival is largely due to Corny Littmann who runs both the Schmidt Theater (with a striking new façade at Spielbudenplatz 24-25), and the Schmidts Tivoli (in the former

Zillertal at Spielbudenplatz 27). Littmann is not just an impresario but an entertainer in his own right. In his spare time he is also a Green political campaigner and gay rights activist, as well as president of FC St. Pauli.

Sandwiched between Littmann's flourishing enterprises and Fritz Schumacher's historic Davidwache police station is the venerable St. Pauli Theater (Spielbudenplatz 29), which has been known by its present name since 1941, but occupies a building whose auditorium dates back a whole century further, to the Urania Theater of 1841. Another popular destination is the Operetta House (Spielbudenplatz 1), an ugly but functional shed in which *Cats* ran uninterrupted for fifteen years. Hamburg is the country's undisputed capital of musical theater, and a large proportion of the Operetta House audience comes from well outside the city. The long line of coaches parked on Helgoländer Allee is testament to provincial Germans' apparently insatiable appetite for undemanding entertainment. Next door, and with a similarly populist appeal, is the country's oldest waxworks, the Panoptikum (Spielbudenplatz 3). It displays wax effigies of 130 personalities over four floors, and claims to have been in the same family's ownership since 1879.

For all the merits of these entertainments, however, it is unlikely they will be able to compete with the variety and color of the street itself. Passionate people-watchers will find plenty of useful vantage points, but the legendary Lucullus fast-food kiosk on the corner of Davidstrasse is hard to beat. There you can tuck into *Currywurst* and chips while observing the madness all around you. If you are not familiar with the post-war, pre-McDonald's cultural phenomenon that is *Currywurst*, it is a sausage smothered in ketchup and curry powder. While it can be bought pretty much anywhere, the recipe used at the Imbiss bei Schorsch (Beim Grünen Jäger 14) since 1961 is particularly admired by connoisseurs. *Currywurst* is no gourmet food, of course, as the German novelist Uwe Timm observes: "none of the Perrier/boutique crowd eat it because you have to do so standing up, between sunshine and showers, alongside a pensioner, a young flipped-out girl, a vagrant reeking of piss who tells you his life story, a King Lear, so there you stand, with that taste on your tongue, listening to an incredible story about the times that gave birth to curried sausage: ruins and new beginnings, sweetly pungent anarchy." Timm's 1993 novella *The Invention of Curried Sausage* offers one engaging, if fanciful, version of "the triumphal march of the curried sausage, starting from Grossneumarkt [in

Hamburg's Neustadt], then to a stand on the Reeperbahn, then to St. Georg, then and only then with Lisa to Berlin, where Lisa opened a stand on Kant-Strasse, then to Kiel, Cologne, Münster and Frankfurt, but strangely enough stopping at the River Main, where *Weisswurst* held on to its territory."

The enduring appeal of the *Currywurst* cannot disguise the fact that the Germans have proved just as vulnerable to the global advance of McDonald's and Burger King as the British or North Americans. It could be argued, however, that in Hamburg the "Big Mac" and "Whopper" have merely returned to their spiritual home. It is certainly the case that in the early nineteenth century a lightly smoked salt beef patty was known as a "Hamburg steak," and it seems plausible that German migrants took the dish with them to the New World, along with frankfurters and wieners, although there is little documentary evidence to back up this assertion.

Less controversial culinary landmarks associated with the city include the oldest Italian restaurant in the whole of Germany (the Restaurant Cuneo at Davidstrasse 11, which opened in 1905 to cater for Italian workers building the Elbe Tunnel) and the first cocktail bar in Germany (the America Bar, which opened on Spielbudenplatz in 1900). The latter has long since disappeared, but Christiansens Fine Drinks and Cocktails (Pinnasberg 60) is a more than adequate replacement, with 150 tempting concoctions on the menu.

No nighttime visit to the Reeperbahn is complete without a stroll down the Grosse Freiheit, Hamburg's number one party street. It is only modest in length, but its narrow confines and the sheer profusion of neon signs—of guitars, elephants and palm trees as well as girls—ensure a welcome sugar-rush of bad taste in a city more generally characterized by sober understatement. This is where to come for live music and dancing, although there is no shortage of sex shows either. These streets on the north side of the Reeperbahn were the location of Hamburg's first Chinatown. Its focal point was the Schmuckstrasse, a side road off Grosse Freiheit, which is now the haunt of transvestites and transsexuals. Chinese sailors and ships' cooks, fed up with the long voyages and poor wages, set up laundries and restaurants here in the early 1900s. At first they catered primarily for other Chinese, but soon Hamburgers developed a taste for Asian cuisine too. As well as these legitimate businesses, however, Chinatown became the center of Hamburg's drug trade in the early decades of the twentieth century.

The restaurants and laundries were connected by a network of cellars and tunnels, which allowed criminals to disappear into thin air. The property at Schmuckstrasse 7, for instance, had no fewer than twelve separate but linked cellar rooms. In 1921 police raided two "opium dens" at Hafenstrasse 126 and Pinnasberg 77, and found dozens of Chinese, Japanese and Germans in a state of intoxication. Stephen Spender became familiar with the area in 1929:

> They walked back to the Freiheit, down a side street. Signs for shops and Lokale were written in Chinese. Joachim told Paul of fights between sailors free with their knives. In some streets it was dangerous to walk alone. Someone might throw a handkerchief over your face, search your clothing for valuables and leave you stripped and beaten, dying perhaps in the gutter. Bars were haunted by drug pushers. All this excited Paul greatly.

The connection between the "Chinese mafia" and drugs was frequently made by Hamburg's newspaper commentators in the 1920s. The reports of the day bear a remarkable similarity to those that dominated the city's press in the 1980s, when the drugs trade was blamed on "black Africans"; and to the present decade, when the spotlight has turned on the "Kurdish mafia." This extract by Ernst Engelbrecht and Leo Heller dates from 1926:

> The Chinese has generally sacrificed his ponytail to civilization, but in his customs he has generally remained very conservative. This is to be seen, if nowhere else, in the Chinese restaurants, which Hamburg, like all of the larger port cities, displays in abundance... Enterprising Chinese have leased dance clubs and cafés in Hamburg, where they offer entertainment of all sorts to their fellow countrymen streaming into the harbour... The enjoyment of opium is probably the most widespread of the Chinese vices, one to which large numbers in China have hopelessly succumbed... The opium scourge is slowly making its way into the life of the German people. And the foreign sailing crews have introduced two other narcotics into Hamburg: marijuana and heroin, two drugs that ultimately seem to be of Spanish or South American origin. Just as cocaine is obtained on the black market under the names "cement," "coke" or "cacao," heroin is widely known in the St. Pauli neighbourhoods favoured by criminals and sailors as "H."

Hamburg's Chinatown was effectively destroyed on May 13, 1944, when all the Chinese people living in the city were arrested on suspicion of "espionage": 165 were sent to a work camp at Wilhelmsburg, where seventeen died. They are among the many "forgotten" victims of Nazism.

Just around the corner, at Simon-von-Utrecht-Strasse 2, is a hospital set up by Salomon Heine in 1841. Originally called the Betty-Heine-Hospital in memory of Salomon's deceased wife, it was the most modern hospital yet seen in northern Germany. It was also one of the most significant charitable foundations of the nineteenth century, not least because its policy was to admit patients on the basis of need rather than religion. Despite this, it quickly became known as the "Jewish Hospital" and was largely ignored by the city's mid-twentieth-century historians as a result. As Matthias Wegner (1998) has highlighted, Percy Ernst Schramm was particularly culpable in this regard. The hospital was at least commemorated in a poem by Salomon's nephew Heinrich, in which he famously commented on the "threefold misery" to be poor, in pain and Jewish: the latter, he suggested, was the worst of the three. As if to confirm that gloomy prognosis, the building was cleared of Jewish patients in the Nazi period and used by the Wehrmacht as a military hospital. Today it houses the local council offices, and its prayer room has been restored.

Many of the hospital's former patients were buried in the nearby Jewish Cemetery on Königsstrasse, where you can see gravestones dating back to the seventeenth century. The cemetery originally maintained separate sections for Sephardic (from Spain and Portugal) and Ashkenazi (Eastern European) Jews, but these were merged to form one of the largest and most important Jewish graveyards anywhere in Germany. It survived the Third Reich relatively intact, but fear of neo-Nazi vandals ironically means it is now only open to the public by prior appointment.

THE HAMBURG SOUND

It was in these streets to the north of the Reeperbahn that Hamburg's principal contribution to the history of popular music was made. "Pop" in Germany during the economic miracle years had meant middle-of-the-road *Schlager* stars like Peter Alexander, Freddy Quinn and Ted Herold. Hip youths liked skiffle and trad jazz: Chris Barber was such a big star in Hamburg that some people dubbed it the "Free and Barber City" in his honor. It was not until the late 1950s that a rock 'n' roll scene began to develop on the Elbe: in October 1958 a concert by Bill Haley in the Ernst-Merck-Halle (St. Petersburger Strasse) led to a riot, in which dozens of seats were broken—the cost of damage was put at 20,000 Marks—and more than a hundred police were deployed to clear the hall. Hamburg's young rockers may have been rebelling against the stifling bourgeois conformism of Adenauer's Germany, but over the coming months they would owe much to two archetypal St. Pauli "entrepreneurs," Bruno Koschmider and Horst Fascher, who became key figures in establishing rock 'n' roll on the Reeperbahn.

Koschmider (1926-2000) was a diminutive, gay ex-circus performer, who walked with a permanent limp after a fall from the high wire. He had purchased the Indra strip club (Grosse Freiheit 64) in 1950. By the end of the decade he was also running a porn cinema, the Bambi-Kino (Paul-

Roosen-Strasse 33), and the Kaiserkeller cabaret club at Grosse Freiheit 36. Sensing the growing appetite for rock 'n' roll, Koschmider began to stage live shows in his clubs. The first British musicians to play the Kaiserkeller were the Jets, from London, in June 1960. Their singer, Tony Sheridan, would go on to become a regular fixture on the Reeperbahn rock scene for many years. A few months later, Derry and the Seniors became the first group from Liverpool to play the Kaiserkeller. They were quickly followed by Rory Storm and the Hurricanes, with a young Ringo Starr on drums. Such were the numbers attending the Kaiserkeller gigs that Koschmider decided to try rock music at the Indra too. It was there, on August 17, 1960, that the Beatles played their first show in Hamburg, arranged by their Welsh agent-cum-manager Allan Williams.

Fascher (born 1936) was a former ship's carpenter, diver, boxer and nightclub bouncer who had served a prison sentence for manslaughter. He recommended the Jets to Koschmider after meeting Tony Sheridan in a Soho coffee bar. Back in Hamburg he became Sheridan's manager and befriended the Beatles, for whom he was to become a minder, gopher and surrogate father figure. The Beatles were not yet the "Fab Four"—their five-man line up included Stuart Sutcliffe on bass and Pete Best on drums—and nor were they yet the "mop-tops": they had Elvis-style quiffs and wore drainpipe trousers and winklepicker shoes. They played four and a half hours a night on weekdays and six hours on Saturdays, for a total of 48 nights. During this first stay in the city, the group slept on ex-army bunks in two dank windowless concrete rooms at the back of the Bambi-Kino, with the cinema's toilets doubling up as the band's bathroom. Stuart Sutcliffe wrote in a letter home: "Hamburg has little quality, except the kind you would find in a test tube of sewer water. It's nothing but a vast amoral jungle." Although the building has now been converted into apartments, a small plaque and a painted Bambi figure can be seen on the Paul-Roosen-Strasse frontage. The back door, used by the Beatles, opens on to Grosse Freiheit and is unchanged today (opposite Grosse Freiheit 84).

Complaints from neighbors about the level of noise led Koschmider to switch the band from the Indra to the larger Kaiserkeller. There the group's initial residency ran from October 4 to 16, but it was extended to December 31, 1960. They alternated with Rory Storm and the Hurricanes on an hourly basis, sustained by Preludin (slimming tablets with a stimulant effect), amphetamines and beer. It was during one of the 58 Kaiserkeller shows that a group of Hamburg art students—including the graphic artist Klaus Voormann, and the photographers Astrid Kirchherr and Jürgen Vollmer—first saw the band. The story of how the Hamburg students came to influence the Beatles' image and outlook has been told many times before, not least in the film *Backbeat* (1994), but it merits brief repetition here. The students, nicknamed "Exis" because of their interest in French Existentialism, became friends with the young Scousers and showed them some of the sights of the city. Kirchherr took photos of the group at the Dom funfair on the Heiligengeistfeld, and began dating Stuart Sutcliffe, who was a more talented painter than he was bass player. She also invited the group for meals at her mother's apartment at Eimsbütteler Chaussee 45a, and broadened their cultural horizons by introducing them to new kinds of books and records, adding a continental sophistication to their Anglo-American tastes.

Under the influence of the "Exis," the band started dressing in black, and one by one they abandoned their greasy quiffs for the "French cut": the forward-combed, fringed style associated with Left Bank intellectuals and French film actors, which Vollmer and Voormann had adopted several years earlier. When Kirchherr made Sutcliffe a collarless jacket, Lennon was initially dismissive, yet before long all the band had one. Indeed, although he was only a Beatle for fifteen months, Sutcliffe's role was crucial. Through his relationship with Kirchherr, he became what Paul du Noyer (2002) refers to as "a vital bridge between the two contrasting and apparently incompatible aesthetics: the cosmopolitan beatnik and the working-class Teddy Boy."

The Beatles' first stay in Hamburg came to a premature end. It was discovered that George Harrison was still a minor and would have to be deported. He left on November 21, and although the rest of the band continued without him, Koschmider terminated their contract with effect from November 30. Frustrated, Paul McCartney and Pete Best hung a condom on a nail in the concrete wall of the Bambi-Kino's back corridor and set light to it. The fire was soon extinguished—there was precious little to burn—but Koschmider accused them of attempted arson and the two lads spent the night in the Davidwache cells. Estranged from Koschmider, the band minus George then played five nights at the Top Ten Club (Reeperbahn 136), which had just been opened by Peter Eckhorn, a 21-

year-old restaurateur with gangland connections. The authorities had discovered, however, that the group had no residence or work permits, so on December 5, Paul and Pete were deported too. John Lennon followed by train a few days later.

Stuart Sutcliffe stayed in Hamburg. He became engaged to Astrid and had moved in to her mother's apartment, setting up an artist's studio in the attic. Although he continued to play with the group until August 1961, he applied for and won a scholarship to Hamburg's College of Visual Arts (Lerchenfeld 2), where his Abstract Expressionist paintings made a lasting impression on his tutor, the Scottish sculptor and Pop Art pioneer Eduardo Paolozzi (1924-2005). He worked feverishly, producing numerous dark and troubling pictures, but was affected by increasingly debilitating headaches. He died of a brain hemorrhage on April 10, 1962, before his potential could be fulfilled.

The Beatles returned to the Reeperbahn in the spring of 1961. On March 27, they began a mammoth season of 98 gigs at the Top Ten Club, playing seven nights a week until July 2. They lived in a spartan apartment above the venue, a former hippodrome, and earned forty Marks each per night. Although owned by the Eckhorn family, the Top Ten was effectively run by Horst Fascher and Tony Sheridan, who was the resident singer. Indeed, one of the group's main duties was to provide the backing music for Sheridan's nightly performances. The Beatles' first participation in a record was the Polydor single *My Bonnie / The Saints*, credited to Tony Sheridan and the Beat Brothers. It was recorded live at the Friedrich-Ebert-Halle in the suburb of Harburg on June 22, 1961, and produced by the famous Hamburg bandleader Bert Kaempfert (1923-80).

The commercial success of the Top Ten Club soon alerted other St. Pauli bar owners to the growing market for rock 'n' roll music. Manfred Weissleder (1928-80), a former electrician who owned several premises around the Paradieshof (a courtyard off the Grosse Freiheit), had more ambition than most. His aim was to turn a former cinema into the ultimate rock 'n' roll venue. In the early months of 1962 he succeeded in converting the Stern-Kino into the Star Club, which opened on Friday, April 13, at Grosse Freiheit 39. The opening night was advertised on bright red posters under the slogan "The Despair is at an End! The Era of Village Music is Over!" Around 1,200 people turned up, with the queue stretching around the corner into the Reeperbahn. The line-up, billed by

Weissleder as a "concentration of Europe's finest talent," was Tex Roberg, Roy Young, the Graduates, the Bachelors and the Beatles.

The Beatles played three seasons at the Star Club in 1962 (April 13-May 31, November 1-14, December 18-31), with their fee rising from 500 to 700 Marks per person, per week during the course of their stay. By the end of 1962 the group were living in comfortable single rooms in the Pacific Hotel (Neue Pferdemarkt 30-31). Midway through their Star Club engagement, with the ruthless Brian Epstein now as manager, Pete Best was unceremoniously dumped from the line-up in favor of that other Reeperbahn veteran, Ringo Starr—a move that prompted protests in Liverpool. At around the same time, John Lennon was alleged to have urinated on Sunday morning worshippers on the way to St. Joseph's Church. There was a visit from the police, and legal papers were drawn up, but the group had left Hamburg before the case could proceed. It was finally dropped, under pressure from Brian Epstein and Manfred Weissleder, in 1965.

Despite this juvenile episode, Lennon famously said of his time on the Reeperbahn: "I grew up in Liverpool, but I came of age in Hamburg." Certainly, it was only during the course of their 200-odd appearances in St. Pauli that the Beatles evolved into the band which conquered the world. Joe Flannery, who managed a number of Merseybeat bands, commented on Hamburg: "That place was the making of so many Liverpool groups. They went out as novices and came back as tight as anything. It was one of the best training grounds." Gerry and the Pacemakers, the Searchers and the Swinging Blue Jeans were among the other Merseybeat bands to play regularly in and around the Reeperbahn. Indeed, there is a school of thought which suggests that the much-fêted "Liverpool Sound" was actually a "Hamburg Sound." A 2006 exhibition at the Museum of Hamburg History under that title suggested as much, as did the accompanying book by Ulf Krüger and Ortwin Pelc (2006). Even the Liverpudlian music critic Paul Du Noyer acknowledges: "For most of us, the Beatles' real career begins in 1962 with their first Parlophone recordings. But there is an argument that as a live act their best days were already over."

Not everyone would agree. Bill Harry, founder of *Mersey Beat* magazine and a close friend of the Beatles, told Spencer Leigh: "Hamburg's importance has been exaggerated by nearly every author. Liverpool is far more important." There were more bands and more venues in Liverpool, to be sure, but the Beatles played many more times on the Elbe than on the Mersey, and this apprenticeship proved crucial in developing not just their visual image, but their sound as well. Playing long hours in an uncompromising atmosphere helped, as did the need to *mach Schau* (put on a good show). The more professional sound equipment in Hamburg helped too: a proliferation of microphones not only enabled the band to work on vocal harmonies, but also enabled them to discover the benefit of placing a microphone in the bass drum, which helped to create the loud, driving rhythm that gave "beat" music its name. The need to share lead vocal duties helped each band member to develop individually, and the group benefited collectively from having to learn hundreds of cover versions. It gave them an understanding of how successful pop songs were constructed: what worked and what did not.

As a city, however, Hamburg has been remarkably slow to cash in on its Beatle connections. It was only in May 2009 that a Beatles Museum, the five-story Beatlemania, opened at Nobistor 10. A few months earlier, after a campaign by a local radio station and contributions from wealthy fans, the city agreed to rename the junction of Grosse Freiheit and the Reeperbahn "Beatles-Platz." It was redesigned in the form of a giant vinyl record, 95 feet in diameter, with stainless steel sculptures of the Fab Four placed in an arc facing Grosse Freiheit, together with one of Stuart Sutcliffe set back from the main group. The first organized Beatles tours of the city were also launched in 2009, devised by the band's former associate Horst Fascher, in conjunction with Peter Paetzold and David Hanowski. Many of the group's original haunts can still be visited today. Their favorite bar, Gretel & Alfons (Grosse Freiheit 29), is still decorated with memorabilia, including a poster signed by McCartney when he finally returned to pay his bar bill in 1989. Their favorite clothes shop was Paul Hundertmark Jeans and Western Store at Spielbudenplatz 9, where they bought cowboy boots, and they drank many a coffee in Café Möller, on the corner of Grosse Freiheit and Beatles-Platz.

As for the Beatles' former venues, the Indra still hosts live music, but mostly jazz and blues these days. The Kaiserkeller operates predominantly as a nightclub, but still hosts occasional live gigs. The Top Ten no longer exists, although it survived into the 1990s. The Star Club, which styled itself as "The Most Famous Beat-Club in the World" at the height of Beatlemania, had a stormy post-Beatles existence: Bill Haley returned to do a

ten-night residency, and it also attracted such luminaries as Ray Charles, Fats Domino, Jerry Lee Lewis and Little Richard; but it was stormed by police in July 1963 and was forced to close down in June 1964. It was later allowed to reopen and staged shows by Jimi Hendrix, the Bee Gees and Eric Clapton among others, but it shut its doors for a final time on New Year's Day 1970. Live music was then replaced by Germany's first live-sex show, Salambo, before the building was gutted by fire in 1983. Its remains were demolished three years later, although a plaque in the court-yard of Grosse Freiheit 39 marks the site of the former stage.

CONTEMPORARY COUNTERCULTURE

In the wake of the Beatles' spectacular rise to stardom, numerous British bands tried their luck in Hamburg. The West Country musician Graham Sclater, who lived and worked in the city during the 1960s, wrote a novel based on his experiences; *Ticket to Ride* (2006) tells the story of one such band, the Cheetahs, who arrive from Devon in January 1966:

> They were stiff, tired and aching after their long journey, but the re-alisation that they were really in Hamburg soon woke them up. They

took it in turns to wash in the basin in the corner of the room, put on their shoes and jackets, and before they knew it they were walking on the streets of Hamburg for the first time in search of something to eat... The traffic raced in every direction and, taking their lives in their hands, they crossed the road into the sunshine on the other side. It helped momentarily, but as the clouds built up and the wind began to strengthen, the euphoria of walking on the streets of Hamburg soon wore off as the ice cold wind began to bite through their thin coats and jackets...

The Cheetahs' dreams of stardom quickly turn into the stuff of nightmare, with drug overdoses, venereal disease and a colorful cast of crooks, pimps and hookers. The extremes and excesses of life in St. Pauli make it an ideal setting for novelists and script writers, of course, but it is important to emphasize that Hamburg's nightlife does not stop and start with the Reeperbahn. In fact, since the 1980s much of the city's coolest nocturnal activity has been centered on two neighboring districts to the northeast: the Schanzenviertel and the Karolinenviertel.

The former takes its name from the Sternschanze, a star-shaped bastion outside the main city fortifications, built in fear of Danish attacks in 1682. There are no traces of the bastion today, but the park where it once stood, Sternschanzenpark, has been dominated since 1909 by a fortress-like water tower. While the tower now contains a four-star hotel, it remains the symbol of the district, which was considered solidly working-class until the 1970s, when its proximity to the university led to a significant demographic shift. Today it is inhabited by a mix of students and young professionals, particularly those working in advertising, graphic design and IT. Most of the local nightlife is located between Schanzenstrasse and Stresemannstrasse, with Schulterblatt being the main drag. The unusual name—*Schulterblatt* means "shoulder-blade"—is said to have come from one of the local hostelries, frequented primarily by whalers, which in the seventeenth century had a painted whale's shoulder-blade as its pub sign. That particular establishment disappeared long ago, but in the 1980s the places to be seen were Subito, Luxor and Kir. Today the bars around the Piazza on Schulterblatt attract the liveliest clientele.

By the 1990s, however, the Schanzenviertel was being overtaken in the hipness stakes by the Karolinenviertel, a short distance to the east.

Taking its name from the Karolinenstrasse, the quarter is squeezed un-promisingly between the municipal abattoir (*Schlachthof*), which opened in 1864, and the large modern halls of the trade fair site (*Messehallen*). It is overshadowed by the 900-foot television tower, named after the Hamburg-born physicist Heinrich Hertz (1857-94), and built between 1964 and 1968 on Rentzelstrasse. Although animals are no longer slaugh-tered in the abattoir, there is still a large wholesale meat market, and large refrigerated trucks are a familiar sight on local roads. An area of low-grade workers' housing since the 1860s, the Karo quarter's much-predicted gen-trification has been slow to materialize, not least because of local hostility to "yuppies" and speculators. It became a center of the city's punk sub-culture in the 1980s and the alternative fashion industry in the 1990s. Today it is a rough-and-ready multicultural district with numerous sec-ondhand shops and independent traders. The main street is Marktstrasse, with lively bars such as Yoko Mono, Egal or the venerable Marktstube.

Between these two districts and the Reeperbahn lies the vast expanse of the Heiligengeistfeld, formerly a meadow belonging to the medieval Hospital of the Holy Spirit, but now the location of three iconic Hamburg institutions: "Hochhaus 1," a vast Second World War bunker and flak tower dating from 1942 (and originally one of a pair); St. Pauli football club, founded in 1910; and the Dom funfair, which used to take place in the vicinity of the cathedral (hence its name), but moved to the Heiligengeistfeld in 1900. In fact, traveling showmen have been setting up their stalls on the field ever since the construction of permanent build-ings forced them away from the Spielbudenplatz. In the late nineteenth century, for instance, the legendary Barnum & Bailey Circus erected its 15,000-seat marquee here, as did Buffalo Bill's Wild West show. There were also temporary ice rinks, panoramas, animal shows and military tattoos, but right up until the 1880s it was still common to see sheep grazing on the field too. The Dom fair was originally a Christmas market, but today takes place three times in the year—spring, summer and winter—and lasts for one month at a time. In 1979 it celebrated its 650th anniversary, and is one of the largest fairs of its kind in Europe, with around 260 attractions and more than four million visitors for each thirty-day stretch. The attractions include all the traditional fairground favorites—bumper cars, ghost trains, waltzers and roller coasters—together with beer tents, restaurants, and a spectacular firework display every Friday

evening. The Dom's big wheel may not be quite the London Eye, but it is the largest mobile Ferris wheel in the world, and its open gondolas are not for the faint-hearted. The Dom also has its own distinctive smell: a mixture of fried almonds, cotton candy and *Glühwein*.

FC St. Pauli, whose ramshackle Millerntor stadium sits on the western side of the Heiligengeistfeld, was founded in 1910 and first started playing on this site in 1921. Although the club have enjoyed brief spells (1977-8, 1988-91, 1995-7, 2001-2) in the highest German league, the Bundesliga, most of their recent existence has been spent in the second or third tier of German football. The club is unusual for two principal reasons: it is one of the few professional teams anywhere in the world to play in an all-brown kit; and its supporters have the reputation for being left-wing or anarchist in outlook, waving pirate flags and anti-capitalist banners at matches. This radical anti-establishment image is in fact quite a recent development: in the early 1980s attendances had dwindled to fewer than 2,000, and it was only in the course of that decade that the club was adopted by many on Hamburg's Green/Alternative and punk scene. Some violent clashes with the right-wing, skinhead followers of other clubs ensued (particularly from the former East Germany), but these days matches at Millerntor are peaceful if noisy affairs. Games are frequently sold out—the stadium is being modernized and its capacity expanded to 27,000 by 2013—and female fans make up an unusually large proportion of the crowd.

Even the most fervent St. Pauli fan would have to concede, however, that in purely sporting terms their club plays second fiddle in the city to the Hamburger Sport-Verein, known simply as HSV (founded 1919). The last of HSV's six German league titles may have come more than a quarter of a century ago, but the club's fans can proudly boast that their team has never been relegated, and even won the European Cup back in 1983. HSV is a multi-sport club in the continental manner, with successful volleyball, baseball and hockey teams, and attracts followers from right across northern Germany. Their impressive modern stadium in the city's northwestern outskirts, now known as the Imtech Arena, often accommodates crowds close to its 60,000 capacity, yet the volume of noise seldom matches the "Millerntor roar." St. Pauli fans may be fewer in number, but they have the better songs. Fittingly, these include the Liverpool anthem "You'll Never Walk Alone," which is sung at every match.

Chapter Seven

THE WORLD CITY

The citizen of Hamburg, it is said, looks outward rather than inward: not to Germany or Central Europe, but to the great wide world. Richard Evans quotes Julius von Eckhardt, the Senate's secretary in the 1870s, who recalled "dozens of older gentlemen who knew 'every town on the Mississippi' from personal experience, and had been 'twenty times in London', but had never visited Berlin at all." The names of shipping companies founded in the city in the nineteenth century testify to this outlook: the Hamburg-America line, the Hamburg-South America Shipping Company, the Hamburg-East-Asia line. They reflect a city that saw itself as a world player, trading not just with other ports but with whole continents. In fact, however, Hamburg's merchants only became truly global in the second half of the eighteenth century: before then, their regular trade routes had been concentrated in the North Sea and the Baltic. Trade with the Americas, for example, was very limited before the United States achieved independence in the late eighteenth century. It was only when European powers found their colonial ties weakening that Hamburg merchants could step in to fill the breach. This is what happened with the USA after 1776, and with the newly independent states of South America in the following century.

It was around this time that people from other parts of Germany began to regard Hamburg as their "gateway to the world." It is a characteristic of all major ports to evoke thoughts of travel and distant parts, and in truth the phrase had become a cliché even before Hitler bestowed it as an official title on the city in the 1930s. In his speech at the opening of the Speicherstadt in 1888, for instance, Kaiser Wilhelm had told the city's merchants: "You are the ones who connect our fatherland with invisible ties to distant parts of the globe, trade with our products, and more than that: you are the ones who transmit our ideas and values to the wider world, and for this the fatherland owes you a debt of special gratitude." One can reasonably assume, however, that transmitting German ideas and values was not top of the merchants' real list of priorities. For people like

Hamburg. Hafen-Kehrwiederspitze

3479

the Godeffroy family, dubbed the "Grab-Alls of the Pacific" by the travel writer Constance Gordon-Cumming (1837-1924), it was the pursuit of profit which came first.

Gateways, moreover, can be approached from opposite directions. It may not have crossed the Kaiser's or Hitler's mind, but Hamburg was not only an exit but an entrance too. When Coleridge referred to the city as "this great mart of nations" in 1798, it was for the goods and ideas coming in as much as those going out. This chapter explores the traces left by these early encounters with overseas territories. This is easier to illustrate with buildings and institutions than with ideas, but the foreign origin of some of the city's most cherished cultural traditions can be readily surmised, as can the provenance of many of Hamburg's leading families: Amsinck (Dutch), Ballin (Danish), de Chateauneuf (French), Sloman (British), Godeffroy and de Chapeaurouge (both Huguenot). For all its restrictions, the city was a veritable melting pot compared to many parts of Germany. "Hamburg readily accepted and even encouraged the immigration of 'desirable' individuals and groups," Mary Lindemann (1990) notes. "It particularly welcomed those who supplied capital, offered trade secrets, or proposed new branches of manufacturing." This was recognized in other parts of Germany too: "I can find next to nothing that is German in Hamburg, apart from the language," complained a Bavarian diplomat in 1845. "There can be no question of any German blood here."

Hamburg has been described as "the most English city on the continent" by the historian Helmut Böhme. In part this was due to its traditions of continuity, gradual reform and free trade, but it was also a consequence of the direct commercial links which can be documented back to the early thirteenth century, and which are probably older still. In 1566 the city succeeded in tempting the Company of Merchant Adventurers, which controlled the English textile trade with the Continent, to leave its previous base in Antwerp and set up court on the Elbe. They did so with promises of a privileged trading position, a new building—the "English House" on Gröningerstrasse—and an Anglican chapel with services in English. Under pressure from the Hanseatic League, the Merchant Adventurers were forced to relocate to Stade between 1587 and 1611, but they returned to Hamburg in 1611 and stayed until 1806, when the occupying French forced the remaining Adventurers out. The company may have been a declining force by this time, but Britain's rise as a maritime power ensured that Hamburg needed to maintain a cordial relationship with its neighbor across the North Sea. Most of the leading Hamburg firms had branches in London, and, as we have seen, the city's own currency had twelve Pfennigs to the Schilling right up until 1873.

Through the centuries visitors have commented on the Anglophile nature of the city, whose inhabitants adopted English customs such as the carrying of an umbrella, wearing tweed clothes and taking tea at 5 o'clock. The Hamburg bourgeoisie was quick to embrace British sports too, notably rowing, golf and equestrianism, and gave their children names such as Percy, Henry, William or John. In 1892 the great German novelist Theodor Fontane (1819-98) observed that the most heartfelt wish of all Hamburg women was to be mistaken for an English lady. He added, moreover, that it was an ideal to which most of them came close.

Great port cities are always more cosmopolitan than their hinterlands, of course, yet it is striking how often writers commented on the contrast between Hamburg and Germany's interior. Examples from two Nobel laureates should suffice. The playwright Gerhart Hauptmann (1862-1946), who won the literature prize in 1912, wrote: "I was born in Salzbrunn in Silesia, but it was in Hamburg that I first saw the light of day: the light of the great wide world." Meanwhile in *The Magic Mountain* the 1929 winner, Thomas Mann, described Hans Castorp's upbringing on the Elbe:

> Yes, he was thoroughly in his element in the atmosphere of this great seaboard city: this reeking air, compact of good living and a retail trade that embraced the four corners of the earth. It had been the breath of his father's nostrils, and the son drew it with profound acquiescence and a sense of well-being. The exhalations from water, coals, and tar, the sharp tang in the nostrils from the heaped-up stacks of colonial produce; the huge steam-cranes at the dock-side, imitating the quiet, the intelligence, and the giant strength of elephants at work... all this he felt, saw, heard, knew.

HAMBURG AND COLONIALISM

Germany's era as a colonial power was brief. It began, somewhat unexpectedly, in 1884 and lasted only until 1919, when all her colonies were lost under the Treaty of Versailles. The historiography of German colonialism was, until recently, similarly modest in scale. As the historian W.

O. Henderson observed in 1962, "there are limits as to what can be said about an empire which lasted only thirty-five years." Even so, recent years have seen a boom in studies of German colonialism, with a particular emphasis on the impact of colonies on social and cultural life back home in Germany. This was probably much greater than the political or economic value of a "disparate and far-flung collection of largely undesirable real estate in Africa and Asia" (Holger Herwig), which always lagged behind the high hopes of colonial activists. The initial expansion (1884-5) consisted of a series of ad hoc initiatives by individual merchants and adventurers. At first these German protectorates were administered privately, through chartered companies, but when this proved unsatisfactory a small Colonial Department was set up in the Foreign Office in 1890.

Further acquisitions followed in the late 1890s, such as the port of Tsingtao on China's Kiao Chow Bay, and a scattering of territories in the South Seas (Papua New Guinea, the Solomon Islands, Samoa), but German colonial rule was increasingly characterized by embarrassing scandals and aggressive confrontations with the native populations. These included the brutal suppression of uprisings by the Herero and the Nama in South West Africa (1904-7), and of some twenty different tribes in East Africa (the so-called Maji Maji Rising of 1905-7). A more subtle and technocratic course, sometimes dubbed "scientific colonialism," was then adopted under the liberal banker Bernhard Dernburg, who was appointed Secretary of State in the newly-created Office for Colonial Affairs in 1907. Dernburg was in the post for less than four years, and German colonial policy remained a haphazard and improvised affair, but his aim of treating the native population as a valuable commodity rather than an obstacle did appear to work. Certainly, there were no more major risings, and the native populations remained largely loyal to the German Empire throughout the First World War.

Short-lived though it was, the German colonial empire undoubtedly stimulated the imagination of writers and artists, from the popular adventure stories of Karl May (1842-1912) to the vivid Expressionist art of Emil Nolde (1867-1956), Ernst-Ludwig Kirchner (1880-1938) or Walter von Ruckteschell (1882-1941), who in 1914 painted "Germany's highest mountain," Mount Kilimanjaro. It inspired imperial Germany's scientists to be at the forefront of a host of nascent academic disciplines such as ethnology, anthropology, zoology and oceanography, and led in 1900 to the founding of Hamburg's Institute of Maritime and Tropical Diseases, a fore-runner of Hamburg University. It encouraged new methods of collection, organization and display in museums such as Hamburg's pioneering Museum for Ethnology, which opened in 1879. It provided entertainment for thousands of paying spectators at the era's many zoos and *Völkerschauen* ("people shows"), such as Carl Hagenbeck's shows on the Reeperbahn and the Heiligengeistfeld, when live human "exhibits" attracted large audiences. Above all, it touched millions through its influence on everyday language, popular culture and advertising. Colonial imagery in the latter field was not confined to so-called *Kolonialwaren*—"exotic" groceries such as coffee, chocolate and bananas—but was also employed to sell products and services ostensibly unrelated to the colonial world (the "whitening" power of soap, toothpaste and washing powder, for instance).

Colonial representations of this kind have been at the forefront of much recent work by Anglo-American scholars in the field of German Studies. It has been argued that the "imperialist imagination" both pre- and post-dates Germany's actual colonial empire. In other words, Germans were constructing "colonial fantasies" well before the acquisition of real colonies, while memories of the colonial experience have continued to echo through works of German art, film and literature long after the territories were lost. This may well be true, but it nevertheless seems unlikely that the Germans were as deeply affected by imperialism as the British or the French, given the brevity of Germany's colonial experience and the relative lack of migration from the empire's periphery to its center. Until the late twentieth century, Africans or Asians were a much rarer sight on the streets of Hamburg than of London or Liverpool, and the favorite trick of postcolonial studies—to focus on "the voyage in" rather than "the voyage out"—is harder to pull off for the German empire than for its British or French counterparts.

As one might expect, Hamburg merchants and scholars feature prominently in the development of an imperialist imagination in nineteenth-century Germany. On the one hand this was through the lobbying of organizations such as the Hamburg Association for Colonization in Central America; the Hamburg Geographical Society, whose leaders Wilhelm Hübbe-Schleiden (1846-1916) and Ludwig Friedrichsen ensured that colonial issues were frequently discussed by the city's economic and intellectual élites; or the German-African Society, which numbered

Hamburg's mayor Gustav Kirchenpauer among its members. On the other hand it was also a consequence of practical action: either privately founded colonial communities, such as Blumenau (1850) and Joinville (1851) in Brazil; or of trading stations established by Hamburg merchants. With regard to the latter, three family businesses stand out: the Godeffroys in the South Pacific, the Woermanns in West Africa and the O'swalds in East Africa.

The Godeffroy merchant house was founded by Johan César Godeffroy IV in 1766 and became J. C. Godeffroy & Son in 1806. Combining shipping, shipbuilding and iron-making interests, the company gradually built up trade links around the world. Even so, by 1836 it possessed only six ships. The rapid expansion that followed—two decades later the company owned 27 vessels—was due largely to the rise in emigration from Central Europe. Godeffroy's ships took people to South America, South Africa and Australia and returned with valuable commodities such as copper and copra (coconut oil). While Chile was an important source of income for the company, their influence was particularly felt in Australia— where they had a stake in the lucrative Burra Burra copper mines—Samoa, Tahiti and Tonga, where coconut plantations were laid out and natives were employed as forced labor.

Johan César Godeffroy VI (1813-85), grandson of the firm's founder, was dubbed the "King of the South Seas" by the British newspapers, but the Godeffroys did not travel to the South Pacific in person. Instead they paid others, such as August Unshelm and Theodor Weber, to act as their agents. On their expeditions they collected skulls and other artifacts which were shipped back to Hamburg. In 1861 a Godeffroy Museum opened in the city to display their finds, and a zoologist, Dr Eduard Graeffe, was employed to evaluate the exhibits scientifically. Private museums of this kind were quite commonplace in the nineteenth century: another Hamburg merchant, Hermann Strebel (1834-1914), assembled a valuable collection of Mexican artifacts which was known throughout Europe for its size and quality. However, neither the Strebel nor the Godeffroy Museum survived the nineteenth century intact: the latter closed in 1885 and the majority of both collections ended up in Leipzig.

Not content with "informal empire," the Godeffroy family became vociferous advocates for the German states to develop imperial policies of their own. Johan's brother Gustav (1817-93) sat in the revolutionary

Frankfurt National Assembly in 1848, where he offered to rename one of the firm's ships *Deutschland* and donate it to the country as part of a fledgling German navy. While that plan failed, the Godeffroys continued to lobby for official protection of their trading interests against growing British and American competition. Gustav became a Hamburg senator in 1854 and was instrumental in establishing a Hamburg consulate in the Samoan capital of Apia in 1861, which was largely under the control of the Goddefroys and was described by eyewitnesses as a "German town." Although the family's fortunes nosedived in the late 1870s as a result of their ill-advised coal mining investments, a separate company was set up to oversee their Pacific interests. This "German Trade and Plantation Society of the South Sea Islands in Hamburg" was offered to the Reich government in 1880 in a move which many see as the start of a more formal era of colonialism. The Australian historian Matthew Fitzpatrick (2008) writes:

> ... the house of Godeffroy illustrates neatly the deep interconnectedness between liberalism, nationalism, and expansionist discourse and praxis. From their support and partial supplying of a national fleet in 1848 through to the establishment of an extensive and highly profitable German Pacific trade empire, Godeffroy & Sohn, like the house of Woermann in Africa, illustrated the extent of the embeddedness of Hamburg's Wirtschaftsbürgertum [bourgeoisie] in the processes of imperialism—whether formal or informal, governmental or private sector.

The story of the rise and fall of the Godeffroys (see Chapter Three) is in some respects reminiscent of the Buddenbrooks in Thomas Mann's classic novel of the same name, which is subtitled "The Decline of a Family." Indeed, Matthias Wegner (1999) points out that there was even a Toni in the Godeffroy clan. Of course, Mann's tale is based in his home town of Lübeck, and many of the characters are drawn from his own family, but it is likely that he was at least aware of the Godeffroys of Hamburg:

> The business was to close, the firm to go into liquidation, and the estate to be settled within a year. This was Thomas Buddenbrooks' wish, as expressed in his will. Frau Permaneder felt much upset... She wept for

hours to think that one should dispose thus summarily of that honourable shield, that jewel cherished by four generations of Buddenbrooks: that the history of the firm was now to close, while yet there existed a direct heir to carry it on. But she finally consoled herself by thinking that the end of the firm was not, after all, the end of the family, and that her nephew might as easily, in a new and different career, perform the high task allotted to him—that task being to carry on the family name and add fresh lustre to the family reputation.

The Hamburg brothers William Henry O'swald (1832-1923) and Albrecht Percy O'swald (1831-99) built up a giant commercial empire in East Africa. It was centered on the island of Zanzibar, where they founded their first trading station in 1849. The brothers took turns as consul general, and in 1859 William was able to negotiate a mutually beneficial trade agreement with the local ruler. As a result, William's profile in Hamburg grew and he was elected to the Citizens' Assembly in 1866. He would later become a long-serving senator and deputy mayor of the city. The O'swald brothers, who expanded their operations on to Madagascar in 1870 and began to establish rubber plantations on the African mainland in 1886, were founder members of the Hamburg branch of the German Colonial Association.

A third and final Hamburg family business to make its mark in the age of imperialism was founded by the son of a Westphalian linen manufacturer, Carl Woermann (1813-80), in 1837. Woermann traded with South America, the West Indies, Australia and India, but it was in the West African state of Liberia that he set up his first overseas office. By the end of the 1850s there were eight Woermann vessels taking regular shipments of arms and spirits to West Africa, and returning with rubber and palm oil to Europe. Further offices opened in Gabon (1862) and at the mouth of the Cameroon River (1868), the latter under the leadership of Woermann's son Adolph (1847-1910). The younger Woermann, who became a partner in the business in 1874, was an energetic, ambitious and ruthlessly aggressive figure, even by the standards of Hamburg's colonial entrepreneurs. As well as his business activities and a seat in the Citizens' Assembly (1880-1904) he also found time to be a National Liberal member of the Reichstag in Berlin (1884-90), where he was a prominent lobbyist for a German colonial empire. A memorandum written by Wo-

The Woermann dynasty

ermann for the Hamburg Chamber of Commerce in June 1883 called on the city's merchants to take advantage of the opportunities presented in Africa, and on the German Reich to protect its citizens who sought to do business there. The memorandum, which was forwarded to the imperial government, also called for the acquisition of a coastal strip in West Africa on which to establish a trading colony.

Woermann was invited to a series of meetings with Chancellor Bismarck, who had previously been a vocal critic of colonial adventures, and as a result of these meetings the battleship *Möwe* was dispatched to West Africa to offer symbolic protection to German traders. Woermann was also asked to brief the newly appointed Imperial Commissioner to Africa, Dr. Gustav Nachtigall, before he embarked on a secret mission to secure a German foothold on the "dark continent." In April 1884 the land holdings of the Bremen merchant Adolf Lüderitz in South West Africa (present-day Namibia) were made a protectorate of the German crown. Other protectorates in Africa quickly followed, including Cameroon where Woermann's own son Eduard had met tribal chiefs in July 1884, securing a contract which handed over full territorial sovereignty to the Woermann concern and its subsidiary Jantzen & Thormälen. Further acquisitions in Africa included Togo (1884) and German East Africa (1885); while Kaiser-Wilhelm-Land (1885) and the Bismarck Archipelago (1885) were added to give Germany an official presence in the Pacific too. When the European powers met in Berlin in the winter of 1884-5 to discuss the division of Africa, Woermann was part of the German delegation.

Historians have long debated what lay behind Bismarck's apparent U-turn on the colonial question. Hans-Ulrich Wehler has argued that in fact there was no sudden change in the chancellor's thinking, but "a remarkable continuity of both the ideas and the methods of free-trade commercial expansionism," dating right back to the 1860s. "There were however some motives, which, contrary to his previous experience and hopes, induced Bismarck for some time to involve the state in the governance of Protectorates." For Wehler, these motives were predominantly socio-economic in character. As a "pragmatic expansionist" Bismarck may have anticipated genuine economic benefits from colonies in Africa, but more importantly their acquisition offered a diversionary escape from the adverse effects of industrialization and recession, and a short-term boost for pro-government candidates in the 1884 Reichstag election campaign.

Not all historians agree, however, that foreign policy objectives or considerations of national prestige "were only incidental" in Bismarck's flirtation with colonialism. Andreas Hillgruber, for instance, acknowledged the domestic considerations, but argued that Bismarck's prime motivation was external: to seek an accommodation with France, in order to take advantage of Britain's difficulties in Afghanistan, Egypt and the Sudan. Edgar Feuchtwanger also favors a foreign policy explanation, but suggests that Bismarck's "immediate aim was to distract French attention from Alsace-Lorraine and put Britain under pressure to tie herself more positively to Germany." A further possibility has been put forward by Seligmann and McLean: that Bismarck's concern over the imminent monarchical succession in Germany led him to seek ways in which to drive a wedge between the Anglophile Crown Prince Friedrich Wilhelm and Great Britain. By developing colonies in Africa, Bismarck "had a ready-made mechanism for generating Anglo-German diplomatic incidents whenever he wished."

Whatever the reasons for Bismarck's change of heart, Woermann won considerable praise in Hamburg for his part in "winning" Cameroon for Germany. It no doubt contributed to his hard-fought electoral victory in one of Hamburg's three parliamentary constituencies later that year. He was appointed to the government's advisory Colonial Board (1890), joined the board of directors of the shipbuilders Blohm & Voss (1891) and became president of the Hamburg Chamber of Commerce (1899-1902). Meanwhile his business interests went from strength to strength. The Woermann Line's green, white and blue livery increasingly adorned steamers as well as sailing ships, and in 1890 he was part of a consortium to set up a new German East Africa Line. Yet, in spite of all these triumphs, Woermann remained a controversial figure, admired and detested in roughly equal measure. The centrality of arms and liquor to his business was frequently criticized, as were the high death rates on his African plantations.

He brushed off such criticisms, but worse was to come. A storm of outrage blew up in Germany over the vast profits he made from the 1904-7 colonial war in German South West Africa, when some 15,000 troops and 11,000 horses were transported to Africa on Woermann ships, at a huge cost to the German taxpayer. He was condemned in the Reichstag as a war profiteer, and the Kaiser pointedly refused to receive him. He even had excrement thrown at him in a Hamburg street. Woermann retired in disgrace in 1910 and died less than a year later. Thus while there is a Godeffroystrasse and an O'swaldstrasse in Hamburg today, you will not find a Woermannstrasse. One man who did stand by him, however, was HAPAG's Albert Ballin. In his obituary he wrote: "Fly the flag at half-mast, you citizens of Hamburg. The greatest of all Hanseatic merchants is dead."

It would be a mistake to regard the Godeffroys, O'swalds and Woermanns as typical of Hamburg opinion as a whole. Until the 1890s the majority of the Senate was opposed to colonialism, as was the city's large socialist milieu. Even within the business community there were many who were skeptical of its benefits, and those who did embrace it were anxious to proceed cautiously, so as not to provoke a protectionist backlash from other colonial powers. Nevertheless, 25 Hamburg merchants were listed as members of the fledgling Colonial Association in 1884, and, as Matthew Fitzpatrick's recent study makes clear, the city was far from insulated against colonial activism: "Hamburg was in many ways the precocious face of German expansionism," he suggests. Nowhere is this more apparent than at Grosse Reichenstrasse 27, which is still the headquarters of the Woermann concern. Afrika-Haus, as it is known, was built in 1899-1901 to designs by Martin Haller and Hermann Geissler. The internal courtyard entrance is flanked by a pair of giant bronze elephants, and guarding over the entrance hall is the muscular figure of a Togo native by the Dresden sculptor Walter Sintenis. The door is decorated with a palm-tree motif. In short, the visitor is left in little doubt where the Woermanns first made their money.

As trade between Hamburg and Africa grew in the second half of the nineteenth century, there was a marked increase in so-called "tropical" diseases. The naval doctor Bernhard Nocht (1857-1945), who acted as an adviser to the city authorities during the 1892 cholera epidemic, was appointed Hamburg's first harbor doctor in April 1893. He developed a plan, backed by the imperial government, to establish an Institute for Maritime and Tropical Diseases in the city. It opened in 1900, located in the administrative building of the old sailors' hostel overlooking the St. Pauli landing stages. The intention was not only to treat tropical diseases, but also to study the colonial sciences more broadly. Civil servants preparing for overseas postings in the German colonial service attended lectures at the institute, which was considered a prestige project by both the Reich Colonial Office and the Hamburg Education Authority. The latter saw the institute as an important advance in the long-running campaign to establish a university in the city. Between 1910 and 1914 a purpose-built home for the institute, adjacent to its existing building, was designed by Fritz Schumacher. Renamed the Bernhard Nocht Institute (BNI) in 1942, it remains Germany's leading research institute for tropical medicine, employing more than 400 people in the city (Bernhard-Nocht-Strasse 74).

If the Bernhard Nocht Institute is one evident legacy of Hamburg's colonial past, another is the Museum of Ethnology, which moved into its present clinker-brick building at Rothenbaumchaussee 64 in 1912. Housing 350,000 objects from around the world, this pioneering museum includes items from both the Godeffroy and Strebel collections. Highlights include a display of masks from the South Pacific and a complete Maori house. Today, of course, the museum is much more than just a collection of curiosities from the world's "primitive" peoples. The introductory exhibition does a good job of contextualizing the objects within the history of trade and colonialism. Moreover, the museum focuses not only on the metropolitan perspective, but also on what non-Europeans made of their white interlopers.

In the same spirit as Godeffroy or Strebel, but without any scientific pretentions, the tradition of the private museum was maintained in twentieth-century Hamburg by the ex-seaman Harry Rosenberg (1925-2000), who inherited a large collection of artefacts from "Captain" Haase's legendary naval bar in the Erichstrasse and supplemented it with his own souvenirs. "Harry's Harbour Bazaar" opened in St. Pauli in 1954 and kept on growing, despite Rosenberg's willingness to sell as well as to buy. Word soon spread that he was willing to pay for curiosities of all kinds, and many a returning sailor raised funds for a night on the Reeperbahn by parting with his more exotic possessions. The bazaar enjoyed something of a peripatetic existence, moving up and down Bernhard-Nocht-Strasse, then to the Grosse Freiheit, before ending up on the corner of Erichstrasse and Balduinstrasse, where the collection of 80,000 objects is now looked after by Harry's daughter Karin. For a small entrance fee you can experience what in the eighteenth century would have been known as a cabinet of curiosities: a jumble of stuffed animals, shark's teeth, ships in bottles, wooden chests and ethnic arts and crafts of all kinds, spread unsystematically over twenty rooms. What is more, if you buy something, your entrance fee will be refunded.

"Around the World for Fifty Pfennigs"

Harry Rosenberg might have been tempted to use this slogan for his St. Pauli bazaar, had it not already been coined by the animal trader, circus impresario and zoo pioneer Carl Hagenbeck. He was the son of a fishmonger, Gottfried Clas Carl Hagenbeck, who in 1848 took delivery of half a dozen live seals along with his usual catch of herring and cod. Hagenbeck decided to show off the creatures in a tent on Spielbudenplatz. The seals in washtubs proved quite a draw, although probably only because the canny Hagenbeck advertised them as "The Six Living Mermaids," and even illustrated them on posters with real girls' faces. With the money he made from showing the seals Hagenbeck purchased some more animals, and before long his career as a fishmonger was at an end. He staged an animal show each year at the Dom fair, and set up an import–export business for exotic animals. From 1863 his "menagerie" had a permanent home at Spielbudenplatz 19. Carl began working with the animals as a teenager, and by the age of twenty he was looking after a rhinoceros, a giraffe, an antelope, a leopard, two lions, two zebras, ten elephants and twelve hyenas. He took over the business from his father in 1866 and relocated to nearby Neue Pferdemarkt in 1874. Ambitious to expand the

African animals flee Hagenbeck's zoo collectors

business, he sent his agents on a series of expeditions to Africa, North America and Asia, capturing animals not only for his own shows, but also to supply a growing number of zoos and circuses around the world. Indeed, it was not unusual for Hagenbeck to dispatch three or four trips to Africa each year.

However, as Hilke Thode-Arora (1989) has shown, Hagenbeck did not stop at collecting animals. As profit margins in the exotic animal trade declined in the late 1870s, so he began experimenting with shows of human beings too. Among the "primitive" peoples he exhibited were Samoans, Laplanders, Inuit and Nubians. The original idea was said to have come from his friend the animal painter Heinrich Leutemann (1824-1905). The natives were to be displayed in a "natural" state, with their children, animals, tools and dwellings, so as to convey the impression of a scene from real life. Just like *Big Brother* and the reality television shows they prefigured, such *Völkerschauen* proved hugely popular—even Bismarck attended one—before the rise of film stole much of their thunder. In another uncanny parallel with reality TV, the shows' promoters often claimed they were not freak shows but had a serious anthropological purpose, but in practice they usually just reinforced existing stereotypes. While Hagenbeck did at least aspire to some kind of accuracy, many of his competitors did not: one group of indigenous people from Tierra del Fuego, for instance, was ordered to eat raw meat simply to satisfy the public's expectation that they were cannibals.

Hagenbeck's program of touring shows, whether featuring animals, humans or both, was hectic. Shows often ran simultaneously on either side of the Atlantic. A particular effort was made for the 1893 World's Columbian Exposition in Chicago, where the 6,000-seat Hagenbeck Pavilion was modeled on the Colosseum in Rome. There was a full program of gladiatorial combat (including man against beast), chariot races and "Bacchanalian dances," but it was the animal performances which captured the popular imagination: bears walking on tightropes, camels on roller skates and a chariot drawn by tigers and driven by lions in regal costume were among the attractions.

Hagenbeck's greatest achievement, however, came in 1896 when he patented a way of exhibiting lions and tigers in enclosures without bars, using only moats and low walls. It is for this reason that the son of Hamburg has gone down in history as the "father of the modern zoo." The invention of the *Freigehege* ("open-air enclosure") came only after years of careful observation of how far and how high the most athletic animals could jump. The first outing for Hagenbeck's open-air enclosure was his Arctic Panorama, which was shown on the Heiligengeistfeld in 1896 and then toured to Berlin, Dresden, Paris and later to the St. Louis World's Fair of 1904. It presented an artificially icy landscape with polar bears, seals and sea lions from the Arctic, but also penguins from the Antarctic. What it lacked in geographical accuracy, it made up for in drama and romance. It even included a replica of the Norwegian explorer Nansen's boat *Fram*, which had captured the public's imagination earlier that year. The Arctic Panorama had phenomenal viewing figures, but Hagenbeck was not satisfied. He dreamed of filling an entire zoo with natural enclosures, embedded in a park landscape and stepped to create a deeper sense of perspective. To this end he began buying up farmland in the Hamburg suburb of Stellingen, then still a rural village in Prussia.

The city already had a traditional "caged" zoo, founded in 1861 and boasting the first sea-water aquarium on the continent, but that did not deter Hagenbeck. By the end of 1897 he had purchased twelve lots of real estate, including all the land between Stellingen and the Hamburg border at Eimsbüttel. This would later enable him to connect the zoo to the suburban rail network. Building work on the enclosures began in 1902: the Swiss artist Urs Eggenschwyler and the landscape architect H. Hinsch were employed to design enclosures which replicated the animals' natural habitat. In the course of the twentieth century it would become something of a zoological cliché to have a flamingo lake or a mini-Gibraltar for Barbary Macaques, but when Hagenbeck's Animal Park opened to the public in 1907 these enclosures caused a sensation. In an era before wildlife television programs or package holiday safaris, they allowed ordinary people the chance to see wild animals in an approximation of their natural habitats for the very first time. The zoo was no longer just a site of urban entertainment but of popular enlightenment too.

Hagenbeck was celebrated as a true hero of his age, and his autobiography *Beasts and Men* (1908) became a best-seller: well over 100,000 copies were sold in the first year alone, and it remained in print until 1967. One of his admirers was Kaiser Wilhelm II, to whom the book was dedicated and who visited the Animal Park on several occasions. The connection was not just coincidental: Hagenbeck's rise was inextricably linked to German imperialism. One of his proudest moments, he claimed, came in 1906 when he was asked by the Colonial Department to supply 2,000 camels for German troops during the war against the Herero in South West Africa. Germany's other zoo owners, however, regarded him as a vulgar upstart, and in 1909 they began a long-running boycott of his enterprises.

In July 1943 the Animal Park was badly damaged by bombing. Four keepers died trying to put out the fires, and five more were killed by a direct hit on the zebra house. In all, some 120 animals perished too. Keith Lowe notes that "curiously, none of the animals was driven wild by its experience, and few tried to escape from their broken cages and enclosures—it is probable that they were every bit as shocked as their human counterparts." The animals were easily rounded up and the most valuable specimens were put on a train for the relative safety of Bavaria. Sadly the story does not have a happy ending: while the train was standing in sidings to the east of the city it was caught in a subsequent air raid and all the animals were killed.

Today Hagenbeck's big set-piece panoramas remain an impressive sight, even to those usually immune to the appeal of zoos. Although the enclosures have been modernized over the years, the zoo retains something of its Wilhelmine character, from the theatrical *Jugendstil* ornamentation of the old main gates (1907) to Josef Pallenberg's life-size dinosaur sculptures (1909), and the many other monuments dotted around the 65-acre site. Several of the enclosures, such as the Polar Sea panorama—a descendant of the 1896 Arctic landscape—are listed in the city's conservation register, and are considered important buildings in their own right. The animal park, which is now run by a sixth generation of Hagenbecks, claims to be the largest family-owned zoo in the world. Nearly 2,000 animals and 210 species have their home in this otherwise unremarkable North Hamburg suburb, including rare Chinese leopards, Indian elephants and Sumatran orang-utans.

The site, which also boasts a hotel in "colonial-exotic" style and stages spectacular "Jungle Nights," attracted 1.5 million paying visitors in 2007. Unlike the zoo in the Bavarian city of Augsburg, which in June 2005 caused controversy by setting up an "African Village," complete with real African natives selling traditional arts and crafts, Hagenbeck has largely managed to avoid accusations of racism. It should not be forgotten, however, that the Hagenbeck family continued to stage "human zoo" shows long after 1907. Indeed they were the undisputed market leaders in Europe, with more than fifty different shows to their name by the time of Carl Hagenbeck's death in 1913. The last such event staged by the family was John Hagenbeck's "Dagoes of the South Seas" show at the Munich Oktoberfest in 1931.

BALLINSTADT: THE WORLD OF THE EMIGRANT

Between 1834 and 1924 a staggering five million people emigrated from Germany to America via Hamburg, with most leaving in the years prior to 1890. For every Levi Strauss or H. J. Heinz who went on to find fame and fortune in the new world, there were thousands more who had to be content with eking out a modest living as a chambermaid or laborer. One in five returned home disappointed, while many others never even made it: estimates suggest that some 7-8,000 German migrants died in transit during the 1830s alone. The flow of migrants through the city fluctuated according to economic and political circumstances, but in a busy year the figure often exceeded 70,000. While the rate of German emigration began to decline in the 1880s, a second wave, from Russia and the Austro-Hungarian Empire, ensured that the city's shipping firms continued to benefit from this lucrative trade in human misery and hope. In 1891, when the total number of migrants leaving Hamburg exceeded those leaving Bremen for the first time, nearly 150,000 waved goodbye to Europe from a ship on the Elbe.

Conditions for migrants in the first half of the nineteenth century were appalling: the cramped sailing vessels were not built for passenger traffic and it took six to eight weeks to cross the Atlantic. The transatlantic travelers who were allowed on board, numbering between sixty and eighty, even had to bring their own mattresses and food. Hamburg had initially regarded this traffic with disdain: indeed it had banned it for a time, fearing that would-be migrants could become a burden on the city's poor relief system. This allowed Bremen, on the River Weser, to take an early lead. It was not until 1850 that the Sloman Line introduced the first regular steam-powered transatlantic passenger service from the Elbe. It was quickly surpassed by the HAPAG, which introduced its first steamers—the *Borussia* and the *Hammonia*—in 1855. These vessels could carry more than 300 people each and took only 13-19 days to complete the crossing. The migration trade in the second half of the century was there-after dominated by HAPAG and its Bremen-based rival Norddeutscher Lloyd, founded in 1857.

Steamers not only slashed journey times but also offered a more comfortable crossing, with HAPAG making much of its high-quality passenger accommodation. Nevertheless crowding, hunger and disease remained the order of the day in the notorious steerage class, and outbreaks of typhoid were not uncommon. In 1898 an imperial Emigration Law was passed, which stipulated that migrants should receive three meals per day, but the reality often looked very different. As late as 1906, the American author Edward Steiner (1866-1956) could write:

> ... the 900 steerage passengers crowded into the hold... are positively packed like cattle, making a walk on deck when the weather is good absolutely impossible, while to breathe clean air below in rough weather, when the hatches are down is an equal impossibility. The stenches become unbearable, and many of the emigrants have to be driven down; for they prefer the bitterness and danger of the storm to the pestilential air below. The division between the sexes is not carefully looked after, and the young women who are quartered among the married passengers have neither the privacy to which they are entitled nor are they much more protected than if they were living promiscuously. The food, which is miserable, is dealt out of huge kettles into the dinner pails provided by the steamship company. When it is distributed, the stronger push and crowd, so that meals are anything but orderly procedures. On the whole, the steerage of the modern ship ought to be condemned as unfit for the transportation of human beings.

Yet for many would-be migrants, an overcrowded or unhygienic ship was the least of their concerns: tragically it was not unusual for their life savings to disappear before they had even set foot on board. Often poorly educated people from rural areas, already exhausted from a long and sometimes perilous journey, they presented Hamburg's landlords, conmen and prostitutes with easy pickings. They crowded into the city's lodging houses, often waiting weeks before they could depart. At busy times emergency accommodation was sometimes made available in the hulks of old sailing ships, but the authorities saw little reason to help. The first office set up to

80 Emigrants Coming to the "Land

help migrants during their time in the city was opened by a charity, the Hamburg Association for the Protection of Emigrants, in 1851. Somewhat belatedly, the city established an Emigration Authority to oversee procedures and regulate disputes four years later. It was not until the early 1890s that one of the shipping lines accepted any responsibility to look after its passengers. The first barrack-style accommodation was built by HAPAG at the America Quay in 1892, but the unhygienic conditions brought only bad publicity to the company: many blamed the Russian migrants for that year's outbreak of cholera.

The very future of Hamburg's emigration trade looked under threat, as both the city authorities and the Prussian government were reluctant to continue to allow thousands of poor Russians through their territory. It was then that Albert Ballin, the company's managing director, began to plan a model "town" for transit passengers. The "emigrants' city" was built on the dockland island of Veddel in 1900-1, to designs by the local architect Georg Thielen. The site was located at Veddeler Bogen 2, just a stone's throw south of Veddel railway station, and a short ferry-ride from the HAPAG departure terminal on Grasbrook Island. The Hamburg authorities gave the land to HAPAG for free, and contributed to the building costs: they saw it as an ideal opportunity to remove migrants and the threat of disease from the city center.

The "emigrants' city," which opened on December 20, 1901, was quickly dubbed "the biggest guesthouse in the world." Even before it was finished, the plans won a prize at the Paris World Exhibition of 1900. Apart from the main reception and departure hall, the site initially consisted of fifteen buildings, including dormitories, a boiler house, canteens (serving up to 3,000 portions per hour), a barber, a general store, a music pavilion, a church (offering both Protestant and Catholic services), a synagogue and a hotel for wealthier emigrants. The buildings were surrounded by well-tended gardens and pathways. There were separate dormitories for men and women, with single beds rather than the bunks usually found in migrants' hostels. Luggage was not allowed in the dormitories: it had to be disinfected and stored separately. The total bed capacity was initially around 1,200, including some in family rooms. The cost of the accommodation was two Marks per night for adults, but those deemed unable to pay were allowed to stay for free. The site was maintained by a staff of around 180 HAPAG employees.

Emigrants from Germany or Austria-Hungary were free to come and go from the site whenever they wished, but until 1909 the US immigration authorities insisted that Russian citizens booked in steerage had to remain for a five-day period of quarantine. Of 72,000 people who stayed in the "emigrants' city" during 1904, some 80 percent were from Russia, including thousands of Jews escaping persecution. In 1906 this figure rose to nearly 102,000, and further dormitories had to be added, bringing the total capacity up to around 5,000. All records were broken in 1913 when 170,000 people passed through the Veddel, but numbers declined rapidly after the First World War when the USA introduced stricter immigration quotas. Only 20,000 people stayed in 1924 and the site's capacity was reduced. After the Great Depression reduced migration to America to a trickle, HAPAG handed the site back to the city authorities in 1934. The main hall was knocked down in 1938 as part of a road-widening scheme; and most of the remaining structures disappeared in 1962.

On July 4, 2007—the choice of date was no coincidence—a major new museum opened on the historic site called BallinStadt: The World of the Emigrant. The three buildings are reconstructions based on original plans, although a small part of Hall 3 is authentic. The museum offers "history at the touch of a button," with many interactive elements and a family history research center boasting an electronic database of 4.3 million migrants' names from the Hamburg passenger lists. Appropriately enough, the main sponsor is the shipping company Hapag-Lloyd, the two former competitors having merged in 1970. As its name implies, Albert Ballin features prominently in the museum's narrative. It suggests that his personal experience of hardship and his social conscience lay behind HAPAG's decision to build the facility. This is, however, somewhat disingenuous.

Ballin was undoubtedly born into modest circumstances, one of thirteen children born to a Danish Jew who had lived in Hamburg since 1830 and founded the emigration agency Morris & Co. in 1852. Following the death of his father, Albert had to become the family's main breadwinner at the age of seventeen, but did so with such success that he was invited to become HAPAG's head of passenger services while still in his twenties. He joined the board of directors at the age of 29, and in 1899 he became managing director of the whole concern. A short, bald man, Ballin was living proof that a "career open to talent" was possible in nineteenth-century Hamburg, even if he did remain something of an outsider. Though he met frequently with Kaiser Wilhelm II, he was more pessimistic than most Jews about the possibility of being fully accepted into German society. He also expressed deep concerns about the direction of the Reich's foreign policy in the decade before 1914, and warned of the dangers of war with Britain. He died from an overdose of sleeping tablets on the day of the Kaiser's abdication, November 9, 1918.

In short, Ballin was a fascinating man who certainly deserves to be remembered by posterity. He was no mindless reactionary, yet to imply he was some kind of philanthropist, motivated by a strong social conscience, seems wide of the mark. As his fulsome tribute to Adolph Woermann suggests, Ballin was no woolly liberal either. He was "a bold business innovator" (Niall Ferguson), motivated primarily by profit and a sense of obligation to the company he developed into the largest shipping line in the world (194 ships and 29,000 employees by 1914). Ballin is often credited with inventing the cruise vacation—as a way of utilizing spare capacity on HAPAG's liners in the 1890s—but he once admitted that "without steerage passengers I would be bankrupt within a few weeks." The truth was that HAPAG did little to help migrants until the company's core business was under serious threat. By constructing the "emigrants' city," Ballin was not only able to save the most lucrative arm of the business, but also secure a great publicity coup over his rivals, and all for a relatively modest outlay. For the first time, moreover, HAPAG gained full control over its passengers. This was important because any would-be migrant denied entry by the US authorities at Ellis Island had to be transported back to Europe at the shipping line's expense. Now such people could be prevented from traveling in the first place. Therefore neither the company's nor the museum's claims regarding the "emigrants' city" should be accepted uncritically. Indeed, when an undercover reporter from the socialist newspaper *Vorwärts* visited the site in 1904, he described having to wait for hours without food, water or adequate sanitary facilities.

It is sometimes said that the defining feature of a metropolis in the years around 1900 was the sense that the whole world could be experienced within the confines of a single city. Hamburg, with its huge flows of mi-

Albert Ballin: a self-made man

grants, its ever-increasing volume of international trade, its celebrated ethnographic collections, its colonial institute, its innovative displays of wild animals and even its shows of native peoples, was arguably the most metropolitan of all the Reich's cities, including the capital Berlin. Germany may have failed in its attempts to become a world power in the early twentieth century, but its principal port had become a world city. As an American *Guide to Great Cities for Young Travelers and Others*, published in 1910, put it:

> Hamburg is, indeed, a very modern and up-to-date city. In every direction electric cabs and taximeter cabs, trams, steamboats and ferries flit hither and thither, making the streets and lakes very gay and full of movement. The city itself is constantly pressing outwards. Beyond rolls the sea where there is room for all nations...

Epilogue

THE FUTURE CITY

Hamburg's center of gravity is shifting back to the Elbe, but this time the emphasis is not only on toil and trade: in the twenty-first century, housing, leisure, education and culture are all part of the plan. As the City Architect Jörn Walter put it on the eve of the new millennium: "Up until now Hamburg has turned its back on the Elbe; that is about to change." The largest inner-city building project anywhere in Europe is currently taking shape on a brownfield site in the former free port, immediately south of the Speicherstadt.

The so-called HafenCity project differs from other post-industrial urban regeneration schemes in two key respects: its vast scale; and its proximity to the existing city center. The 400-acre site incorporates three historic docks—the Sandtorhafen (1866), Baakenhafen (1887) and Magdeburger Hafen (1888) —and is fifteen times larger than Berlin's Potsdamer Platz redevelopment of the 1990s. It is on a similar scale to London's Docklands, yet is only half a mile from the town hall, and less than a mile from the main railway station. When complete, it will almost double the size of the city center.

The official announcement of the project by Mayor Henning Voscherau (SPD) in 1997 came after months of discussion held in secret so as to avoid land speculation. Construction began in 2001 and is scheduled to be finished around 2020. Building work is proceeding from west to east and from north to south across the site, which has been divided into ten "quarters." Each quarter is further subdivided into small plots to ensure architectural variety. Renzo Piano, Richard Meier, Philippe Starck and Beth Gali are amongst the leading designers to become involved. The first quarter to be built, Sandtorkai, was completed in 2005, and the second, Dalmannkai, in 2009. As a result, nearly 2,000 people are already living in HafenCity, and more than 200 businesses have settled within the project's boundaries. Eventually it will house 12,000 inhabitants and offer workplaces for 40,000 more: the German headquarters of Unilever, Kühne & Nagel logistics, China Shipping, Greenpeace and the Spiegel media group will all move to HafenCity.

Some 70,000 Hamburgers are already employed in the media or in information technology. The city is a major center of film and television production, and more than half of all the newspapers and magazines on German newsstands are published here, including the mass-market *Bild-Zeitung* (founded 1952), *Stern* (1949) and *Der Spiegel* (1952). IT employers range from market-leading multinational companies such as IBM and SAP to small start-up businesses. The city hopes that the embryonic district will help it to consolidate its position as a major center of the so-called "new economy." Indeed, those familiar with the rather sclerotic nature of German economic life are often taken aback at the dynamism of business on the Elbe, which is arguably closer to the Anglo-American brand of capitalism than the Bonn or Berlin model. It was no coincidence that the villain in *Tomorrow Never Dies*, played by Jonathan Pryce, was a Hamburg-based media tycoon who employs new technology to "make" the news.

The heart of the project is the Übersee quarter, with sixteen main buildings adjacent to the new Cruise Liner Terminal. Construction began in 2007 and is due to be finished in 2012. A new pedestrian boulevard already links the quarter to the Speicherstadt and the city center, while an underground car park offers room for 3,400 vehicles. Typical of HafenCity as a whole is the quarter's diverse mix of residential, commercial and leisure functions, and the attempt to create new public as well as private spaces.

Unusually, plots have been sold and building contracts awarded on the quality and sustainability of the proposed concept, rather than on price alone. Reasonably priced rental accommodation and housing for families have been included, as well as luxury apartments. The intention is to prevent the over-concentration of "yuppie" apartments and offices that have characterized dockland developments elsewhere.

It remains to be seen, of course, whether HafenCity will live up to these lofty ambitions, but the plans are certainly impressive. Work on the transport infrastructure, including a new U4 underground line, is well underway (due for completion in late 2011), and a school to serve the new community has recently opened next to the attractive Sandtorpark. The HafenCity University, an amalgamation of the architecture, planning and engineering schools from three existing institutes (the College of Visual Arts, the College of Applied Sciences and the Hamburg Technical University), will move into a new purpose-built campus between Magdeburger Hafen and Baakenhafen in 2011-12; and an interactive Science Center, with an eye-catching O-shaped building by the Dutch architect Rem Koolhaas, is due to be completed at the same time.

HafenCity is already home to an International Maritime Museum (Koreastrasse 1), which was built up by the late Peter Tamm in the 1970s and 1980s, and was formerly based in the village of Övelgönne on the Elbe. It opened in its new venue—a converted 1878 red-brick warehouse—in 2008. It documents 3,000 years of nautical history over nine "decks," with 36,000 scale models, ships' compasses, naval uniforms, and the largest Lego boat in the world. Since 2008 a number of actual boats of historical interest can be seen nearby, permanently moored to a floating pedestrian walkway in the middle of the historic Sandtorhafen basin.

The aspect of the project that really catches the public imagination, however, is the Elbphilharmonie (Elbe Philharmonic Concert Hall), which is scheduled to stage its first concerts in 2012. This spectacular building in a prominent position at the western tip of Grasbrook Island is intended to be Hamburg's equivalent of Sydney Opera House. It has been designed by the Swiss firm of Herzog and de Meuron, who also created Tate Modern in London. As with that scheme, the Elbphilharmonie involves gutting an industrial building—a squat brick warehouse formerly known as Kaispeicher A (1963-6)—and turning it into an instantly recognizable cultural icon. A sculptural glass "tent," with a roof-line resembling a frozen ocean wave, will be built on top of the old warehouse. It will house a main concert hall with 2,150 seats and a smaller hall with 550 seats, together with a viewing platform, luxury hotel and 700 parking spaces.

Hamburg's leaders hope that the new concert hall will finally lay to rest the city's reputation as a community hostile to culture. Those who have had the good fortune to live in this city of 259 libraries, 150 bookshops, 40 theaters, 60 museums and 160 art galleries may need little convincing, but a city's image is shaped as much by myth as reality. The predominantly private financing of the Elbphilharmonie—like so many of the city's cultural institutions—will probably ensure that outsiders continue to view Hamburg as a city of *Pfeffersäcke* and philistines rather than poets and painters. Yet even the most cynical of cultural commentators must surely be impressed by the sheer scale of the HafenCity project.

For now much of it remains a building site, but an old boiler house at Sandtorkai 30 has been converted into an information center with a huge 25x12-foot scale model of the entire scheme. In 2012, when the development will be more or less half-finished, Hamburg had hoped to be staging the Olympic Games. That dream was quick to fade, of course, but HafenCity's goal of being "green and metropolitan at the same time" may well be achieved. If it is, then Hamburg looks set to remain a "livable metropolis" for many years to come.

Further Reading

As the preceding chapters suggest, Hamburg has long regarded itself as different from the rest of Germany. Given the troubled course of that nation's history, it is not surprising that Hamburg's alleged exceptionalism has generally been portrayed in a positive light. What might be dubbed "the Whig interpretation of Hamburg history" began with the works of the one-time City Archivist Johann Martin Lappenberg (1794-1865), and reached its apogee with Percy Ernst Schramm (1894-1970). Schramm, the son a Hamburg senator, argued in the essay *Hamburg: ein Sonderfall in der Geschichte Deutschlands* (Hamburg, 1964) that the city's traditions of freedom, tolerance and cosmopolitanism made it a "special case" within Germany—more akin to Britain or the Netherlands than to Prussia or Bavaria. Schramm's first name may have testified to the city's Anglophile outlook, but subsequent research has tended to show that much of his thesis was based on little more than wishful thinking: Hamburg's history cannot be detached from the history of the territories which surrounded it, and certainly not after the foundation of the German Empire in 1871.

The darker corners of the city's past began to be probed by Germany's critical social historians of the late 1960s and 1970s, but it was left to a British academic, Richard J. Evans, to write the most damning indictment of the city and its rulers. *Death in Hamburg: Society and Politics in the Cholera Years 1830-1910* (Oxford, 1987) was ostensibly about the devastating cholera epidemic of 1892, but the book's scope was broader than this might imply. By the end of the nineteenth century, Evans concluded, Hamburg was no less authoritarian than the rest of Germany, and its much-vaunted liberalism was largely moribund.

Some of the themes of Evans' book have since been taken up in Niall Ferguson's *Paper and Iron: Hamburg Business and German Politics in the Era of Inflation, 1897-1927* (Oxford, 1995); Jennifer Jenkins' *Provincial Modernity: Local Culture and Liberal Politics in Fin-de-Siècle Hamburg* (Ithaca and London, 2003); and Mark A. Russell's *Between Tradition and Modernity: Aby Warburg and the Public Purposes of Art in Hamburg* (New York and Oxford, 2007). While anxious not to revive the "mythical" Hamburg of Schramm's account, these historians suggest there was more zest left in the city's élites than Evans was willing to acknowledge. Jenkins, in particular, offers a fascinating series of vignettes, highlighting the ways in which civic associations and new cultural institutions were at the heart of middle-class efforts to create educated and cultivated citizens, even at the height of the "cholera years." Where Evans emphasized the centrality of class conflict in late nineteenth-century Hamburg, Jenkins' focus is on attempts to bring about social reconciliation. The ultimate success of such efforts remains open to debate, but Jenkins does show that at least parts of the city's bourgeoisie were willing to consider strategies of integration rather than exclusion.

In the two decades since Evans' book first appeared, Anglo-American historians have continued to be at the forefront of research into Hamburg's history. As Jenkins notes, "outsiders have traditionally been good observers of Hamburg's particular personality." A conference was held at Cornell University in 2001, for instance, to reconsider Percy Schramm's thesis of Hamburg's exceptionalism. The papers were published in a book edited by Peter Uwe Hohendahl, *Patriotism, Cosmopolitanism and National Culture: Public Culture in Hamburg, 1700-1933* (Amsterdam and New York, 2003), which includes essays on aspects of the city's musical life, literary and print culture, art and architecture, as well as its politics. As one would expect, however, the majority of books published about Hamburg are in German. These are only mentioned below if they are directly referred to in the main text. All translations in this book are mine unless otherwise stated.

INTRODUCTION

As noted in the main text, one of the first attempts to write a cultural history of Hamburg came from the lawyer and art collector Gustav Schiefler, although in the end his book *Eine hamburgische Kulturgeschichte 1890-1920: Beobachtungen eines Zeitgenossen* (Hamburg, 1985) was not published until half a century after his death. Other overviews of Hamburg's cultural history include Volker Plagemann's *Kunstgeschichte der Stadt Hamburg* (Hamburg, 1995), with an emphasis on the visual arts; and Hermann Hipp's *Freie und Hansestadt Hamburg: Geschichte, Kultur und Stadtbaukunst an Elbe und Alster* (Cologne, 1996), which focuses primarily on architecture and town planning. The quotes in this chapter come from Mark A. Russell, "The Building of Hamburg's Bismarck Memorial, 1898-1906," *The Historical Journal*, 43 (2000); the exhibition catalogue *Als Hamburg noch nobel war— Widersprüche einer Zeit* (Hamburg, 1974);

Celia Applegate, *Bach in Berlin: Nation and Culture in Mendelssohn's Revival of the St. Matthew Passion* (Ithaca and London, 2005); Kurt Hofmann, "*Sehnsucht habe ich immer nach Hamburg,*" *Johannes Brahms und seine Vaterstadt: Legende und Wirklichkeit* (Reinbek, 2003); and Eckart Kleßmann (ed.), *Hamburg: Eine Städte-Lesebuch* (Frankfurt, 1991).

CHAPTER ONE

Despite the loss of much of the city's archival records in the conflagrations of 1842 and 1943, Hamburg has always attracted historical researchers. Although no general histories of the city are available in English, several of the themes and periods discussed in this chapter have been the subject of detailed monographs. These include: Katherine Aaslestad, *Place and Politics: Local Identity, Civic Culture, and German Nationalism in North Germany during the Revolutionary Era* (Leiden, 2005); Mary Lindemann, *Patriots and Paupers: Hamburg, 1712-1830* (New York and Oxford, 1990); Joachim Whaley, *Religious Tolerance and Social Change in Hamburg 1529-1819* (Cambridge, 1985); and the aforementioned Richard J. Evans, *Death in Hamburg: Society and Politics in the Cholera Years 1830-1910* (Oxford, 1987). Among the German titles cited are: Jörgen Bracker, *Hamburg von den Anfängen bis zur Gegenwart: Wendemarken einer Stadtgeschichte* (Hamburg, 1989); Martin Krieger, *Geschichte Hamburgs* (Munich, 2006); Christian Schnee, *Hamburg: Eine kleine Stadtgeschichte* (Erfurt, 2003); and Matthias Wegner, *Hanseaten: Von stolzen Bürgern und schönen Legenden* (Berlin, 1999).

The literary quotes are taken from: W. G. Sebald, *Austerlitz* (London, 2001); Samuel Taylor Coleridge, *Biographia Literaria*, vol. 2, (Oxford, 1958; first published 1817); Thomas Mann, *The Magic Mountain* (first published 1924, translated by H. T. Lowe-Porter, 1928); Stephen Spender, *World within World* (Berkeley, 1966; first published 1951); Arnold Zweig, *The Axe of Wandsbek*, translated by Eric Sutton (New York, 1947); Bill Bryson, *Neither Here nor There: Travels in Europe* (London, 1991); and A. Kaes, M. Jay and E. Dimdenberg (eds.), *The Weimar Republic Sourcebook* (Berkeley, 1995), from which the Larissa Reissner and Heinrich Hauser quotes are taken.

CHAPTER TWO

On monuments in Hamburg in general see Volker Plagemann, *Vater,*

Vaterstadt, Vaterland... Denkmäler in Hamburg (Hamburg, 1986). On the Bismarck monument see Jörg Schilling, *"Distanz halten": Das Hamburg Bismarckdenkmal und die Monumentalität der Moderne* (Göttingen, 2006); Mark A. Russell, "The Building of Hamburg's Bismarck Memorial, 1898-1906," *The Historical Journal*, 43 (2000); or the same author's *Between Tradition and Modernity: Aby Warburg and the Public Purposes of Art in Hamburg* (New York, 2007). The Samuel Beckett quote comes from *First Love and other Novellas* (first published 1973); the Alfred Andersch quote comes from his essay "Nördliche Republik"; and the Alfred Kerr quote from Eckart Kleßmann (ed.), *Hamburg: Eine Städte-Lesebuch* (Frankfurt, 1991).

CHAPTER THREE

On the Speicherstadt see Karin Maak, *Die Speicherstadt im Hamburger Freihafen, eine Stadt an Stelle der Stadt* (Hamburg, 1985). The literary quotes in this chapter come from: Robert Muller, *The World that Summer* (London, 1994; first published 1959); Thomas Mann, *The Magic Mountain* (first published 1924, translated by H. T. Lowe-Porter, 1928); Roswitha Quadflieg (ed.), *Beckett Was Here: Hamburg in Samuel Beckett's Diary of 1936* (Hamburg, 2006); Heinrich Heine, *Deutschland: A Not So Sentimental Journey*, ed. and translated by T. J. Reed (London, 1986; first published 1844); Heinrich Heine, *Schöne Wiege meiner Leiden: Hamburgische Miniaturen*, ed. by W. Vontin (Hamburg, 1981); Heinrich Heine, *From the Memoirs of Herr von Schnabelewopski*, translated by C.G. Leland (New York, 2008; first published 1834); Stephen Spender, *The Temple* (London, 1988); and Samuel Taylor Coleridge, *Biographia Literaria* vol. 2 (Oxford, 1958). The extracts by John Strang, Joseph von Eichendorff, Gustav Falke and Detlev von Liliencron are all taken from Eckart Kleßmann (ed.), *Hamburg: Eine Städte-Lesebuch* (Frankfurt, 1991). The guide to Hamburg's famous no. 36 bus route is Rainer Elwers, *Linie 3: Hamburg Bus Tour in 38 Minuten vom Rathaus bis Blankenese und zurück* (Hamburg, 2000).

CHAPTER FOUR

On "Operation Gomorrah" see Jörg Friedrich, *The Fire: The Bombing of Germany 1940-1945* (New York, 2006); Keith Lowe, *Inferno: The Devastation of Hamburg 1943* (Harmondsworth, 2007); W. G. Sebald, *On the*

Natural History of Destruction (London, 2003). For the aftermath of the bombing see Jeffrey M. Diefendorf, *In the Wake of War: The Reconstruction of German Cities after World War II* (New York, 1993); and Bill Niven (ed.), *Germans as Victims: Remembering the Past in Contemporary Germany* (Basingstoke, 2006). The quote by Friedrich Hebbel comes from Eckart Kleßmann (ed.), *Hamburg: Eine Städte-Lesebuch* (Frankfurt, 1991). The quote by Robert Koch and the anonymous poem about Hamburg's water supply are taken from Richard J. Evans, *Death in Hamburg: Society and Politics in the Cholera Years 1830-1910* (Oxford, 1987). The quotes from Hans Erich Nossack, Wolf Biermann, Franz Termer and Joseph Goebbels are all taken from Lowe, *Inferno*. Other extracts come from Heinrich Heine, *Schöne Wiege meiner Leiden Hamburgische Miniaturen*, ed. by W. Vontin (Hamburg, 1981); Heinrich Heine, *Deutschland: A Not So Sentimental Journey*, ed. and translated by T. J. Reed (London, 1986); Stephen Spender, *World within World* (Berkeley, 1966); and Boris Meyn, *Die rote Stadt* (Reinbek, 2003).

CHAPTER FIVE

The quote by Fritz Höger is from Carl Westphal, *Fritz Höger, der niederdeutsche Backstein-Baumeister* (Wolfshagen, 1938); those by Rudolf Binding and Hermann Sörgel are taken from Harald Busch and Ricardo F. Sloman, *Das Chilehaus in Hamburg* (Hamburg, 1974). Nikolaus Pevsner is quoted from *An Outline of European Architecture* (Harmondsworth, 1942). The quote from Alfred Lichtwark is from Dörte Nicolaisen, *Studien zur Architektur in Hamburg, 1910-1930* (Hamburg, 1985). For Paul Bröcker, see my essay "A City in Distress? Paul Bröcker and the New Architecture of Hamburg," in M. Gee, T. Kirk, J. Steward (eds.), *The City in Central Europe: Culture and Society from 1800 to the Present* (Aldershot, 1999), from which parts of this chapter are taken. The Schumacher quote is from Hermann Hipp, "Fritz Schumachers Hamburg," in V. M. Lampugnani and R. Schneider (eds.), *Moderne Architektur in Deutschland 1900 bis 1950: Reform und Tradition* (Stuttgart, 1992). The quotes from Maiken Umbach come from her *German Cities and Bourgeois Modernism, 1890-1924* (Oxford, 2009). Bröcker's quote on the symbolism of the DHV building is cited in an unpublished essay by Jörg Schilling, "Zwischen den Zeilen. Paul Bröcker und die Einweihungsschrift zum Verwaltungshochhaus des DHV in Hamburg 1931."

The issues in this chapter are explored in more detail in Umbach's *German Cities and Bourgeois Modernism*. In particular she emphasizes the very different ideological visions which underpinned Schumacher's and Höger's use of red brick architecture. Other sources include Ralf Lange, *Architekturführer Hamburg* (Stuttgart, 1995); Hermann Hipp, *Freie und Hansestadt Hamburg* (Cologne, 1996); Alan Tate, *Great City Parks* (London, 2001); Jennifer Jenkins, *Provincial Modernity: Local Culture and Liberal Politics in Fin-de-Siècle Hamburg* (Ithaca and London, 2003); Hartmut Frank (ed.), *Fritz Schumacher: Reformkultur und Moderne* (Stuttgart, 1994); and Jürgen Tietz, *Von der Schönheit des Ziegels: Bernhard Winking, Bauten und Projekte* (Hamburg, 2003).

CHAPTER SIX

The quotes from Curt Moreck and Ernst Engelbrecht / Leo Heller come from A. Kaes, M. Jay and E. Dimdenberg (eds.), *The Weimar Republic Sourcebook* (Berkeley, 1995). The quotes from Stephen Spender are from *World within World* (Berkeley, 1966) and *The Temple* (London, 1988). The quotes from Ronald Gutberlet, Johannes Meyer, Jeremias Gotthelf and Stefan Becker are all from Gutberlet, *Die Reeperbahn: Mädchen, Macker und Moneten* (Hamburg and Vienna, 2000). Other quotes are taken from Bill Bryson, *Neither Here nor There: Travels in Europe* (London, 1991); Julia Bruggemann, "The Business of Sex: Evaluating Prostitution in the German port city of Hamburg," in R. Beachy, B. Craig and A. Owens (eds.), *Women, Business and Finance in Nineteenth-Century Europe* (Oxford, 2005); Richard J. Evans, "Prostitution, State and Society in Imperial Germany," *Past and Present* 70 (1976); and Uwe Timm, *The Invention of Curried Sausage*, translated by Leila Vennewitz (New York, 1995).

On the Beatles in Hamburg see Ulf Krüger and Ortwin Pelc, *The Hamburg Sound* (Hamburg, 2006); Ulf Krüger, *Beatles in Hamburg: Ein kleines Lexikon* (Hamburg, 2007); Paul du Noyer, *Liverpool: Wondrous Place* (London, 2002); and Spencer Leigh, *Twist and Shout: Merseybeat, The Cavern, The Star Club and the Beatles* (Southport, 2004). On the city's drug scene in the 1960s see Robert P. Stephens, *Germans on Drugs: The Complications of Modernization in Hamburg* (Ann Arbor, 2007). The Stuart Sutcliffe quote is from Alan Clayson and Pauline Sutcliffe, *Backbeat: Stuart Sutcliffe—The Lost Beatle* (London, 1994). The chapter also cites Graham Sclater, *Ticket to Ride* (Flame Books, 2006).

CHAPTER SEVEN

The quotes from Julius von Eckhardt, the Bavarian diplomat von Homayer, and Helmut Böhme all come from Richard J. Evans, *Death in Hamburg: Society and Politics in the Cholera Years 1830-1910* (Oxford, 1987). The extract from a speech by Kaiser Wilhelm II is taken from Maiken Umbach, "The Vernacular International: Heimat, Modernism and the Global Market in early twentieth-century Germany," *National Identities*, 4 (2002). Constance Gordon-Cumming's quote comes from Matthew Fitzpatrick, *Liberal Imperialism in Germany: Expansionism and Nationalism 1848-84* (New York and Oxford, 2008), which offers useful insights into early German colonial activism. The Gerhart Hauptmann quote is taken from Eckart Kleßmann (ed.), *Hamburg: Eine Städte-Lesebuch* (Frankfurt, 1991). The literary extracts are from Thomas Mann, *The Magic Mountain* (first published 1924, translated by H. T. Lowe-Porter, 1928); idem, *Buddenbrooks: The Decline of a Family* (first published 1901, translated by H. T. Lowe-Porter, 1924); and Edward Steiner, *On the Trail of the Immigrant* (New York, 1906).

Other quotes in this chapter are taken from: Mary Lindemann, *Patriots and Paupers: Hamburg, 1712-1830* (New York and Oxford, 1990); W. O. Henderson, *Studies in German Colonial History* (London, 1962); Holger H. Herwig, "Industry, Empire and the First World War," in G. Martel (ed.), *Modern Germany Reconsidered*; Hans-Ulrich Wehler, "Bismarck's Imperialism, 1862-1890," in J. J. Sheehan (ed.), *Imperial Germany* (New York and London, 1976); Andreas Hillgruber, *Otto von Bismarck: Gründer der europäischen Großmacht Deutsches Reich* (Göttingen, 1978); Edgar Feuchtwanger, *Imperial Germany 1850-1918* (London, 2001); Matthew Seligmann and Roderick McLean, *Germany from Reich to Republic 1871-1918* (Basingstoke, 2001). These quotes can also be found in my *Contesting the German Empire, 1871-1918* (Oxford, 2008), which explores this period of German history in more depth. Ballin's obituary for Adolph Woermann is quoted from Matthias Wegner, *Hanseaten: Von stolzen Bürgern und schönen Legenden* (Berlin, 1999).

On the Colonial Institute in Hamburg see Jens Ruppenthal, *Kolonialismus als "Wissenschaft und Technik": Das Hamburgische Kolonialinstitut 1908 bis 1919* (Stuttgart, 2007). On Carl Hagenbeck and his animal park see Nigel Rothfels, *Savages and Beasts: The Birth of the Modern Zoo* (Baltimore, 2002); and Eric Ames, *Carl Hagenbeck's Empire of Entertain-*

ments (Seattle, 2009). Hagenbeck's "people shows" are explored by Hilke Thode-Arora, *Für fünfzig Pfennig um die Welt: Die Hagenbeckschen Völkerschauen* (Frankfurt, 1989). The quote from Keith Lowe is from *Inferno: The Devastation of Hamburg 1943* (Harmondsworth, 2007). On Albert Ballin see Lamar Cecil, *Albert Ballin: Business and Politics in Imperial Germany 1888-1918* (Princeton, 1971); and Niall Ferguson, *Paper and Iron: Hamburg Business and German Politics in the Era of Inflation, 1897-1927* (Oxford, 1995). The chapter closes with an extract from Esther Singleton, *A Guide to Great Cities for Young Travelers and Others: Northwestern Europe* (New York, 1910).

Index of Historical & Literary Names

Index of Places & Landmarks